Surprised by
the LORD'S
PRAYER

GARY TABER

WESTBOW
P R E S S®
A DIVISION OF THOMAS NELSON
& ZONDERVAN

WestBow Press books may be ordered through booksellers or by contacting:

WestBow Press
A Division of Thomas Nelson & Zondervan
1663 Liberty Drive
Bloomington, IN 47403
www.westbowpress.com
1 (866) 928-1240

ISBN: 978-1-5127-5230-4 (sc)
ISBN: 978-1-5127-5231-1 (hc)
ISBN: 978-1-5127-5229-8 (e)

Library of Congress Control Number: 2016912840

Print information available on the last page.

WestBow Press rev. date: 9/27/2016

This book is dedicated to the memory of Pastor Lloyd Ellison, my wife's father. I was blessed and privileged to have him in my life. He impacted me so much in a few brief years. Dad taught me so much. We spent hours talking about God, ministry, and life. I am forever indebted to him for sharing with me his faith and his philosophy of ministry. His courage and refusal to be defined by the physical challenges he faced due to polio have inspired, challenged, and humbled me. The impact he has had on my life and ministry has been immeasurable.

Acknowledgments

I want to acknowledge some of the key people in my life who have profoundly influenced me, encouraged me, and stuck by me.

I am most grateful and appreciative for my wife of over forty years, Vivian. Her love, encouragement, and help in my ministry have been invaluable.

Thank you to my children, Julie and Mark, and his wife, Brianne, who have made me a proud father and who have provided Vivian and me with great memories of life as a pastoral family.

I have been blessed with a number of mentors in my academy (high school), college, and seminary years. The following educators were used by God:

Pastor Carl Ashlock, my academy (high school) and college dean who taught me grace by extending it to me long before I understood the word.

Dan Shultz, my academy band director, who taught me more than notes. He taught me the importance of excellence and challenged me to see beyond the limits I saw for myself.

Dr. Douglas Waterhouse, professor of religion, whose love for God's Word and insights into the Old Testament gave me a desire to continually learn and seek the truth of God's Word for my life.

Dr. Raoul Dederan, whose teaching style and desire for his students to grasp the subject enabled me to remember what he taught in his classes long after other class materials had been forgotten. I will never forget the lessons he taught in Revelation and Inspiration class.

Dr. Ivan Blazen, college and seminary professor, who taught by his example a love of scripture, especially the Pauline letters, and whose concern for his students and faith in God was evident.

Finally, to my staff, Pastor Gilbert Del Vecchio, Kelly Pick, and Pastor Josie Asencio, who prayed for me and bore with me as I took time to write this book. To my Corona Church family for their support and encouragement as I took time to write.

I am eternally grateful to each one.

Epilogue

What? An epilogue at the beginning of the book? No, this is not a misprint. The publisher did not misplace the epilogue. I chose to write the epilogue at the beginning of the book. Actually, it is my real purpose that there will not be an epilogue to this book. For an epilogue is considered to be the concluding remarks that bring closure to a book. It is my hope, prayer, and desire that after reading this book about the Lord's Prayer, you will not have closure but a continuing renewal of more meaningful prayers in your life and your journey with God.

Let me share with you both my experience of taking a new look at the Lord's Prayer along with my hopes and desires for you as you read this book. I had been in the ministry for almost forty years and had never given a sermon series or study on the Lord's Prayer. I had been praying about what to preach on when the suggestion was made to me to do a short series on the Lord's Prayer. Immediately I knew that was the answer to my prayer. Little did I know, at the time, how much my study, preparation, and sermon presentations of the Lord's Prayer would change *me*. My prayer life would *never* be the same. As a result, my relationship with my heavenly Father would never be the same either.

My prayer is that the Lord's Prayer will become a source of hope, help, and inspiration that will add new depth to your prayers and enable you to live and serve as Jesus did. He was able to live for God and serve God and others because he lived a life of prayer. And that must be our reality, too!

The prayer Jesus taught to his disciples has been called by various names: the Lord's Prayer, the Our Father, the Disciples' Prayer, and the Model Prayer. And each name fits the purpose of the prayer Jesus taught. It is the prayer Jesus gave us. It is a prayer addressed to our

Father. It is the pattern for prayer that Jesus taught to his disciples. And it does contain the elements of meaningful prayer for us to include in our prayers.

There have often been two approaches to the Lord's Prayer in the worship services of the church. Many churches pray the Lord's Prayer every week in their worship services. It is sometimes assumed that when it is repeated so often, it is said out of habit, without thought or meaning. While that can happen, that does not automatically have to be the case. Many of those who repeat the Lord's Prayer on a weekly basis can, *and do*, find meaning in the Prayer and spiritual help in their relationship with God. It never becomes old or mechanical to them.

On the other hand, there are churches that repeat the Lord's Prayer in worship just occasionally, perhaps two or three times a year. It is assumed that since it is repeated only infrequently, it is said with more meaning and held in higher esteem. Such may not automatically be the case either.

I would like to suggest that this prayer, which most Christians learn early on in their Christian lives, continues to offer us lessons in how to pray. It gives us opportunities for developing a more meaningful prayer life that will:

- impact our relationship with God
- impact our relationship with others
- impact how we live
- give us a pattern for avoiding our own clichés or worn-out phrases
- enable us to focus more on God and others than ourselves
- enable us to focus more on the desire of His heart for us rather than on the desires of our hearts

I have gone from being familiar with his prayer to being deeply affected by his prayer. From saying the words now and then in church to having my prayers shaped by his prayer! Not by merely repeating it but by using it as pattern for who is the focus of my prayers, what I focus on in prayer, the frequency of my prayers, and the insights I have received while praying.

The Lord's Prayer is so simple a child can learn and understand it—yet so profound the brightest mind can never plumb its depths. There is a simplicity in the prayer that can be understood by people of any age, educational level, cultural background, or stage of spiritual maturity. And at the same time, we will never get to the point where we will master the principles Jesus gave us when he taught the disciples how to pray.

I came across the following quotations quite early on in my study of the Lord's Prayer:

> I used to think the Lord's Prayer was a short prayer; but as I live longer, and see more of life, I begin to believe there is no such thing as getting through it. If a man, in praying that prayer, were to be stopped by every word until he had thoroughly prayed it, it would take him a lifetime.[1]

> (The Lords Prayer) "can be repeated in less than a minute. Despite its brevity, it has been an enormous benefit to multitudes of men and women. Many of them knew little or nothing else about the Scriptures. Yet there is inherent in this prayer all the strength and compassion of our Father in heaven. There moves through it a beauty and serenity which no mortal man can fully explain. It reassures our hearts, strengthens our resolve, and leads us into personal contact with God, our Father."[2]

I must admit, at first I did not understand these statements. I thought they were overstatements. The more I studied the Lord's Prayer, meditated on the Lord's Prayer, and applied the Lord's Prayer in my own prayer life, the more I saw these quotes as understatements. I have become committed to learning and applying the Lord's Prayer as a

---

[1] Henry Ward Beecher, *Life Thoughts Gathered from Extemporaneous Discourses* (Boston: Phillips, Sampson and Company, 1858), 132.

[2] Phillip Keller, *A Laymen Looks at the Lord's Prayer* (Chicago: Moody Bible Institute, 1976), 9–10

regular pattern and way of life. And it is my desire and hope that anyone who reads this book will do the same.

The very brief summary of chapter titles and a brief description of their contents are provided below:

The Priority of Prayer. Jesus's prayer life, which included regular times of solitude, meditation and listening to God, was the key to his life and his ministry.

The Pattern of Prayer. Jesus gave the disciples, including us, a pattern or outline to follow in our prayers. In some ways, it is like a pathway. The pathway begins with acknowledging God. Along the path are waypoints that keep our prayers in focus and guide us as we submit our lives to God. It leads to exalting and glorifying God.

The Privilege of Prayer. We discover the privilege of prayer in knowing that we are in the presence of our heavenly Father who is the Almighty God of the universe.

The Purpose of Prayer. The life, ministry, and teaching of Jesus enables us to more fully understand what it means to pray, "your kingdom come, your will be done." This phrase reveals the purpose of prayer, to enable us to know God and to seek His purpose and plans for our lives and for others, too.

The Provision of Prayer. God provides the necessities of life, including our physical, emotional, relational and spiritual needs. Jesus is the ultimate provision for our lives.

The Pardon of Prayer. Forgiveness is the essence of living in the kingdom that must be experienced and expressed. We first receive forgiveness from God for our sins. And then we are enabled to express forgiveness to those who offend or hurt us.

The Protection of Prayer. The parallelism of this phrase reveals that it is about times of testing versus day-to-day temptation. Deliverance from evil (or the evil one) comes from God, not from us.

The Praise in Prayer. The results from prayer will always focus on God and give glory to Him.

Persistence in Prayer. Luke's parabolic conclusion is more about a life of prayer than getting results from prayer. It is a challenge to us to apply the Lord's Prayer to our lives. And it is a promise of God's willingness to give us what we need the most as we minister to and serve others.

Are you ready to be surprised? This book on the Lord's Prayer contains perspectives that will enlighten you. It has insights that will challenge you. And it contains suggestions that will help you. You will never think of the Lord's Prayer in the same way again!

Chapter 1

The Priority of Prayer:
As Revealed in the Life of Jesus

Now Jesus was praying in a certain place, and when
he finished, one of his disciples said to him, "Lord,
teach us to pray, as John taught his disciples."
—LUKE 11:1, ENGLISH STANDARD VERSION[3]

Note: Throughout this book, personal pronouns that refer to Jesus while he lived
and ministered as the Son of Man, that is in his humanity, will not be capitalized.
Personal pronouns that refer to God or to Christ in his pre-incarnate state or
resurrected state will be capitalized.

Who was your superhero when you were growing up? That usually
depends on the decade(s) in which you grew up. People love stories about
heroes. Hollywood and comic books have thrived—and still do—on the
stories of superheroes. From Superman to Spiderman! From Batman to
the Green Hornet! From the Lone Ranger to Bat Masterson! From Neo
of the Matrix to Mr. Spock! Superheroes capture our imagination. Why?
Because they can do things we can't. They can leap buildings with a
single bound, ride white horses across wide-open prairies, and capture
the bad man. Above all, they triumph over evil.

However, only Jesus could provide the greatest triumph over evil,
the greatest triumph over sin and Satan. Some skeptics see Jesus as just

---

[3] Unless otherwise noted, all biblical references are taken from the English
Standard Version.

another superhero that humans have added to their collections. From the gods of Greek mythology to the heroes of the silver screen, they lump them together. But there are two major differences between Jesus and the imaginary superheroes of literature, drama, or even our own imagination.

First, of course, is the fact that Jesus did indeed live! There are recognized historians, primarily Josephus and Tacitus, who wrote about his miracles and his death and resurrection.[4] He is not the imaginary creation of some person's mind. He is the real revelation of the heart and character of God.

There is a second difference. A huge difference! Superheroes don't share their "magic powers." They may for a short period of time, but they always seem to take them back. Jesus said he *wants us* to have the same power for living and for ministry that he had. He promised, "Truly, truly, I say to you, whoever believes in me will also do the works that I do; and greater works than these will he do, because I am going to the Father" (John 14:12).

Sadly, I must confess that I, along with most Christians, have a hard time really believing that Jesus meant *me* when he said, "whoever ..." We think only the "super spiritual" have the chance to live and minister effectively as Jesus did. In this passage, Jesus tells us that he wants us to minister effectively to others. In his life, through his teaching and ministry, he has given his disciples—and that includes us—the secret of his life and ministry.

The disciples recognized the secret of Jesus's life and ministry. One day, one of Jesus's disciples found him praying alone and asked him, "Lord, teach us to pray, just as John taught his disciples" (Luke 11:1).

Ellen White elaborated on this event. She makes some very strong points about Jesus's prayer life being the source of his effectiveness in his ministry. "The hearts of the listening disciples were deeply moved. They saw how he spent long hours in solitude, in communion with his Father. His days were passed in ministry to the crowds that pressed

---

[4] Information on Tacitus and Josephus can be readily found on the Internet and in the books *Evidence that Demands a Verdict* (San Bernardino: Here's Life Publisher's, 1979) by Josh McDowell and *The Case for the Christ* (Grand Rapids: Zondervon Publishing House, Grand Rapids, MI, 1998) by Lee Strobel.

upon him, and in unveiling the treacherous sophistries of the rabbis. And his incessant labor often left him so utterly wearied that his mother and brothers and even his disciples had feared that his life would be sacrificed. However, as he returned from the long hours of prayer that closed the toilsome day, they marked the look of peace upon his face, the sense of refreshment that seemed to bathe his presence. It was from hours spent with God that he came forth morning-by-morning to bring the light of heaven to men. *The disciples had come to connect his hours of prayer with the power of his words and works.* Now, as they listened to his supplication, their hearts were awed and humbled. As he ceased praying, it was with a conviction of their own deep need that they exclaimed, 'Lord, teach us to pray'" (emphasis mine).[5]

In response to the request to "teach us to pray," Jesus repeated, in essence, the prayer he had taught when he had given the Sermon on the Mount. He taught them the same prayer because they had failed to understand the depth of that prayer. Unfortunately, it is a depth that we have failed to grasp, too. Therefore, we need to reconsider the Lord's Prayer so that we can learn and apply the deeper principles to be found to our lives.

Before we look at the Lord's Prayer, let's ask for God's guidance as we seek to understand the prayer life of Jesus. May the desire the disciples had to learn how to pray from Jesus become our desire, too!

---

[5] Ellen White, *Thoughts from the Mount of Blessing* (Boise, ID: Pacific Press Publishing, 1956), 102–103.

Prayer

> Our Father in heaven! Thank You for the privilege of prayer. As we look at the prayer life of Jesus, we are amazed! May we learn important lessons from the example of the One who came to live for us, die for us, and who was resurrected and ascended to heaven where he continues to pray for us. We ask for Your forgiveness for failing to pray as often as we should. May his life of prayer inspire us to pray.
>
> In Jesus's name, we pray. Amen.

Examples in Prayer

As we begin to consider the priority we give to prayer in our lives, we must admit that all too often our prayers lack the proper perspective.

The story is told about a young boy who was being sent to his room after he had misbehaved. Soon after, when the time was up and his punishment was over, he told his mom: "I have been thinking about what I have done, and I prayed about it."

"That's wonderful, son! Then you learned your lesson. When you pray, God will help you!" his mother said.

"Oh! No! I did not pray for me! I prayed for you! I asked God that you would put up with me better!" [6]

We all laugh! However, if we are going to be honest about it, so many of our prayers are not too different from the prayer of this young boy. When we pray, all too often our concerns are for ourselves.

- We pray out of obligation or guilt.
- We pray to ask God to make our lives better.

---

[6] Taken from *Our Daily Bread*®, © 2011 by Our Daily Bread Ministries, Grand Rapids, MI. Used by permission. All rights reserved.

- We pray to ask God to change the physical, emotional, and/or spiritual circumstances of our lives that are causing us pain and heartache, some of which are beyond our control. Too many are the results of the mistakes and messes *we* have created.
- We pray to ask God to change those who give us problems.
- We pray to ask God for wisdom to make right decisions to improve our lot in life.
- We pray to ask God to bless our lives.

Of course, it is appropriate to pray about those things—and much more!

However, when we offer *only* the kinds of prayers as mentioned above, we are reducing our prayers to wish lists, crisis requests, or selfish desires in order to remove the difficulties from our lives or receive something we want or need. We then deprive God from accomplishing what *He* longs to do in us, to recreate us in His image and to transform us and give us the mind and heart of Christ. We also deprive God of what God can accomplish through us in ministry to other people!

The number-one purpose of prayer is that we experience and know God more fully in every area of our lives. That should be our priority in prayer, as stated in John 17:3. "And this is eternal life, that they know you the only true God, and Jesus Christ whom you have sent."

That was the obvious result of the prayer lives of some of the most loved and honored Bible characters! Those who made some monumental contributions to our faith and to the faith of millions through the years! They have one thing in common:

They knew how to pray because they knew God.

And ...

They knew God because they knew how to pray.

Abraham would set up altars everywhere he went in his journey to the land of promise. Not just altars of sacrifice but also altars of memorial. They were aids to remind him of God's faithfulness and goodness and the encounters he had with his God. No wonder he was called a friend of God!

Moses is another example of what it means to be a person who prays. From the burning bush to Mount Pisgah, throughout the time when the plagues were falling on Egypt, at Sinai, in times of battle and conflict, and throughout the Exodus, God spoke with Moses and Moses with God. When he would appear after talking to God, his face was shining with a radiance and a peace that others could not deny. He was referred to as the meekest man because in prayer he had learned where he stood in relation to Jehovah.

King David's many psalms were nothing less than his prayers that were put into music. His prayerful statements became songs of praise and supplication. He was so honest about his feelings toward his God. At the same time, he was honest about his feelings toward his enemies. Through his prayers, he became a man after God's own heart. He's not the only one.

Prayer was a prominent part in Daniel's distinguished life of serving God and kings. It impacted who he was and affected what he did. His first response to any situation was to pray—to request God's intervention or to thank God for His answers. In fact, when his enemies scrutinized his life, the only fault they could find with him was his devotion to his God as exhibited by his life of prayer. It is not a coincidence that Daniel is one of the very few Bible characters who lived a totally exemplary life! The list could go on.

There were other noteworthy prophets, such as Elijah, Elisha, Nehemiah, Ezra, Ezekiel, and so many more.

Their successes came not because of what they had done on their own but because they knew God and trusted God to work through them. They believed in the power of prayer. Thus, God's involvement in their lives and ministries was evident to all.

I believe that through listening to the stories of scripture, Jesus learned from the patriarchs, prophets, and kings of Israel. And he learned well. The gospels have much to tell us about the high priority Jesus placed on prayer in his life. Let's discover what they say.

Prayer, the Key to His Life and Ministry

It is of the utmost importance for us to understand that *the life of Jesus Christ was a life of prayer.* He could not have fulfilled his mission of being the Messiah without having a constant and focused life of prayer. For he lived and ministered as the Son of Man, which was his favorite title for himself, for it stressed his humanity.

As already mentioned, his disciples recognized and understood the importance of prayer to Jesus's life and ministry. They recognized that everything he had accomplished in his ministry was a direct result of his time spent with God in prayer. Even after Jesus had been preaching, teaching, and healing all day, he would often get away and spend all night in prayer, communing with his heavenly Father. They observed his exhaustion as he would go out to a solitary place to pray. Then they were amazed when he returned refreshed and energized to minister again. At the same time, they recognized how ineffective their prayers were.

Luke 11:1 tells us what happened one time when they found him praying alone. "While he was praying in a certain place, after he had finished, one of his disciples said to him,

'Lord, teach us to pray
just as John also taught his disciples to pray.'"

Some of Jesus's disciples had also been disciples of John the Baptist. They had seen the effects of John's prayers on his life and ministry. They had listened to him teaching about prayer and repentance. It is obvious, isn't it, that they saw Jesus's prayers resulted in more power than John's? John had performed no miracles (John 10:41). John's ministry had been limited to the desert. Jesus's ministry was reaching more people, in cities and towns. So it was natural for them to ask Jesus to teach them the secrets of his prayers! They wanted to have the same power and ability to perform miracles that they saw in Jesus's ministry.

However, they did not know *what* it was in Jesus's prayers that made a difference in his life and especially in his ministry. Yet their request seemed like an odd one! Jesus was entering the third year of his ministry. He had already given the Sermon on the Mount. In the middle of that sermon, Jesus had already taught the disciples the Lord's Prayer. But at that time, the two primary lessons he pointed out to them were:

- Prayer needs to be more than a mere ritual, more than repetitive words, and certainly more than a means to impress others of one's own piety.
- Those who receive God's mercy and forgiveness must be willing to express mercy and forgiveness to others.

If he had already taught them how to pray, why did they ask him to teach them again?

Perhaps they had linked what he had taught them about prayer in the Sermon on the Mount with prayer for personal holiness. They may have thought that to perform such miracles as healing the deaf, blind, and lame, the casting out of demons, and multiplying bread and fish required a different kind of prayer than the one he had taught them in the Sermon on the Mount. After all, the Lord's Prayer contains no words about miracles, requests for power, or even for faith to perform them. No wonder they asked him to teach them to pray!

What they did not realize is that Jesus, in his teaching and by his example, had already been teaching them how to pray. Later, the gospel writers, including two of his disciples, would relate how prayer was a top priority in the life of Jesus. Not because he said it was but because they saw him praying daily. Furthermore, they observed the effects of his life of prayer on his life and ministry.

Jesus's Consistent Prayer Life

Have you ever noticed how often the gospels mention that Jesus prayed? Let's look at what the gospels tell us about this important aspect of Jesus's life and ministry.

A careful study of the gospels reveals fifteen specific occasions when Jesus prayed. These do not include all the allusions to other times when he prayed. When we read that he was out alone in the mountain, we can almost add the word praying, and we would know that we are right. There were times when he performed a miracle, and Jesus said that his Father had heard him. Obviously, Jesus had been praying. Other times he mentioned that he did the things his Father told him to do. Certainly this indicates that Jesus prayed often. On a regular basis!

Even in his daily interactions with people he was in an attitude of prayer, listening for guidance from his Father.

Let's look at the gospels and the insights they give us regarding the prayer life of Jesus.

In his gospel, Matthew detailed three times when Jesus prayed. One of Matthew's main themes is focusing on how Jesus would fulfill the Old Testament prophecies of the Messiah. His prayer life enabled him to maintain God's plan for him as the Messiah and not to go along with the commonly accepted misunderstanding of the Messiah's mission as an earthly king.

The gospel of Mark specifically mentions four times when Jesus prayed. Mark's primary interest was to unveil Jesus as the suffering Messiah. He recorded how Jesus continually attempted to change people's focus from the Messiah as an earthly king to the Messiah as a saving King. This became even more pronounced as he neared the time of his crucifixion. Jesus wanted his disciples and the people in the crowds to understand his mission of seeking and saving the lost.

I was surprised to discover that the book of John mentions Jesus praying only four times! It would seem that John would have written about it more often. After all, John's is the more "spiritual" and theological gospel. However, John focused on Jesus primarily as the divine Son of God.

Luke's focus was predominantly on the humanity of Jesus. Therefore, it should not surprise us that Luke would speak of Jesus's prayer life more than the other gospel writers. For Luke wants us to know that Jesus's sinless life was lived in dependence on his Father. His ministry, including his miracles, was performed by the power of the Spirit. The fact that prayer was vital to the life and ministry of Jesus in the eyes of this gospel writer is more than obvious.

Some scholars/authors/commentators refer to Jesus praying eleven times in Luke, while others mention him praying fifteen times. The difference is explained by how they viewed his prayers while on the cross. Some count each individual plea Jesus stated on the cross as a prayer. Others said that he was praying to his Father the entire time while he was on the cross, thus counting it as one prayer. There is something to be said for both ways of evaluating what took place. It makes sense that

Jesus was in constant communion with his Father while on the cross. At the same time, there is much to learn from each separate plea that was preserved in the gospel accounts of the crucifixion.

Only the communication (prayer) Jesus had with his Father enabled him to endure the physical, emotional, and spiritual pain. Only the communication he had with his Father enabled him to remain on the cross. Only the communication he had with his Father enabled Jesus to fulfill his mission as the saving Messiah.

Thus, it is apparent that the prayer life of Jesus was the most prominent aspect of his life and ministry. Because of prayer:

- Jesus performed the miracles of healing, casting out demons, and raising the dead.
- Jesus's preaching had the authority that even his accusers could not deny.
- Jesus did not wilt under the personal attacks of the religious leaders.
- Jesus withstood the relentless temptations of Satan.
- Jesus stayed focused on his mission that would lead him to Calvary.

As we think about his temptations, sometimes, they were obvious. Many times they were subtle. Often they were deceitful! But they were ever present. They were always difficult. No wonder the disciples wanted Jesus to teach them to pray! And we should, too!

In his classic book on prayer, Andrew Murray wrote, "Would that we might learn from our Lord Jesus how impossible it is to walk with God, to obtain God's blessing or leading, or to do his work joyously and fruitfully, apart from close unbroken fellowship with him who is ever a living fountain of spiritual life and power!"[7] (Murray uses the word fellowship as a synonym for prayer.) He is right! We need to learn how to pray from our Lord Jesus!

Let's take a brief look at the specific occasions when the gospel writers mention that Jesus prayed to his Father in the gospels.

---

[7] Andrew Murray, *The Prayer Life,* Charles Rivers editors, e-book, 34.

Jesus Prayed in the Assurance of His Father's Love

The first time the gospels record Jesus in prayer is at his baptism in Luke 3:21–22. Notice what it says:

> [21]Now when all the people were baptized, and when Jesus also had been baptized *and was praying,* the heavens were opened, [22]and the Holy Spirit descended on him in bodily form like a dove; and a voice came from heaven saying: 'You are my beloved Son; with you I am well pleased.' (Italics are mine.)

What was the first thing Jesus did after his baptism? He knelt down on the bank of the Jordan River and prayed. It was *while he was praying* that he received the anointing of the Holy Spirit, in the form of a dove. It was *while he was praying* that he received the verbal confirmation of his relationship with his Father, "You are my beloved Son." Those words were in response to Jesus's prayer! They were the words of God the Father speaking through the Spirit while Jesus listened.

The words of divine approval and familial tenderness were key words, for throughout his ministry he clung to them. The devil's greatest temptation was to try to get Jesus to doubt his relationship with his Father. That was *the* main temptation in the wilderness. It was often repeated through the scribes and Pharisees during times of confrontation. It was shouted to him in mocking tones from the foot of the cross. It was whispered to him by Satan and his hosts during the physical darkness of the noonday and the spiritual darkness of abandonment. Yet Satan could not get Jesus to distrust in the love, acceptance, and approval of his heavenly Father.

It was from Jesus's life of prayer we learn that one of the primary effects of prayer is to know we belong to God. We are His beloved children. While Jesus was the unique Son of God, we are God's children, too. And the temptation to doubt our relationship as God's children is one of the devil's most successful ploys in getting us to distrust God. We all need to know that we belong to God. For a long time, I did not truly know this to be true for me. From scripture, I learned to believe I am

His son. Frequently during times of solitude and prayer I have sensed it. I once heard His voice telling me, "You are my son."

This is extremely important because we can only live joyous, satisfying, and peace-filled lives as Christians when we know that we are the children of God. When we know that:

- we belong to Him
- not just by knowing it intellectually in our heads
- but by knowing it experientially in our hearts

And when that happens, we are enabled to live our lives in the confident assurance of His presence in our own life. We can live our lives in the awareness that we are the recipients of His grace and love. Jesus's example of developing this sense of belonging is what enabled him to effectively minister God's grace to others. God wants us to have the same sense of belonging, too.

Jesus's Ministry Guided by His Father

In fact, Jesus's ministry begins with an incident that reveals how prayer was an integral part of his blueprint for ministry. It was a Sabbath, and Jesus was in the synagogue at Capernaum. Talk about a busy Sabbath! First Jesus taught (preached) in the synagogue with an amazing, divine authority. Then while still in the temple, Jesus was accosted by a man with an evil spirit. He cast the evil spirit out. Jesus left the synagogue and went to Peter's house, where he healed his mother-in-law of a high fever. After the sun went down, the crowds found out where Jesus was, and they brought all kinds of sick people to Jesus, who laid hands on every sick person and healed them (Luke 4:31–42; Mark 1:21–37).

I am sure he was exhausted. Yet he rose early in the morning and went to a desolate place. Luke stopped there. But Mark added one vital piece of information. Mark wrote that Jesus went to a desolate place to pray. In fact, Peter and the disciples had to go in search of him because people were storming Peter's house looking for him. They wanted Jesus to perform more miracles. They wanted more healings. They wanted

Jesus to cast out more demons. But when the disciples told him about the crowds waiting back at Peter's house, Jesus looked at them and told them, "We are leaving to preach in other towns" (Mark 1:29–39).

Now by most standards of public ministry, when you have a crowd calling for you to preach and minister to them, you stay to establish that ministry. You don't leave a successful ministry while there are still people flocking to hear you. Yet Jesus was different. Jesus was ready to move on to the next town. How did he know what he was supposed to do? He had been praying:

- He had been talking to God.
- And he had been listening to God for his guidance.

From Jesus's prayer life we learn the importance of prayer as a means of guidance for our lives and especially for our ministry to others. This is true whether we are involved in formal ministry as pastors or informal ministry as disciples of Jesus Christ.

Luke wanted us to know something extremely important. He wanted us to know that this was not one isolated instance in which Jesus withdrew to a desolate or solitary place to pray.

After his disciples returned from their missionary venture and just prior to the miracle of the feeding of the five thousand, Jesus took them to a deserted place (Luke 9:10–ff). While Luke did not specifically mention that Jesus prayed, it is quite reasonable to conclude from other instances in the gospel record that when Jesus went to a deserted place, he went there to pray. Mark included the additional information that they were so pressed by the people that they did not even have time to eat (Mark 6:30–32). Jesus's constant practice in ministry was that of going off by himself to pray. This often took place in the nighttime and early morning hours. We often make excuses about being too busy to spend time with God. No one was busier than he was! Yet Jesus regularly withdrew to pray.

Ellen White gives us further insight into Jesus's practice of spending time with God in prayer. She wrote: "All day he toiled, teaching the ignorant, healing the sick, giving sight to the blind, feeding the multitude; and at the eventide or in the early morning, he went away to the sanctuary of the mountains for communion with his Father. Often he passed the entire night in prayer and meditation, returning at daybreak to his work among the people."[8] (Ellen White had much to say about Jesus's prayer life. See appendix 1).

Jesus's Prayer Life Included
Times of Solitude and Intercession

Jesus prayed for his disciples. From Jesus's life of prayer we learn the importance of taking time to pray about those we mentor in ministry and those we love.

Luke recorded another time when Jesus prayed. Jesus's ministry had been effective. Too effective for the scribes and Pharisees! Crowds were coming to hear him, to be healed by him, and hoping to crown him the Messianic King. His popularity was rising. The religious leaders were both jealous and alarmed (Luke 6:1–16).

It is important to note that Jesus often healed the sick on Sabbath. This was considered a breach of the Sabbath by the scribes and Pharisees. And it infuriated them. They then "discussed with one another what they might do to Jesus" (Luke 6:11). The scribes and Pharisees were plotting his death. In the midst of these disparaging remarks concerning his mission and ministry, he went away to the mountain and prayed to God. In the face of conflicts and confrontations, he sought solitude and quietude in communion with his Father.

- This was not an hour of prayer.
- This was not a season of prayer.
- This was an all-nighter!

He prayed all night after ministering all day! And what was the result of that entire night spent talking to God and listening to God? New ways to deal with his distracters? Perhaps! Better ways to explain his methods? Maybe! Reminders of God's presence and love for him? Of course! However, none of these were the primary result.

---

[8] Ellen White, *The Desire of Ages,* (Boise ID: Pacific Press Publishing Assoc., 1940), 259–260.

The ultimate result is unexpected! The ultimate result is found in verse 13. Notice what it says: "When day came, he called his disciples and chose from them twelve, whom he also named apostles." Then Luke listed them by name. Mark's gospel says in chapter 3 that it was at this time that Jesus "appointed them to be with him."

Most of us have the idea that this took place at the very beginning of Jesus's ministry. It is true that Jesus first called his disciples shortly after his baptism. And it is true that they witnessed much of his early ministry. But they also spent time away with their families and their previous occupations (see The Desire of Ages 246). This final call to the disciples occurs, according to the timeline chart of Christ's ministry in the *Adventist Bible Commentary*,[9] over one and a half years after Jesus's baptism. Over halfway through his ministry! Only after a night of prayer does Jesus appoint them as his disciples who would become the apostles. He dared not rely on his human judgment to prepare those who would fulfill his ministry after his death, resurrection, and ascension. He had to depend on his Father's guidance.

Jesus's Prayer Life Enabled Him to Handle Success in Ministry

John gave another snapshot to place in Jesus's prayer album. In John 6:1–15, John wrote the story of how Jesus fed the five thousand men, plus women and children. Verses 12–15 give us the final conclusion to the familiar story:

> [12]And when they had eaten their fill, he told his disciples, "Gather up the leftover fragments, that nothing may be lost." [13]So they gathered them up and filled twelve baskets with fragments from the five barley loaves left by those who had eaten. [14]When the people saw the sign that he had done, they said, "This is indeed the Prophet who is to come into the world!" [15]Perceiving then that they were about to come and take him by force to make

---

[9] Francis D. Nichol, *Seventh-day Adventist Bible Commentary*, v. 5, (Washington, DC, 1956), 230–231.

him king, Jesus withdrew again to the mountain by himself.

Although this event is recorded by all four gospel writers, John is the only one who noted that Jesus went to the mountain by himself to be alone. Matthew and Mark wrote that he went there to pray (Matthew 14:23; Mark 6:46).

It is interesting that Jesus prayed *after* one of his most "successful" miracles. The crowd saw him as the long-awaited Messiah, fulfilling the role of Moses, who provided manna in the wilderness. The crowd had been ready to take him by force and make him king. But Jesus recognized the temptation inherent in success and power, and so he withdrew to pray.

He withdrew to the mountain by himself. Why? Because he needed to reaffirm with his Father the true nature of his messianic role. He needed to receive the divine approval and not settle for human approval. He needed to be reassured that he was to be a Messiah who would wear a crown of thorns and not one wearing a crown of royalty. He needed to be reminded that he would one day reign as King of Kings and Lord of Lords, but he could do so only if he became the Lamb of God who would take away the sins of the world.

Jesus spent time praying to find out what his Father wanted him to do. He followed God's plan, and it also became his plan. "But the Son of God was surrendered to the Father's will, and dependent upon His power. So utterly was Christ emptied of self that he made no plans for himself. He accepted God's plans for him, and day-by-day the Father unfolded His plans."[10]

Jesus's Prayers Teach Us to Persistently Pray for Others

One of Jesus's most powerful prayers was recorded by John in the story of the raising of Lazarus (chapter 11). Mary and Martha sent word to Jesus that Lazarus was ill. Jesus told those present that Lazarus's illness would not lead to death but to the glory of God. Jesus delayed going to Bethany for two days. When he told his disciples they were

---

[10] Ellen White, *The Desire of Ages,* 208.

going to Judea, they argued with him, fearful of what the religious leaders might do to him. Jesus answered them and divulged to them the real reason he was going to Jerusalem. He told them that Lazarus was sleeping, meaning he had died.

By the time Jesus arrived in Bethany, Lazarus had already been buried for four days. Martha heard that Jesus was coming and went out to meet him. There Jesus gave her some of the most comforting words in all of scripture when he said, "I am the resurrection and the life" (verse 25). These words filled her with hope for the second coming.

Martha sorrowfully commented to Jesus that if only he had been there, her brother would not have died. She even expressed hope that Jesus would still do something. When Jesus told her that Lazarus would rise from the dead, Martha acknowledged that he would be raised in the resurrection on the last day. After their conversation was finished, Martha sent for Mary to come and meet Jesus. Jesus was filled with compassion for Mary and Martha and asked them to take him to where Lazarus has been entombed.

When he arrived at the tomb, Jesus commanded them to remove the stone. The objection is raised that Lazarus has been in the tomb for four days and there would be a stench. Jesus reminded them that he had said they would see the glory of God.

Then Jesus prayed a surprising but powerful prayer. He did not say, "Father, please raise Lazarus from the dead." He did not say, "Father, please resurrect Lazarus so everyone will know and believe that I am the Son of God." He didn't even ask God to raise Lazarus to relieve the grief of Mary and Martha. Here is what happened:

> [41]And Jesus lifted up his eyes and said, "Father, I thank You that You have heard Me. [42]And I know that you always hear Me, but because of the people who are standing by I said this, that they may believe that You sent Me." (John 11:41–42)

Jesus's prayer was a prayer of gratitude. He said, "Father, I *thank You*." Furthermore, Jesus did not say, "Father, I thank You that You *hear* me." Rather, he said, "Father, I thank You that You *heard* me." Notice he used the past tense. I think it is fairly safe to assume that Jesus and God had been talking together about Lazarus, Mary, and Martha for four days. Jesus went to Bethany to do what his Father had told him to do.

How did he know that Lazarus had already died if God had not told him? Some might say that he knew because he was the Son of God. Therefore he was omniscient. But remember, Jesus's life and ministry were lived in his humanity. His miracles, his authoritative preaching, his casting out of demons—all were done not through his own divine power but by the power of God through the Holy Spirit.

Jesus acknowledged that it was the power of God that was behind his ministry of teaching, healing, and restoring people to God and to one another. Jesus said:

> [19]"Truly, truly, I say to you, the Son can do nothing of his own accord, but only what he sees the Father doing. For whatever the Father does, that the Son does likewise. [20] For the Father loves the Son and shows him all that he himself is doing." (John 5:19–20)

This aspect of Jesus's prayer life is powerfully illustrated by three other times when Jesus prayed for others during the events of his Passion.

- At the Last Supper, he prayed for Peter that "his faith would not fail and that when he had turned again (repented) he would strengthen the other disciples" (Luke 22:31–22). That prayer was answered!
- Just before entering the Garden of Gethsemane, he prayed his High Priestly Prayer (John 17). The majority of the prayer was focused on the disciples of all ages, including you and me. It was a prayer for unity among the disciples and that they would have the desire and ability to continue his ministry after he would return to heaven.
- While he was being nailed to the cross, he kept on praying, "Father, forgive them, for they do not know what they are doing."

As you can see, it appears that Jesus spent more time praying for others than he did praying for himself.

Summary

Jesus's prayer life made a difference. It enabled him to fulfill his mission as the Messiah his Father had planned. It kept him from becoming the Messianic King humanity was looking to receive. And his prayer life enabled him to be the Messiah God had planned to send.

- His life of prayer made a difference in knowing that he was God's beloved Son.
- His life of prayer made a difference in love and compassion for the lost.
- His life of prayer made a difference in receiving God's guidance for his ministry.
- His life of prayer made a difference in the authority behind his teaching.
- His life of prayer made a difference in receiving the power to perform miracles.
- His life of prayer made a difference in victory over temptation, including both the temptations associated with apparent failure and those associated with apparent success.
- His life of prayer made a difference in wisdom and endurance when being confronted by his critics and those who saw him as an enemy.
- His life of prayer made a difference in providing him patience for dealing with his disciples.
- His life of prayer made a difference that enabled him to accept the cup of suffering for a lost world. He was willing to be abandoned by his Father on account of our sins that he might offer redemption to a lost world.

We have been given the privilege and responsibility of being modern-day disciples whose lives are transformed to reflect the character of our

Lord. Our prayer life should make a difference and enable us to fulfill our mission as modern-day disciples of Jesus!

- Our life of prayer will make a difference by reinforcing our awareness that we are God's beloved son or daughter.
- Our life of prayer will make a difference by giving us a greater love and compassion for the lost.
- Our life of prayer will make a difference that will result in receiving God's guidance for our ministry to others.
- Our life of prayer will make a difference and have a greater impact when we teach others God's Word.
- Our life of prayer will make a difference and provide more opportunities for God to perform miracles—big and small.
- Our life of prayer will make a difference and impact how we deal with temptation. This includes both the temptations associated with apparent failure and those associated with apparent success.
- Our life of prayer will make a difference and provide us with divine wisdom and endurance when being confronted by those who criticize our faith and beliefs.
- Our life of prayer will make a difference and generate patience for dealing with difficult people. This includes family, friends, and church members.
- Our life of prayer will make a difference and will enable us to face the uncertain future of end-time events.

It is no wonder that Jesus taught the Lord's Prayer to his disciples. Are we willing to learn?

Prayer

Our Father in heaven, You are an awesome, compassionate, and patient God. Forgive us for using prayer as primarily a wish list to fulfill our needs and wants. Please continue to reveal Yourself to us. May we be open to hearing You speak to us at the level of our deepest needs. May we be willing to receive Your gracious provisions. But above all, may we recognize prayer as an awesome privilege to have an audience with the King of the universe. To learn Your heart, Your compassion, and Your concern for each of us as Your children. May we seek Your guidance for how to serve others and touch their lives for You on a daily basis.

In the name of Jesus. Amen.

Chapter 2

The Pattern of His Prayer:
An Outline to Integrate

Whenever you pray, do not be like the hypocrites, because
they love to pray while standing in synagogues and on
street corners so that people can see them. Truly I say to
you, they have their reward. But whenever you pray, go into
your room, close the door, and pray to your Father in secret.
And your Father, who sees in secret, will reward you.
—Matthew 6:5–6, New English Translation

Reality shows are popular on television today, especially ones that include celebrities along with "regular" people! In some of them, the celebrities coach the contestants in their areas of expertise—music, cooking, dancing, interior design, and so on.

Can you imagine being a contestant in a competition that would establish you as a master chef? Suppose that in the show, a master chef would give advice to all contestants on how to improve their cooking skills. What would you think of a contestant who ignored the advice of the master chef? To do so would be to invite failure. What would be the likelihood of such a contestant winning the prize? We would shake our heads at them in utter disbelief, at their refusal to listen to the advice of the master chef, wouldn't we?

On the other hand, what a fantastic opportunity to be coached by someone who would dramatically improve the chances for you to win the prize! To have your lifelong dream fulfilled of becoming a world-renowned master chef! You would think someone with a dream of becoming a master chef would jump at the chance to be mentored by a master! Right?

Sadly, most of us who have spent a lot of time in prayer have spent little time studying the Lord's Prayer. We have spent little time meditating on the Lord's Prayer to understand its principles. And we are in a much more important venture than a reality television show contest! We are in a contest that will determine our eternal destiny.

You and I have been given the most wonderful teaching and mentoring by *the* Master of the universe! Prayer is one of the key spiritual ingredients for living the Christian life. Jesus wants to coach us in our prayer lives. He taught his disciples—including you and me— how to pray. Not once but twice he gave the model prayer we call the Lord's Prayer. The first time he taught it as part of the Sermon on the Mount (Matthew 6:9–12). At that time, it was *his* idea to teach the people how to pray. The second time he taught the Lord's Prayer was in response to a request by one of his disciples (Luke 11). Jesus, who was *the* Master Pray-er, taught his prayer twice. Therefore, don't you think we should study it and learn from Him? Don't you think following the principles of *his* prayer will enable us to know how to pray and those things for which we should pray? Let's begin by asking Him to teach *us* to pray!

Prayer

> Our Father in heaven, what a privilege it is to come before Your throne of grace. In order to understand the lessons Jesus gave his disciples on prayer, we must recognize that our thoughts are not Your thoughts, and our ways are not Your ways. You view life from the perspective of Your kingdom of righteousness and grace. We view life from our kingdom of selfishness and rights.
>
> Open our eyes, including the eyes of our hearts, so that we might see and grasp the transforming power of prayer. We especially want to learn how to pray in the spirit of the Lord's Prayer. Open our ears that we might hear Your voice speaking to us in the depths of our being.
>
> May each reader be moved to look at his/her prayers in the light of the prayer Jesus taught us to pray. Thank You that You reveal Yourself to us.
>
> In Jesus's name. Amen.

The Value of the Lord's Prayer

The Lord's Prayer is a part of scripture that we know so well, and yet we know so little. We know it by heart, but we know it so superficially. Many of us learned the Lord's Prayer when we were children. We can and do say it word for word. Too often we repeat it without giving any thought to the depth of its meaning. Whether we repeat it in worship regularly or infrequently, how often do we reflect on the meaning to be found in each phrase? And when we do say it publicly, does our concern for saying it properly keep us from saying it with meaning? For example, what happens when you are reciting the prayer in a public meeting and you come to the words about forgiveness? Does the concern for whether you are using the right words for forgiveness get in the way of understanding what you are saying? Are you more concerned about whether to use the words "debts and debtors" or "trespasses and trespass against us" than in seeking forgiveness? To our detriment, we have failed to see, understand, and apply the principles of the Lord's Prayer in our prayers, in our lives, and in our ministry to others.

There are those who have seen the value of utilizing the Lord's Prayer as a pattern or model for Christians to incorporate in their prayers. When I use the word pattern, it is not to be understood in the sense that it is a rigid, inflexible, and tedious format that must be repeated to be effective. The pattern of Jesus's prayer does not include a mantra to be chanted or a magic formula to be repeated. Rather, it is an orderly arrangement for making requests to meet our spiritual, physical, and emotional needs, concerns, and desires. When we follow the pattern of the Lord's Prayer, it encourages us to discover a process of meaningful and effective prayer. At the same time, there is room to be creative and extemporaneous when you pray using the Lord's Prayer as a pattern or guideline for your prayers.

Here are a few quotes about the wealth of instruction and the practical qualities of the principles to be learned from the prayer that Jesus taught us.

> He presents his own ideal of prayer, words so simple that they may be adopted by the little child, yet so comprehensive that their significance can never be fully grasped by the greatest minds. We are taught to come to God with our tribute of thanksgiving, to make known our wants, to confess our sins, and to claim his mercy in accordance with his promise.[11]

> The Lord's Prayer is the prayer you would want to offer if you loved God with all your heart.[12]

---

[11] Ellen White, *Thoughts from the Mount of Blessing* (Mountain View, CA: Pacific Press Publishing Assoc., 1956), 103.
[12] Archbishop William Temple, *Christian Faith and Life* (London: Student Christian Movement Press, 1957), 111.

Just as the Decalogue is the summary of all laws and the Sermon on the Mount is the whole gospel in miniature, so the Lord's Prayer is the sum and perfection of all prayer. Everything needed by alienated mankind is included in this brief petition.[13]

This prayer embraces the needs of all mankind and should therefore be a model for all our praying, both private and public.[14]

The Lord's Prayer is prayer reduced to the essentials.[15]

In praying this prayer we become the people God has called us to be in Jesus.[16]

Did you notice that Taylor Bunch, Adventist author, pastor, teacher, and theologian of the thirties, forties, and fifties, stated that the Lord's Prayer should be a model for all our prayers? Is he overstating it, or is his insight something we should take to heart, learning how to apply the model prayer when we pray? To do this, we need to understand the ways in which the Lord's Prayer is a pathway for our communication with God.

Perhaps an illustration by Charles Spurgeon, English Baptist minister often referred to as the "prince of preachers," will help us understand in what way the Lord's Prayer is a model. An architect builds a model to help others envision that which he intends to create, but no one expects to live or work in the model building. The building includes much more than the model portrays. So the Lord's Prayer is a model to give us the essence of prayer. The model prayer should be used to develop that which it was intended to create—personal prayers,

---

[13] Taylor G. Bunch, *The Perfect Prayer* (Takoma Park, MD: Review and Herald Publishing, 1939), 14.

[14] Ibid., 17.

[15] Elton Trueblood, *The Lord's Prayers* (New York: Harper and Rowe Publishers, 1965), 50.

[16] William Willimon and Stanley Heauerwas, *Lord, Teach Us: The Lord's Prayer and the Christian Life* (Nashville: Abingdon Press, 1996), 19.

which includes our relationship with God and with others and our own ongoing growth in grace.

We have seen the example of the priority of prayer in Christ's life and ministry. Jesus taught the Lord's Prayer because he wanted his followers to learn how to make prayer a focused, meaningful priority in their lives, too. He wants us to experience the beauty and grandeur of this compact yet comprehensive prayer. He doesn't want us to merely recite words; he wants us to offer our hearts. He doesn't want us to come and merely bow our heads; he is more interested in whether or not we yield our lives. He is not looking for us to come to God in prayer saying the exact *right words*; he is looking for us to come having a correct *right attitude* toward God and others. He is not just waiting to hear what we have to say to God; he is also eager for us to hear what is on God's heart and mind for us and for our lives.

Attitudes toward Prayer

The Sermon on the Mount largely deals with our attitudes toward God and people and subsequently with our relationships between God and man. Jesus pointed out that for too many people, prayer had become more of a means of parading their righteousness before other people than being with God. In Matthew 6:5–6, Jesus said, "When you pray, you must not be like the hypocrites. For they love to stand and pray in the synagogues and at the street corners, that they may be seen by others. Truly, I say to you, they have received their reward. But when you pray, go into your room, shut the door and pray to your Father who is in secret. And your Father who sees in secret will reward you."

In the time of Jesus, Jews had several required types of prayers and times when they were to be said. The first one was the "Shema." It was taken from three passages of scripture, especially Deuteronomy 6:1–4, and it was to be said the first thing in the morning and the last thing at night. It was to be repeated absolutely no later than nine o'clock in the morning and absolutely no later than nine at night. And they were to be prayed, word for word, as written or as recited from scripture. No extemporaneous thoughts, requests, or even words of thanksgiving! No paraphrasing of the words! Strict repetition was expected!

The second prayer that every Jew had to repeat was called the "Shemoneh 'esreh," which means The Eighteen. It consisted of eighteen blessings, mostly short, all based on scripture and quite impressive for their beauty. This prayer was to be repeated three times a day at nine in the morning, at noon, and three in the afternoon. (It is still recited daily by Orthodox Jews today.)

People were expected to stop wherever they were or whatever they were doing to pray. Without any exceptions! Those who wanted to show off their piety to others could be found at the street corners at these times of prayer. They wanted to make sure that others could see their religious zeal and hear their impassioned prayers. Now, it would be one thing if you were on the street corner because you were on your way to meet someone or to conduct some business. It would be another thing if you said, "Hmm! The prayer trumpet is about to sound. I think I will go out to the street corner so people can see and hear me pray and know how devoted I am to God." For too many, especially among the religious leaders, it had become a means of parading their superior righteousness before others and attempting to curry favor with God.

More likely than not, the prayers they prayed were good prayers. The words used were meaningful words. However,

- when they were said as one's obligation to be accomplished instead of one's privilege to be appreciated,
- when they were said to get the requirement out of the way,
- when they were said to let others know that you have done your duty and to show that you are a good and upright person,
- when prayers are said for any or all of these reasons ...

the purpose of prayer becomes tainted. The experience of prayer becomes selfish. It becomes arrogant. It takes a person from praying with the intention of opening their lives to God for His purposes to attempting to use God for their purposes!

The Jews also had set prayers for every occasion. If the lightning flashed, there was a prayer to say to God, thanking Him for the lightning. If it rained, there was a prayer to God giving thanks for the rain. If it was a sunny day, there was a prayer thanking Him for the shining of the sun.

These were prayers that they knew they were expected to pray. Word for word! They were prayers being said from memory and not from the heart. No wonder Jesus spoke against repetitive prayers!

On top of that, there were personal, lengthy prayers that were spoken as another proof of their piety. Long, flowing prayers that would heap adjective upon adjective in describing God! The Old Testament, and especially the psalms, reveals how appropriate it is in prayer and worship to refer to God's qualities and characteristics. To use the titles for God, the metaphors that describe God and adjectives that honor and glorify God! However, too often it had become another means to draw attention to themselves. The religious leaders heaped up adjectives upon adjectives, not to honor God in prayer but in order for others to notice them and observe how spiritual they were. They knew how to pray, and they wanted everyone else to know how well they could pray!

Another common practice that diminishes the meaning of prayer is using the same words over and over again in such a way that they lose their significance. When:

- we let the words flow from our lips without reflecting on their meanings,
- we say the same prayers in the same way day after day—religiously,
- we reduce prayers to spiritual clichés and phrases without any thoughts behind them …

are *we* perhaps near the threshold of reciting habitual prayers? Are *we* piling up empty phrases by repeating the same words in a thoughtless manner?

What Jesus was trying to get people to see is that when people pray those kinds of prayers—required prayers, regulated prayers, verbatim prayers, lengthy prayers, cliché-ridden prayers—they were saying hollow prayers. They had become empty prayers that had lost their meanings. Instead of prayers being said to connect people with God, their prayers were given to win God's approval. Or even worse, their prayers were said to win the approval and admiration of other people. They were to impress rather than commune with God. And those prayers always failed to fulfill either the heart of the God who heard their prayers or the hearts of the people who were saying the prayers.

It is easy to shake our heads and ask, "Why didn't the people of Jesus's day get it?" We should be careful about passing judgment on them. We too can be just as guilty of repeating the same words and phrases in our prayers day after day. How many times do your prayers begin something like this: "Father in heaven, thank you for the nice day and the blessings you give us. Thank you for my family ..." We often start and end our prayers in much the same way. Not that we don't mean the words we say. Not that it is wrong to say them, but how easy it is to get caught in the rut and routine of using familiar words and phrases when we pray! Isn't it?

How often do our prayers focus on asking God to get us out of the messes and mistakes we have made or to provide the pressing needs or even the wants we have?

Lord!

Help me!

Please help me!

All too often, our prayers become something similar to what we do at a fast-food drive-through. We go to fast-food places to get a quick meal on the run. We place our orders and expect to receive our food in a few minutes. We do much the same with our prayers. We drive through the divine fast-prayer chain, give God our requests, and expect Him to answer in a brief period of time, giving us exactly what we requested. There is one difference, however. No one expects a gourmet meal from a fast-food chain. Yet how often do we expect miraculous answers from fast prayer requests?

- How often do we say our prayers out of obligation and duty instead of the anticipation and privilege of being in the presence of God?
- How often do we use the same trite sayings and clichés in our prayers without thinking about them?
- Or how many times do we pray in a hurried manner?

I heard Morris Venden describing this type of prayer many years ago. "For many people a devotional time is a text or story for the day with the hand on the door knob. Lord, a quick prayer this morning because I just don't have time."

Pastor Louie Giglio made the following transparent and vulnerable observation about his prayers as a teenager in his DVD, *How Great Is Our God!*

"Most of my praying had been made up of advising God, correcting God, suggesting things to God, drawing diagrams for God, reviewing things with God, and counseling God."[17] Through the years, I have observed too many adult prayers doing the same kind of things. In fact, all too often our public prayers turn into sermons aimed not just at people within earshot of the prayer but at God Himself!

You see, the Lord's Prayer was given as a model prayer by Jesus to get us away from all these kinds of prayers—rote, ritualistic, routine, obligatory, lengthy, selfish, self-centered, demanding, and even mindless prayers.

Timidity in Prayer

However, some people have other attitudes toward prayer. Some Christians approach prayer more out of fear or feelings of inadequacy. There are some who avoid praying because they are afraid they are not good enough to pray. Others are concerned that their prayers may be stated inappropriately or they may not be eloquent enough. Or they may feel that prayer to God is private. Throughout my ministry, I have been amazed at how many people have come to me and said in one way or another, "Pastor Gary, I am just not comfortable praying in front of other people." They are afraid they are not going to say the right words or say it in the right way, or that other people will think their prayers aren't good enough.

One of the things I have done in my churches is to begin each board meeting with time in the Word and in prayer. Not just a quick thought or story and a quick prayer to ask God to guide and direct our decisions but a time in the Word and in prayer asking for Him to prepare us to be the

---

[17] Louie Giglio, *How Great Is Our God* (Nashville: Capital Christian Music Group, DVD, 2008).

people of God before we attempt to do the work of God. Then we divide into groups to pray together before we conduct the church business.

Thelma Ritchey was our church treasurer when I began my pastorate at my current church in Corona, CA. Thelma told me, "I can't do it. I can't pray in front of other people. I will just be silent." I told her that was all right, she could pray silently. But I also told her not to worry. No one was going to judge her prayers. No one was concerned if she said the right words. God was concerned that she had the right heart. Over a period of time, I watched and observed her as month by month we prayed together as a church board. One night, Thelma told me, "I can pray now." And she did. Once again, it's not about the right words and/ or the right form. Prayer is about the right heart, the right desire, and the right attitudes. Focusing on God makes prayer meaningful!

A Blueprint for Focused Prayer

That's why Jesus gave us this guideline or outline for us to follow in our prayers. He wants us to see and know that more than anything else prayer provides us with the opportunity to talk to God and have meaningful, intimate interaction with our heavenly Father. And it provides our heavenly Father the occasion to interact and communicate with us!

In the Lord's Prayer, Jesus gave us some key indications of what meaningful prayer is all about. First and foremost, we must have an appropriate focus in our prayers. It should not be a surprise that the focus of our prayer should be on God and not on us. Jesus, before giving the Lord's Prayer, said that when we pray, we should go into our room, shut the door, and pray to our Father in secret. *Prayer is about being with God!*

Jesus then taught us to begin our prayer by addressing God as "Our Father, who is in heaven, holy is your name."

The primary focus of our prayers should be on God. Period!

It is too easy to briefly acknowledge God at the beginning of our prayers and then move on to our list of concerns for our lives ... our requests, our failures, our worries, and our needs.

In order for us to begin our prayers with a focus on who God is, we must spend time in His Word to learn about Him. According to 2 Timothy 3:16–17 (NRSV), the purpose of scripture is to be: "[16]useful for teaching, for reproof, for correction, and for training in righteousness, [17]so that everyone who belongs to God may be proficient, equipped for every good work."

When we read scripture, we need to ask what this passage, what this teaching, this doctrine says about God and His character. How does God want to make these principles or characteristics part of my life and my character? When we ask these questions, we allow the scriptures to inform both the focus of our prayers and those issues that we bring to God in prayer.

When God is the focus of our prayers, our prayers become meaningful. When we pray with a focus on God, we listen to God, we talk to God, and we are with God, who is love. His love is unconditional! We are brought to admit that our love is all too often conditional. When we pray to the omnipotent God, we recognize that we are impotent to become the person He has asked us to be. We are impotent to live the life He has called us to live. And we are incapable to serve others in the ways He asks us to serve. There are no other words to describe it.

In prayer, we are in the presence of the loving, holy, and righteous God. In prayer, we are in the presence of the omnipotent God whose power is directed by His love, justice, and faithfulness. Therefore, He is our God in whom we can entrust our lives. It is this experiential knowledge of the character of God that enables us to be in His presence.

Then we will have meaningful times in prayer that enable us to experience Him in our lives. To trust in Him to transform our lives and recreate us in His image! God created us, redeemed us, and is coming back for us because He wants us to be with Him!

In teaching us the Lord's Prayer, Jesus not only taught us the importance of having the right attitudes and focus, he also taught us a prayer with an important progression or outline to help us maintain a meaningful and effective prayer life. This progression is not merely an order of thoughts or topics. It is a flow in conversation that builds and enhances our relationship with God. The progression of his prayer first recognizes whom we are conversing with and how we relate to Him. When this occurs, it will appropriately shape the ideas, requests, and focus of what we say when we pray and our attitudes toward God and others.

I have summarized the sequence of the Lord's Prayer briefly below. Each successive chapter in the book will deal with each phrase in the progression of the prayer Jesus taught. Thus, we will be enabled to be involved in a process of the worship of God in our prayers as we pray with:

- an awareness of what it means trust Him as Our Father
- a desire to explore what it means to accept the invitation to belong to Him and live in His kingdom and to seek His will
- a concern for the necessities of our physical *and* spiritual lives
- a desire to maintain our relationship with God and our relationships with others through receiving and giving forgiveness
- an acknowledgment of our need for spiritual power to overcome temptations and testing and the evil one
- an attitude of humility and gratitude that gives God the glory for what He accomplishes in our lives

Did you notice the flow of that outline? The prayer begins with a focus on God. *Then, the requests made will be in keeping with who He is and what He does within His will.* The requests we make will demand that we depend and rely on God for the answers. I am not referring to just the answers to our requests. More importantly, I am referring to receiving the answers for how we live our lives before God and how we minister to others in His behalf. If that is done, our prayers will end with humility and a deep sense of gratitude as we give God the credit and honor for what is accomplished in our lives.

This progression is also found in three of the best-known prayers of the Old Testament. These include the prayer of Solomon at the dedication for the temple (2 Chronicles 6:14–14), the prayer of Daniel when he was seeking to understand the dream God had given him in Daniel 8 and his concern for Israel (Daniel 9:14–19), and the prayer of Nehemiah when he was concerned that the Israelites had returned to Jerusalem from captivity and had not rebuilt the temple (Nehemiah 1:5–11). All of them clearly followed the same pathway or flow of phrases Jesus gave us in the Lord's Prayer. They began with a focus on God, and then they made requests that would keep their lives aligned with God's will. They ended their prayers with a concern for God's character to be vindicated.

The Purpose of Prayer

The Lord's Prayer ends with a reminder that whatever takes place in our lives, whatever transformations occur, whatever answers we receive, God receives the honor, the glory, and the praise. He is acknowledged as the ultimate provider of every good and perfect gift. If God is the focus of our prayers, then every single prayer will be meaningful, even those that, at times, do not seem to get any further than our upper lip—as happens with all of us from time to time.

A number of authors have suggested that the first part and the last part of the prayer are focused on God. The petitions in the center of the Lord's Prayer are focused on us. As we will see when we look at each phrase in depth, every single phrase, each petition or request, is ultimately designed to keep our focus on God and away from ourselves! After all, He is the provider of our daily bread. He forgives us and provides us with the desire and ability to forgive others. Only He can deliver us from evil and the evil one (Satan). The Lord's Prayer teaches us that our lives are not compartmentalized into spiritual and secular activities, events, and needs. As followers of Christ, our lives are to be lived in the awareness that whatever we are, have, or do, God is to be the ultimate focus of our lives. Therefore, we depend on Him in every area of our lives, not just in those things that are considered sacred.

Taylor G. Bunch wrote the following powerful observation: "The purpose of prayer is to unite man with God. If it fails here, it has lost its mission."[18] Please note first what he did not say. He did not say that the purpose of prayer is to get answers to our requests. He did not say

---

[18] Taylor G. Bunch, *The Perfect Prayer,* 10.

that the purpose for prayer is to have a good life. He did not say the purpose for prayer is to get us out of the messes we make of our lives or the failures we encounter. The purpose of prayer is to unite us with God. Anything else is secondary! Anything else is a bonus!

That's why Jesus said in his Sermon on the Mount, the sermon in which he first gave this Prayer: "Seek ye first the kingdom of God and His righteousness and everything else will be added unto you" (Matthew 6:33). That is, everything else will be above and beyond what we should expect. That does not mean it will be easy. That does not mean you will always get the answers you thought you would get. It simply means that the most important priority of our lives is to be united to God. We are constantly learning about who He is and what He longs to be to us, to do in us, and to do through us as we serve others.

This will not happen if our prayers begin with us—our needs, our desires, our thoughts, and our opinions. If we do not know God as He is revealed in the Bible as
the God of love,
    the God of mercy,
        the God of compassion,
            the God of faithfulness,
                the God of goodness,
                    the God of righteousness,
                        the God of justice,
                            the God of truth, and, above all,
the God of grace,
you will not be united with God! And your prayers will be misguided and misdirected. You will not be united with God if the God you worship is One who is primarily a judge sitting up in heaven on His throne waiting to see if you measure up before He will claim you as His beloved son or daughter.

That is not the character of God the Bible portrays.

- He is the God who "loved us while we were yet sinners, dead in our trespasses and sins" (Ephesians 2:4–5).
- He is the God who "sent His Son into the world, not to condemn the world, but to save the world through Christ" (John 3:17).

- He is the kind of God who waits patiently for prodigal children to come home. When they do, He throws a party to celebrate and honor them (Luke 15:11–32).
- He is the God who, much like earthly parents, cares for His children at each stage of their development (Ephesians 4:12–16).
- He willingly changes the spiritual diapers of baby Christians. God is waiting for the right moment to teach them the next step in the process of their spiritual maturity. He wants to make them new creatures as He transforms their lives. He does it gladly (1 John 2:1–13)!
- He is the God who stays up all night waiting for spiritual teenagers to come home when they have disobeyed and try to sneak in late. He anxiously awaits their safe return.
- He is the God who anxiously awaits communication from His adult children whose lives have gotten so busy and focused on the responsibilities and cares of life that they have forgotten His love and care for them.
- He is the God who cares and watches out for elderly parents whose best years are behind them and who question their continued purpose and worth in life.
- He is the God who knows us better than we know ourselves and who loves us in spite of all our short-comings, failures, and sins.

His unconditional love is always available, waiting for us to recognize it, accept it, and receive it. That is the kind of God to whom we can pray. Even before we acknowledge a single need we have, a single request we want to make, or a single sin for which we need to ask forgiveness. That is true even when our requests are in behalf of others.

Jesus Lived His Prayer

Yes, Jesus gave us the Lord's Prayer as a pattern of prayer that focuses on God because he wants us to encounter God in prayer and to experience *effective* prayer. There is something amazing and wonderful that helps us to understand how this takes place!

The Lord's Prayer describes the life of Jesus and his ministry!

"Jesus lived this prayer. It was wrought out in his life before it became articulate upon his lips."[19] When I first discovered this connection, I was astonished. It was an "aha" moment! New insights into the meaning and purpose of the Lord's Prayer flooded my mind. The Lord's Prayer is really a revelation of the life of Jesus, his ministry, and his relationship with his Father. *Jesus did not just say His prayers; he lived his prayers!* It wasn't something he merely recited. It wasn't something he said and then went on his way. Jesus lived this prayer. I know you are already thinking ahead. What about the plea for forgiveness? After all, Jesus didn't need forgiveness, since he never sinned. Remember, I said it was about his life *and* his ministry. Jesus's entire ministry was a ministry in which he offered forgiveness. His greatest ministry, his death on the cross, is the provision of forgiveness for sinners. We will see how he did this as we focus on each phrase in the following chapters.

N. T. Wright made the following observation about Jesus and his prayer: "This prayer serves as a lens through which to see Jesus himself and to discover something of what he was about. When Jesus gave his disciples this prayer, he was giving them part of this own breath, his own life, his own prayer. The prayer is actually a distillation of his own sense of vocation. His own understanding of his Father's purposes! If we are to truly enter into it (the Lord's Prayer) and make it our own, it can only be if we first understand how he set about living the kingdom himself."[20]

Some have said that Jesus's prayer life, or rather his life of prayer, impacted both how he lived his life and how he went about ministering to others. Others have indicated how he lived his life and how he conducted his ministry impacted his prayers. These two are not at odds with each other. They are both right. They are looking at opposite sides of the same coin. And that is an important point. Jesus spent his time in ministry between the mountain of solitude and the valley of ministry. Ellen White made the following observation:

[19] Clovis G. Chappell, *Sermons on the Lord's Prayer* (Nashville: Cokesbury Press, 1934), 28.

[20] N.T. Wright, *The Lord and His Prayer* (Grand Rapids: Erdman's Publishing, 1996; and Cincinnati: Forward Movement Publications, 1997), 2.

> All day he (Jesus) toiled, teaching the ignorant, healing the sick, giving sight to the blind, feeding the multitude; and at the eventide or in the early morning, he went away to the sanctuary of the mountains for communion with his Father. Often he passed the entire night in prayer and meditation, returning at daybreak to his work among the people.[21]

So many people think that they cannot witness or serve until they are good enough and/or until they know enough. On the other hand, others think they have all the answers and jump right in. Christian discipleship, to which we are all called, is a life of praying that we might serve and serving that we might know what to ask for in our prayers. It is a life of continual growth and development for us and through us to others.

Jesus's life and his prayer life were merged into one. He lived his life dependent on his Father. His life was lived in a struggle against the temptation to rely on himself and not on his Father. His life was lived in a struggle against sin and its effects on this world. His life was lived under the shadow of suspicion, criticism, and conflict of the deepest, darkest kinds.

The source of his power and strength was in knowing his Father so well, that the words he spoke were the Father's words, the works he did were his Father's works. The character he revealed in his words and actions was the Father's character (John 8:28–30). Therefore, he could say that, "He had come to glorify the Father" (John 17:4).

The results of Jesus glorifying the Father were twofold. First, Jesus was glorified, too. And secondly, we were enabled to have a unity with God and with other believers (John 17:4–5, 22–23)!

Experiences, Reflection, and Application

After preaching the sermon series in our church, I observed how the Lord's Prayer made a difference in my life and the lives of others when they used it as a pattern or outline or model for their prayers.

---

[21] Ellen White, *The Desire of Ages,* 259–260.

- Several members used the Lord's Prayer as a pattern when giving the morning prayer in our worship services.
- Some church leaders followed the pattern when they prayed at the church board meetings and other various church committee meetings.
- One father of three children told me he had begun following the pattern of the Lord's Prayer when he said grace for the family meal. He told me saying grace before meals had more meaning and depth.
- Yet another member told me that she has continued following the pattern Jesus gave in his prayer. It has totally changed the focus, purpose, content, and the spiritual depth of her prayers. And it has added a depth and quality to her walk with God!

Recently I had an experience that opened up another way to apply the Lord's Prayer to my prayer life. When faced with a situation of a person I needed to pray for, I began to pray using the various phrases as my guide on how to pray for them. When I was done, I experienced greater peace than previously. More importantly, I had much more to say to God about them. At the same time, I sensed a deeper appreciation of God's love for them. And I saw them in a different light.

As I have been studying the Lord's Prayer, as I have meditated on the Lord's Prayer, and as I have been modeling my prayer after the Lord's Prayer, the fact that Jesus lived his prayer has become more obvious and essential to me. I have been focusing on the Lord's Prayer as a description and explanation of Jesus and his ministry. At the same time, the relationship of Jesus with his Father has impacted me. Profoundly! I have a greater sense of my Father's love for me! A greater awareness of His compassion and mercy! A greater appreciation of His power at work in my life! My prayer life has been deeply enriched! And my desire and prayer are that you can have the same experience, too!

Having seen the pattern or outline for prayer that Jesus gave in the Lord's Prayer, perhaps it would be helpful if you asked yourself the following questions about your own prayers:

1. To what extent do my prayers consist of meaningful words and thoughts?
2. To what extent do my prayers keep God as the focus?
3. To what extent do my prayers reflect, as Jesus's prayers did, my relationship to and with God?

Applying the Lord's Prayer as a pattern for your prayers will enable you to pray more meaningfully and effectively.

Allow me to make a few suggestions of ways you can apply the Lord's Prayer in your prayers.

- Use the Lord's Prayer as a model to be followed, not a prayer to be recited.
- Recognize you do not need to use it every time you pray. But I have found it most meaningful to apply it in my prayers on a regular, consistent basis. I suggest you try it, too.
- Be willing to try different ways to apply the Lord's Prayer in personal prayers, your public prayers, and in your prayers for others.
- When you recite it verbatim, pause to silently reflect on each phrase.
- Paraphrase each phrase as you pray, using your own words to convey the meaning in your own situation.
- Focus on just one phrase in a prayer.
- Before praying, ask the Holy Spirit to guide you as to which part of the Lord's Prayer you need to prayerfully reflect upon that day.

The above suggestions will become easier to apply as we do an in-depth study of each phrase in the remaining chapters.

Are you willing to apply the principles of the Lord's Prayer? After all, the Master of Prayer taught it to his disciples. And that includes you.

Prayer

Our Father in heaven, I am amazed that a holy and righteous God living in the perfection of His universe waits to hear from me! May the reader of this book, Your child by creation and redemption, be aware of the privilege of praying to our Father in secret and find the reward of being united with You.

May the reader long for Your kingdom of righteousness and peace to be established in their life now as they wait to experience it ultimately and forever when Jesus comes again. May that day be soon!

Father, thank You for the many ways You give meaning to our lives. You sustain us with Your love and with the love of others. You uphold the universe with Your laws of nature. You provide rain and sun to nourish our earth and provide for us. May we never take your generosity and kindnesses for granted!

May each reader receive the forgiveness provided through the sacrifice of Your Son and extend that forgiveness to those who have offended or hurt them. Even when it is costly to them!

Father, may a greater understanding and appreciation for the pattern of the Lord's Prayer lead them to apply it in their prayer life! May they experience Your power in their lives as they seek to overcome sin and are delivered from Satan and his attempts to keep them from following You.

Thank You for Your desire and ability to do exceedingly abundantly above all we could ask or think. We trust in You as the God of all compassion and mercy.

In Jesus's name. Amen.

Chapter 3

The Privilege of Prayer:
An Audience with Our Father, the King

Our Father in heaven, hallowed be your name.
—Matthew 6:9

John Dominic Crossan made a rather astute observation about the Lord's Prayer in his book *The Greatest Prayer*. He said, "It is a strange prayer. Because much of what we believe as Christians and what we hold dear isn't found there."[22] If you think about it, he is right. It doesn't mention the death or the resurrection of Christ. It doesn't mention the Bible. It doesn't mention the church. It doesn't even mention the Holy Spirit, His gifts, or His fruit, which is love. However, what *is* in the Lord's Prayer, what Jesus wanted us to know and understand, is that prayer is designed to bring us into God's presence. Prayer gives us the opportunity to linger in God's presence. He has invited us there so that our relationship with Him might continually deepen and grow. As that relationship grows, what we believe and hold dear will be viewed and reviewed by those things that Jesus taught and how he lived. At the same time, as the song says, "the things of earth grow strangely dim, in the light of his glory and grace."

Could it be that our familiarity with the words of the Lord's Prayer keeps us from understanding the deeper meanings and the purpose of the Lord's Prayer? Could it be that what we include in our prayers keeps

---

[22] John Dominic Crossan, *The Greatest Prayer: Rediscovering the Revolutionary Message of the Lord's Prayer* (New York: Harper One Publishing, 2010), 1.

us from applying what Jesus taught us in his prayer? If this is true, could we be missing out on the benefits and blessings Jesus intended for us to receive from him and the blessings and benefits he wants us to give to others?

Let's begin by taking a deeper look at the first phrase of the Lord's Prayer. Before we do, I invite you to repeat the first phrase,

"Our Father, who is in heaven, hallowed be Your name."

Now take a few minutes to meditate on that phrase. Get a piece of paper and a pen or your computer/tablet and jot down what it means to you *before* you read this chapter. Go ahead and close the book. I'll wait for you …

Welcome back. Let's ask God to prepare us to learn new meanings of this phrase, to gain new insights into the Lord's Prayer.

Prayer

> 🙏 *Our Father in heaven, what a privilege to be in Your presence, to know Your peace and above all to have time with You. May each reader grow in their understanding of this part of the Lord's Prayer.*
>
> *May they be inspired by knowing You and by being known by You. May they recognize the privilege they have of speaking with the Almighty God of the universe, who is also their heavenly Father.*
>
> *In Jesus's name. Amen.*

Now! Are you ready to apply this portion of the prayer in new and meaningful ways to your own prayer life?

Jesus's Life and Ministry Were Expressions of This Phrase

It is so easy to read or recite this phrase quickly without giving it a second thought. After all, it is the way we start our prayer, by addressing the person to whom we are speaking! Our heavenly Father!

It seems so obvious to those of us who have, from the very beginning of our Christian experience, heard God being called our heavenly Father. However, when Jesus spoke of God as Father in the first century, it was at best shocking and scandalous to many people. In fact, when in the context of referring to God as his Father, Jesus said, "Before Abraham was I am," (John 8:58) the Jewish leaders wanted to stone him on the spot for blasphemy. They would have if God had not intervened.

But Jesus revealed his awareness of his relationship with his heavenly Father early on, even before his ministry had begun. Luke 2:41–52 tells us that when Jesus was twelve years old, he went with his parents to attend the Passover. When it was over and his parents were on their way home, they missed him and went back to Jerusalem looking for him. After searching for three days, they found him in a side room involved in deep discussion with the rabbis and teachers. They approached him and said, "Where have you been? Don't you know that we have been looking for you?" The words contained a verbal scolding. And a heartfelt belonging!

Jesus's reply was, "Did you not know that I must be about My Father's business?" (Luke 2:49 NKJV). Most translations say house. It literally reads, "the things of My Father," thus referring to his Father's affairs or business.

Have you ever thought about that phrase, "My Father's business?" We rush past it because to us it means he was to accomplish the mission of the Messiah. He had come to seek and save the lost. Of course, that is true. However, we miss something very special because the culture we live in is very different from that in which Jesus lived. In Palestine, in the first century, as well as in much of the world until the Industrial Revolution and in many third world countries today, the role of father and son had an added dimension we rarely consider.

One of the primary roles of a father was what we would today call a master trainer or mentor. Children, especially sons, were expected to work with their fathers in the family trade or business until their fathers handed their businesses over to them—usually just prior to their death. During their youth and young adult years, they were in the role of an apprentice. They were expected to learn from their father the skills and methods used in their family trade by observing how their fathers worked.

Do you get a sense of the depth of what Jesus was conveying to Joseph, Mary, and to the religious leaders? They were both puzzled and amazed at what he said. He was telling Joseph that while he was currently learning to be a carpenter, it was his heavenly Father's business that would be his vocation. He was telling the religious leaders that when he began his ministry, it would be on the basis of being trained by his heavenly Father and not by them!

Once we acknowledge this aspect of the father/son relationship in that culture, many of Jesus's statements take on another dimension! Some very familiar verses gain additional new meaning, both in terms of what Jesus was saying and how we are to apply it to our lives. With this aspect of the human father/son relationship in mind that was in effect in the first century, let's look at three examples of the relationship Jesus had with his Father. So Jesus said to them:

> Truly, truly, I say to you, the Son can do nothing of his own accord, but only what he sees the Father doing. For whatever the Father does, that the Son does likewise. (John 5:19)

> [25]So they said to him, "Who are you?" Jesus said to them, "Just what I have been telling you from the beginning. [26]I have much to say about you and much to judge, but he who sent me is true, and I declare to the word what I have heard from him." [27]They did not understand that he had been speaking to them about the Father. [28]So Jesus said to them, "When you have lifted up the Son of Man, then you will know that I am he, and that I do nothing on my own authority, but speak just as the Father taught me." (John 8:25–28)

> [49]For I have not spoken on my own authority, but the Father who sent me has himself given me a commandment—what to say and what to speak. [50]And

I know that his commandment is eternal life. What I say, therefore, I say as the Father has told me. (John 12:49–50)

Do you see the father/apprentice relationship Jesus had with the Father? How did he maintain it? The obvious answer is the one we saw back in chapter 1. It was through Jesus's prayer life. Jesus heard his Father speak to him during times of prayer and solitude, which often occurred throughout the night or in the early morning. Jesus was being trained to carry on the work of salvation by his Father in heaven. In other words, throughout Jesus's ministry, he maintained the role of apprentice to his Father through his life of prayer.

Ellen White supports this understanding. Let's look at statements she made about the success of Christ's ministry:

> But the Son of God was surrendered to the Father's will, and dependent upon his power. So utterly was Christ emptied of self that he made no plans for himself. He accepted God's plans for him, and day-by-day the Father unfolded his plans. So should we depend upon God, that our lives may be the simple outworking of his will.[23]

> From hours spent with God he came forth morning by morning, to bring the light of heaven to men. Daily he received a fresh baptism of the Holy Spirit. In the early hours of the new day the Lord awakened him from his slumbers, and his soul and his lips were anointed with grace, that he might impart to others. His words were given him fresh from the heavenly courts, words that he might speak in season to the weary and oppressed.[24]

It is not surprising that Ellen White wrote: "Christ's most favorite

---

[23] Ellen White, *The Desire of Ages,* 208.

[24] Ellen White, *Christ's Object Lessons* (Mountain View, CA: Pacific Press Publishing Association, 1941), 139.

theme was the paternal character and abundant love of God."[25] Perhaps we need to ask the question, why was that his favorite theme?

Because Jesus maintained the role of apprentice throughout his life and ministry, it was only natural that his ministry would be conducted in such a way that his Father would be the theme and focus of his teaching, his miracles and his mission. Throughout his ministry, Jesus would refer to God as his Father—over and over again. This is especially true in the gospels of Luke and John. Notice what Jesus said:

> [21]In that same hour he rejoiced in the Holy Spirit and said, "I thank you, Father, Lord of heaven and earth, that you have hidden these things from the wise and understanding and revealed them to little children; yes, Father, for such was your gracious will. [22]All things have been handed over to me by my Father, and no one knows who the Son is except the Father, or who the Father is except the Son and anyone to whom the Son chooses to reveal him. (Luke 10:21–22)

> All that I have heard from my Father I have made known to you. (John 15:15)

For Jesus to call upon God as Father, to pray to God as Father, and to encourage his followers to call upon God as Father was quite revolutionary, even scandalous. In the Old Testament, God is described as Father just fifteen times. There are places where He is alluded to or referred to indirectly as Father. But only seven times is He directly called Father. In the gospels alone, He is referred to as Father 165 times. According to the *Baker Evangelical Dictionary of the Bible* the word Father "appears on his lips some sixty-five times in the Synoptic Gospels and over one hundred times in John."[26]

---

[25] Ellen White, *Testimonies to Ministers* (Mountain View, CA: Pacific Press Publishing Association, 1962), 192.

[26] Walter A. Elwell, *Baker Evangelical Dictionary of the Bible* (Grand Rapids: Baker Books, a division of Baker Book House Company), http://www.biblestudytools.com/dictionaries/bakers-evangelical-dictionary/fatherhood-of-god.html.

The word for Father that Jesus used in teaching the Lord's Prayer, as found in both Matthew and in Luke, is the Greek word, *pater*. However, Jesus most likely spoke Aramaic. The common word for father in Aramaic is *abba*. Therefore, to understand the relationship Jesus had with God as his father and the relationship he wants us to have with our heavenly Father, it is important we understand how these words, the Aramaic word, *abba*, and the Greek word, *pater*, were used in the time of Christ. According to the *Theological Dictionary of the New Testament*, we discover the following:

> This Aramaic word is a familiar term for "father"; it is also a title for rabbis and a proper name, but is almost never used for God ... Jesus probably used *Abbá* for God whenever the Greek, *patér*, occurs. It denotes childlike intimacy and trust, not disrespect.[27]

The following is added in regards to the meaning of *pater*, especially when it is used as, "our Father in the heavens."

> [T]he (above) formula suggests sovereignty but also implies perfect fatherhood. The use of "your" or "our" denotes the status of sonship.[28]

The "perfect fatherhood" of God would include more than just the intimacy between a small child and his father. It would include the father's authority in the home, his responsibility to provide, protect, guide, and discipline his child. And as we shall see, all of these elements of perfect, divine Fatherhood are elements found in the Lord's Prayer. No wonder Jesus taught us to begin our prayers by addressing God as our Father!

Included in the many times when Jesus referred to God as Father were the instances where Jesus referred to God as the Father of others.

---

[27] Gerhard Kittel and Friedrich, Gerhard, eds., W. Bromily, trans., *Theological Dictionary of the New Testament: Abridged in One Volume* (Grand Rapids: William B. Eerdmans, 2003), s.v. WORD*search* CROSS e-book.

[28] Gerhard Kittel and Friedrich, Gerhard, eds., W. Bromily, trans., *Theological Dictionary of the New Testament: Abridged in One Volume.*

Over twenty times in the gospels he told others that God was their Father. In so doing, Jesus was letting them know that they had the same Father. They belonged to God, just as he did! Therefore, they were also united to one another because they had the same Father. Here are two examples:

> Fear not, little flock, for it is *your Father's* good pleasure to give you the kingdom. (John 12:32)

> Jesus said to her (Mary), "Do not cling to me, for I have not yet ascended to the Father; but go to my brothers and say to them, I am ascending to *my Father and your Father,* to my God and *your God*." (Luke 20:17)

Jesus wanted them and us to see that since we belong to the same Father, we will view and treat one another differently. Especially when we reflect on the character and the characteristics of our Father!

Not only did Jesus live his life and carry out his ministry in the awareness of God as Father, he did so with the awareness that his Father was in heaven. Actually, Jesus used the plural form of heaven—heavens—when he taught the Lord's Prayer. It is interesting what some commentators have to say about heaven. They usually write about trying to establish where the heavens are located. A number of them refer to the fact that the three heavens were mentioned in the Bible. There is the atmospheric heaven or the air that we breathe. There is the heaven we can see with our naked eye, the sun, moon, and stars. And then there was the heaven, the place where God dwells, where his throne is and from where He rules.

Why did he use the plural form? Could it be that Jesus wanted to remind us that God is Spirit, and He is omnipresent? We often think of heaven as a place where God dwells, a specific location that He inhabits. Jesus wants us to be aware when we pray that since God is Spirit He can be found in all three of the heavens: He is beyond us in the divine heaven, above us in what we call outer space, and as near to us as the air we breathe.

Jesus knew the Jews saw God as being so holy, so powerful, so all in all that He was unapproachable. The Jews were afraid to say the name Yahweh, the primary Old Testament name for God, so they called Him Jehovah instead. It was for these reasons that Jesus prayed and taught the disciples to pray to our Father in the heavens, the Father who is as close to us as the air we breathe and as far from us as the heavens where He dwells in His unapproachable holiness—and everything in between!

Jesus recognized that God is both far beyond us and near to us at the same time. His incarnation, his baptism, his transfiguration, and his high priestly prayer in John 17 all reveal this truth. Notice what he said in verse 21: "(I pray) that they may all be one, just as you, Father, are in me, and I in you, that they also may be in us, so that the world may believe that you have sent me" (John 17:21).

Here Jesus stresses the closeness of their relationship, both in terms of the Father's presence in him and the closeness of their thoughts and actions. He is also aware that he had been sent from God, from His dwelling place in heaven.

I believe the order in which Jesus addressed God is also important for us. He addressed God first in terms of intimacy, and after that, he addressed Him in terms of His holy, transcendent attributes. He began with coming to God first as our Father. This emphasized the love, care, and compassion of God. Only then did Jesus acknowledge Him as the God of power, might, and even holiness. To do so in the reverse order would make it more difficult to approach God in a close, familial relationship.

He taught us to pray by addressing God as Father first so that we might know that He is approachable. He longs for us to come to Him. At the same time, we must recognize that our heavenly Father is also the holy, awesome, and powerful God who is over all things. It is only as we approach God with this healthy tension in mind that we are able to pray in the same manner as Jesus prayed.

Finally, Jesus lived in the awareness of his Father's awesome, powerful, and holy character. When Jesus taught us to pray "hallowed or holy is your name," it was not just to remind us that we are praying to a holy God. He wanted to help us keep in mind the character of God in its totality as we pray. In the Bible, very often a person's name stands for his character. God's character is holy. His holiness constrains His omnipotence, omniscience, and omnipresence so that all His actions are righteous and carried out through His unconditional love. Therefore, Jesus was teaching us that our prayers are to be in keeping with the character of God. This will change what we pray for. This will impact how we pray for others. This will affect our lives and the lives of those for whom we pray.

Jesus's life and ministry were filled with the results of living in such a way that God's character was revealed in his life. Just before his crucifixion, in response to Phillip's request for Jesus to show them the Father, Jesus replied, "Whoever has seen me has seen the Father" (John 14:9). In other words, they had the same character! His prayer life had indeed formed and shaped his life and ministry!

Jesus's life and ministry were made possible because he knew to whom he belonged. He had come from God and he was going back to God. The realization that he was going back to his Father defined who he was and what he had accomplished. How he lived and how he ministered!

Now that we have seen how Jesus's life and ministry exemplified the first phrase of the Lord's Prayer, let's take another look at this phrase to see how it can transform our prayers and in so doing transform our lives.

For Us

There are many Christians who still see God as being so holy, so powerful, so all in all that they feel as if they cannot approach Him. As already stated, Jesus prayed and taught the disciples to pray to our Father in the heavens because he wanted the disciples, and that includes us, to know Him. God wants us to know that He is not only approachable, but like our earthly fathers, He is eager to listen to what is going on in our lives and to share with us His desires and plans for us. He wants us to know that we belong to our Father in heaven. He also wants us to remember that our heavenly Father is also the Almighty, holy God of the universe who lives in the heavens. He is the God who created us, who sustains us, who redeemed us, and who will judge us. This almighty, powerful God who inspires awe within us is also our Father who motivates us by His grace to love and worship Him.

Therefore, we come to Him as the Creator who made us. We come not in fear and cowering. We do not approach Him out of a fatalistic, resentful submission to His unbending will. Instead, we come out of love and admiration, out of a hope-filled, thankful submission to His unconditional love and grace.

This is the tension we experience between the transcendence and immanence of God! It is a healthy tension we need to keep in mind when we pray. This paradox between the God who is all-powerful, all-knowing, and beyond our human understanding and the God who is so loving He comes near and even dwells within us through His Spirit. Jesus did not begin by teaching us to pray, "Our God in the heavens who is our Father." Rather he taught us to pray, "Our Father in the heavens." Jesus wanted us to understand the importance of intimacy with God as preceding our awe of God. He wants us to respond to God first out of love, then out of honor, respect, reverence, and wonder. That order is important, because it gives us a healthy balance between intimacy with God and amazement and awe of His Majestic Being. To respond to Him with loving awe gives us the proper perspective as we pray.

That balance is also important because it will impact not only how we view God but also how we introduce Him to others.

It is important because it will impact our view of so many areas of the Christian life, such as answers to our prayers, how we tell others the good news of the gospel, evangelism, and our own view of the judgment and other doctrines we believe and teach. Imbalance on either side distorts God's character and harms our relationship with God and others.

When Jesus taught this prayer, he gave it to us so we can pray in the same way he prayed. He was not teaching it for us to use it as the only form of prayer. He was not teaching it so that we would know the right words or even the exact order to make it possible for God to hear us. After all, there are times when circumstances, emergencies, and dire situations dictate a brief and concise prayer as simple as, "God help me!" Most of the time, learning to pray in the manner Jesus prayed will change our prayers as we pray, our attitudes as we pray, and in the process, it will change *us* to become more like Him! And isn't that what the Christian life is all about?

Let's begin by once again admitting that all too often we begin our prayers by addressing God as our Father, without really thinking too much about what it means. May I suggest to you that if we pray in the manner that Jesus taught us, we would slow down at the beginning of our prayer so that we might ponder and focus on *Whom* we are addressing. *Whom* we are communicating with. To *Whom* we are revealing:
the deepest needs and longings of our hearts and lives,
    the greatest joys and accomplishments of our lives,
        the most perplexing and distressing problems we face,
            those circumstances that create fear within us as well as
                those accomplishments that bring deep satisfaction.

When our prayers begin by focusing on Him, it will affect what we say to Him in the rest of our prayer.

In order to begin with that focus, it is imperative that you first answer the following question: *How easy is it for you to call upon God as your Father?*

For many, that may seem like a silly question. If that is true for you, then you should pause and thank God. But for too many people, it is a question that creates emotions that range from a small dust eddy to a giant tornado in their emotional and spiritual life. If you had a father who loved you, encouraged you, affirmed you, stuck by you, nurtured you, and guided you as you were growing up, then relating to God as Father comes rather easily. However, there are fathers who have made it difficult for their children to think of God as their heavenly Father.

It is so hard to trust in a heavenly Father when your earthly father loved you conditionally! Or he neglected you! Or he abandoned you! Or he beat you! It is so hard to trust in a heavenly Father when your earthly father abused you emotionally and/or physically! Or, as is the case with far too many children, those whose father sexually abused them! Unfortunately, it happens in homes claiming to be Christian homes more often than we want to admit.

During the nearly forty years that I have served as a pastor, I have spoken with far too many men and women whose earthly fathers made it difficult for them to look upon God as a heavenly Father, let alone pray to Him. They find it easier to address Him as God or to pray to Jesus. Or sadly, they have difficulty praying at all. They have a hard time relating to Him intimately. To trust Him totally! To submit their lives to His care and keeping! After all, where was God when all those terrible things were happening to them? (Chapter 6 will deal with this more in depth.)

I find it fascinating that the first time the Bible mentions our relationship with God as a Father is in Exodus. When God tells Moses he must go to Pharaoh to ask him to "Let us (Hebrews) go three days' journey into the wilderness, that they may sacrifice to the Lord our God" (Exodus 4:18). Moses was to tell Pharaoh that Jehovah would send plagues if he did not let the Israelites go. When Pharaoh refused, Moses was to tell them, "Thus says the Lord, Israel is my firstborn son, and I say to you, let my son go that he may serve me" (Exodus 4:22–23).

Pharaoh saw the Israelites as his slaves. God saw Israel as His children, His sons and daughters. Which means God saw Himself as their Father. God wanted Pharaoh to know that the Israelites were not slaves; they were His children. While they had been mistreated by Pharaoh, God was stepping in to free them to His own care and keeping—to teach them to trust in His unconditional love and His ultimate plans and goals for their lives. It was at this point that God revealed Himself as their Father and spoke of them as His sons or children.

Jesus portrayed God as Father, prayed to God as Father, and taught us to do the same. He did this because he wants us to know that God desires us to relate to Him as sons and daughters. He does not want slaves rendering begrudging, fearful, and/or resigned obedience forced upon them by an overbearing taskmaster. He wants us to relate to Him as a compassionate, caring Father who desires to be deeply involved in our lives. He does not even want us to relate to Him as children living in fear but as children living in trust. We need to see Him as our Father, filled with love and compassion and as our Father who cares for us, provides for us, teaches us, guides us, and protects us. Our Father has our best interests on His mind and in His heart. Our Father knows when to allow us to struggle with trials, temptations, and difficulties as we mature spiritually. God as our Father is both the starting point of our prayers *and* the goal of our prayers.

There is a very insightful statement about Jesus and his relationship to his Father and what he wants us to know and apply to our relationship with God, our Father.

> In order to strengthen our confidence in God, Christ teaches us to address Him by a new name, a name entwined with the dearest associations of the human heart. He gives us the privilege of calling the infinite God our Father. This name, spoken to Him and of Him, is a sign of our love and trust toward Him, and a pledge of His regard and relationship to us. Spoken when asking His favor or blessing, it is as music in His ears. That we might not think it presumption to call Him by this name, he has repeated it again and again. He desires us to become familiar with the appellation.[29]

Have you ever thought that when you call upon God as your Father, you are blessing Him? Did you notice Ellen White wrote that when we call God our Father it is "music to His ears"? Just as an earthly parent's heart is moved and filled with love when their child greets them with arms wide open, so is the heart of our heavenly Father. Just as earthly parents' hearts are filled with love and tenderness when their children call to them, especially in those times when they are hurting, so our heavenly Father responds to us. If that is the case, why are we so often hesitant to call Him "Father" when we pray?

Jesus's life and ministry were about knowing he belonged to his heavenly Father. So we are to live our lives trusting that we belong to God. I spent the first half of my Christian life and ministry trying to prove that I belonged to God. I knew in my head that He was my Father. However, I didn't know it in my heart. I knew it intellectually, but I didn't know it experientially. Therefore, my prayer life was a mirror of my "successes or failures" in my struggle with sin and overcoming or in my on-again-off-again devotional life or in what was taking place in my relationships with other people.

However, when I learned that I am the son of the King of the Universe, an abiding, growing, and deepening sense of security, trust, and peace

---

[29] Ellen White, *Christ's Object Lessons,* 141–142.

began to define and affect my walk with God. My relationship with God as my Father became more focused on who He is and His promises of never leaving or forsaking me than on the circumstances of the moment or what was happening in my life. Over and over again, I have tried to convey to others the difference that has made in my relationship with God. Words fail me. Knowing I belong to Him, knowing that He is my heavenly Father, has removed the angst, fear, and lack of peace from my spiritual life. And in talking with others who have come to the same realization, it has done the same for them.

It is imperative that we notice the pronoun Jesus used when he taught us to pray to the Father in heaven. When Jesus taught this prayer, he did not teach us to begin by saying, "My Father," although that would be appropriate. Rather, he taught us to begin by calling upon God as *Our* Father. I believe there are at least two reasons for this. First, if Jesus had said, "My Father," people would think that perhaps Jesus had a corner on that relationship with God. After all, Mary conceived him through the Holy Spirit. Jesus used the word "our" because he wanted us to know that his Father is our Father, too. We belong to God, as His sons and daughters. Yet, we must ever keep in mind that Jesus is the unique, only begotten—that is, one of a kind—Son. He was fully God and fully man.

Second, Jesus taught us to pray to our Father because he wants us to recognize when we pray that we are not alone. We are praying to a Father who has *many* other children. Jesus died to make us part of a family. He did not send His Son to die just so that we could be reconciled to God individually. He sent Jesus to die so that we could and can be reconciled to one another, too. Chapters 2 and 3 of the book of Ephesians reveal that one of the greatest miracles God ever performed was when He created the church. The church is made up of people who, from a human perspective, have no expectation or hope of getting along. Our various cultural, social, educational, and even religious backgrounds all work against our being united as family. Our union with Christ creates unity and fellowship with one another. While there are fights and misunderstandings from time to time, as happens in families, people in the church generally get along together. When we are in Christ, we have a common purpose, a common goal. This is true because we have a common heritage, the heritage of the same Father who created and redeemed us out of love.

An interesting statement reminds us about our relationship with our heavenly Father:

> In calling God our Father we recognize all His children as our brethren. We are all a part of the great web of humanity, all members of one family. In our petitions we are to include our neighbors as well as ourselves. No one prays aright who seeks a blessing for himself only … As children of God you will hold His honor, his character, His family, His work as your highest interest. It will be your joy to recognize and to honor your relationship to your Father and to every member of His family. You will rejoice to any act, however humble, that will tend to His glory or to the well being of your kindred (or family).[30]

Every week when you are worshipping your Father in heaven in church, you are worshipping Him along with others who belong to God. Since that is true, you belong to each other. Think of people in your church, not just those you normally talk with, do things with, and feel comfortable being around. There are also those in the church that can annoy, frustrate, and even irritate you. There isn't a perfect person in the place! Look around and acknowledge that they belong to God, too. We need to think of Christians from other denominations in the same way. After all, Jesus said that he has many sheep in other folds (John 10:10).

When you pray to our Father, you are admitting that you are not alone as a Christian. Not only do you belong to God and to His family, but you also belong to others who are His children. When we pray, "our Father," we are admitting that we need the other members of *our* family to encourage and enable us to live the life God has called us to live. Others also need us for the very same reason.

Praying for others takes on a whole different dimension when we remember that we are praying for others whom God calls His children,

---

[30] Ellen White, *Thoughts from the Mount of Blessing,* 156.

whether they are His children by creation or redemption. When we intercede for others as we pray, we are bringing them into the presence of our heavenly Father. This also gives us a different perspective and enables us to see them through their Father's eyes!

There is yet another facet of this phrase we need to understand—"hallowed be thy name." We don't speak of things as hallowed anymore. It means to be holy. In the original Greek, the word "name" precedes the word "hallowed." The name is the subject. It might be easier to understand it if we were to say, "May your name be hallowed." In other words, it is not to be said in recognition that God is holy; rather it is the expression of a desire that in our prayer, and in our lives, God's holiness will be seen and upheld.

I can't emphasize enough that throughout the Bible when God's name is referred to, it is almost always a reference to who God is in His being. It also refers to what His character is like. In fact, when reading the Bible, I have found it helpful to replace the word *name* with the word *character* in a text when it refers to a member of the Godhead. For example, to pray in the *name* of Jesus is to pray in His character. This means much more than making sure I say Jesus's name at the end of my prayer. It means I am saying my prayer in keeping with what I know to be true about Jesus and asking for that which is consistent with Jesus's character. When reading the third commandment, taking God's name in vain is more than swearing. It is taking the character of God, claiming to be a follower of Christ, and continually living in a way that denies His character. To baptize in the name of the Triune God is to immerse a believer in the very character of God!

The story is told of a college student who was the first person in his family to go to college. One day someone offered this student some illegal drugs, saying, "Go ahead, try it. It'll make you feel good."

To which the student replied, "No."

"Don't be so uptight," said the pusher. "Nobody is going to know that you tried a little dope, got a little high."

"That's not the point," said the student. "The point is that my mother cleaned houses and washed floors to send me to this college. I am here because of her. I am here for her. I wouldn't do anything that might tarnish her sacrifice for me."[31]

This young man was so appreciative of his mother and her love that he could not bear the thought of doing something that would deny her love for him. He would not consider betraying her sacrifice on his behalf.

Putting all three aspects together, Jesus is telling us that in our prayers we are addressing God as our Father, whose love, provision, and protection is like those of our earthly father. We are praying to God, who is our Father in the heavens and who has the divine attributes of omnipresence, faithfulness, omniscience, and omnipotence, among others. We are praying to our Father in heaven who is the holy God. It simply means He always does that which is right. He always does what is just. He always acts in truth and honesty. Since this is true:

- We can come boldly before the throne of grace knowing that we will find acceptance.
- We can come boldly before the throne of grace knowing we will be received in love.
- We can come boldly before the throne of grace because we know He desires the best for us.

This is because He has given us the most stupendous gift of all, His own Son.

Reflection and Application

In the Lord's Prayer, Jesus was not giving us a verbatim form of how to address God. He was giving us three facets of God's character that reveal in broad strokes the character and personality of God. He is a God who wants us to see Him and relate to Him as our divine Father. He is the God who is beyond our understanding. He is the God whose character we can trust and whose character He wants to recreate in us.

---

[31] William H. Willimon and Stanley Hauerwas, *Lord, Teach Us: The Lord's Prayer and the Christian Life,* 48.

He did this in order that we might be mindful and aware of the God we worship and to whom we pray.

As you seek to apply this phrase to your prayers, take time to reflect on the following:

- In your prayers and in your journey with God, do you relate to Him more as the transcendent God or as a personal God who is your Father?
- Do you believe in your heart that you belong to God? Why or why not?
- How does understanding the Father/apprentice role of Jesus's culture impact you as you think of your relationship with God?
- How has your relationship with your earthly father affected your relationship with your heavenly Father?
- How well do you see others as sons and daughters of God who belong to Him?

God deserves our love, honor, respect, adoration, and gratitude. I invite you to begin using the Lord's Prayer as a pattern or model for your personal prayers and reflections.

- Take more time to dwell on what it means that God is *your* Father. Talk with Him about the relationship you have with Him, the relationship you want to have with Him.
- Take time to reflect on the person of God. Talk with God about His divine attributes, those characteristics revealed in the Bible that describe both who He is and how He relates to fallen humanity.
- Listen for Him to reveal the aspects of His character you need to understand, experience, and express to others.

When you do, it will change your desire to pray. It will change how you see yourself. It will change how you see other people and how you pray for them. It will change the requests you make and the focus and content of your prayers. It might be awkward at first, but I guarantee it will do more than change how you pray. It will transform you.

Prayer

Our Father in heaven, what a privilege to be in the presence of the God of the Universe, who is our Father. We are humbled that You call us Your children. We are grateful for Your love, care, concern, and compassion for us. We echo the thoughts of the psalmist: When we think of the heavens, the sun, the moon, and the stars, when we think of the power that sustains and orders the laws of nature, who are we that You should care about or even notice us? But Your Word, which we believe, tells us that we are the apple of Your eye and that You carry us on Your heart. Your Son told us that since You care for the birds and flowers, Your love and care for us are far greater. And we are grateful.

Thank You that You are our rock. You are always dependable and provide a place of shelter and protection. Knowing we can depend on You gives us the security and trust we need.

As we continue to study the Lord's Prayer, may our understanding of its depths give us a desire to pray more, affect our attitude in prayer, and change the purpose and focus of our prayers.

In the character of Jesus. Amen

Chapter 4

The Purpose of Prayer:
Living in the Kingdom

Your kingdom come,
your will be done,
on earth as it is in heaven.
—Matthew 6:10

My wife, Vivian, was born in Canada. At the age of ten, her father, Pastor Lloyd Ellison, accepted a call to become a district pastor in Wisconsin, and the Ellison family moved to the United States. Her parents, her brother, and Vivian all obtained green cards. Vivian grew up in the States, received her education in the United States, got married in the United States to an American, and gave birth to our two children, who are Americans. However, she remained a Canadian.

When our son was in eighth grade, she decided to go with him and his class as a chaperone to Washington, DC. While she was there visiting places like the Capitol, the Space museum, Gettysburg, and the Holocaust Museum to name a few, she began to realize that she had already become an American in her heart. She realized that she needed to act. She came home with a new goal: to become a naturalized citizen of the United States of America and to officially become what she already had become in her heart.

She began the somewhat lengthy process of becoming a naturalized citizen. She made the appropriate application. She took and passed the test for citizenship. She finally received the notice in the mail of the day she would be sworn in as a citizen of the United States. She would have a new allegiance to a new country whose laws and constitution she would be expected to uphold and obey. Then, she stood and took the oath of citizenship, along with hundreds of others. She became an American!

The second phrase or petition in the Lord's Prayer is about recognizing that we must change our spiritual allegiance from one kingdom to another, from one ruler to another, from one purpose in life to another, and from the kingdom of darkness into the kingdom of light. This change of allegiance will result in the transformation of our lives!

Prayer

Our Father, Who surrounds us with Your presence and watches over us with unconditional love, Who is our Creator and the sustainer of our lives, whose power and might uphold the universe and Who is holy, faithful, and true, we invite You to inhabit our lives with Your Spirit. As we consider what it means to belong to Your kingdom and seek to understand and do Your will, speak to each reader in the context of their lives and their relationship with You and with others. In the character of Jesus, I pray. Amen.

Before you read this chapter, please spend a moment in prayer and meditation on the second phrase Jesus taught us to use in our prayers:

> "Your kingdom come, Your will be done,
> on earth as it is in heaven."

Jot down some of the thoughts you have about the meanings and implications of the above phrase before reading any further. What does this phrase mean to you? When you repeat the Lord's Prayer, what are you asking from God when you pray, "Your kingdom come, Your will be done"?

Prior to my study of the Lord's Prayer, I had a shallow understanding of these words. Therefore, I moved quickly past this expression to the next one. Since looking at this phrase in depth, there were times I could not get past it. That still happens! I have to admit that this sentence is often the hardest part of the Lord's Prayer to pray. I often find myself lingering as I talk with God about the implications of His kingdom on my life and as I struggle with yielding to His will. Consequently, I have come to believe that it is this portion in the Lord's Prayer that prepares and enables me to pray humbly, boldly, and effectively all at the same time! And it is this phrase that enables me to pray the rest of the prayer!

There are actually two concepts included in this phrase. The first is the concept of the kingdom. What does it mean when we pray for the kingdom of God to come? What did Jesus have in mind when he taught his disciples to pray, "Your kingdom come"? What is included in the kingdom?

The second is the concept related to the will of God and how we understand and respond to His will. We learn more about the meaning of these two phrases when we observe what Jesus taught about the kingdom of God and God's will and how Jesus applied the concept of the kingdom to his life.

Before we do, however, we need to clarify how we are applying the term. There are times Jesus simply refers to the kingdom. Other times he refers to the kingdom of God, and still other times he refers to the kingdom of heaven. While there are some commentators and scholars who try to differentiate between these terms, it seems to me that they are simply interchangeable and will be treated as such throughout this book.

If we are going to pray for the kingdom to come, we need to know when we can expect it to arrive. If you were to get a phone call from a family member stating they are coming to visit, wouldn't you want to know when they are planning to come? How much more imperative it is for us to know when God's kingdom is coming!

When you think about the kingdom of God, what comes to your mind first? Is your focus about being in God's kingdom in the present or being in God's kingdom in the future? Is His kingdom at this moment, or is it at the brink of eternity? Is it in my life in the here and now, or is it in heaven in the then and forever?

This is not a trick question. It is an extremely, vitally important question we need to answer if we are going to live the life God has called us to live. When Jesus taught us to pray, "Your kingdom come, Your will be done on earth as it is in heaven," Jesus was giving us a key for what it means to be his disciples, to be one of his followers through what he taught and what he did. In life and in his ministry, Jesus revealed key aspects of the kingdom that we must keep in mind and consider when we pray this phrase.

The Kingdom Is Future

Most Christians primarily think of the kingdom of heaven as coming in the future. The parables of Jesus often do clearly teach this aspect of the kingdom. In the parable of the net (Matthew 13:47–51), Jesus said that the kingdom of heaven is like a drag net that would be thrown out and catch all kinds of fish. The fish will be sorted into two categories, the good and the bad, with the good being saved and bad being destroyed. Angels will do this sorting at the close of the age or at the second coming of Christ.

Other passages refer to the future coming of the kingdom. These include the parable of the fig tree (Luke 19:11–28), the promise to the disciples that they will eat and drink at his table in the kingdom (Luke 22:29), and in the teaching given just before his ascension that it is the Father that sets the times that we know to be in the future (Acts 1:3, 6–7).

In Matthew 24, the disciples of Jesus asked him what would be the signs of his coming and the end of the age. The term "end of the age" was synonymous with the messianic kingdom.

Jesus had more to say about the coming kingdom than just giving us signs that would indicate he is coming back. In addition, he also gave some advice about what to do while we wait for that glorious event. It is important to realize that Jesus revealed the signs that would precede his Second Coming at the request of the disciples. Jesus quickly followed that teaching with parables about how we should live while we wait for the Second Coming to take place.

Jesus taught a number of parables immediately after he talked about the signs. They are found at the end of Matthew 24 and the beginning of Matthew 25. They all teach us about the delay in the expected, future coming of the kingdom. These included:

- the parable of the evil servant who mistreats others while waiting for the master to return;
- the parable of the ten virgins, five of whom are unprepared for the delayed arrival of the bridegroom;
- the parable of the talents in which the master expects his servants to use their talents wisely until he returns;
- and the parable of the separating of the sheep and the goats based on how they serve others as God has transformed them into His character of love.

His primary purpose was to let us know what is most important for us to do while we wait for Jesus to return. The final parable of the sheep and the goats gives us the primary purpose Jesus had in mind for all of the parables. That parable includes the teaching that those who live during the delay of the coming of the kingdom will be found caring for and ministering to the needs of others. They will be carrying on Jesus's ministry of compassion. We lose much if we *only* focus on the kingdom of God as a future event without an awareness of the present reality that Jesus lived and taught. When Jesus taught us to pray, "Your kingdom come," he wasn't just pointing forward to the time of the end when the Second Coming will take place. He wasn't teaching us to pray a "get us out of here" prayer so that God will come quickly. He had something more in mind. He had something more pressing that demands our attention. He had something that was the focus of his life and ministry.

The Kingdom Is Present

Even before Jesus was born, God's kingdom was a part of Jesus's life. When the angel Gabriel came to Mary, he told her ...

> [30]"Do not be afraid, Mary, for you have found favor with God. [31]And behold, you will conceive in your womb and bear a son, and you shall call his name Jesus. [32]He

> will be great and will be called the Son of the Most
> High. And the Lord God will give to him the throne of
> his father David, ³³and he will reign over the house of
> Jacob forever, and of his kingdom there will be no end."
> (Luke 1:30–33).

In other words, before Jesus was born, it was prophesied that he would
be a king over a kingdom.

When the magi came to Jerusalem looking for the Jewish Messiah,
what was the question they asked? "Where is he that is born king of the
Jews?" (Matthew 2:2). Notice they did not ask, "Where is he that is to
become king of the Jews some day?" Rather they asked, "Where is he
that *is born* king of the Jews?" They believed this newborn baby to be
royalty. From their perspective, Jesus was born to be King of the Jews,
to establish an earthly kingdom.

Just before Jesus began his ministry, John the Baptist was in the
wilderness proclaiming, "Repent for the kingdom of heaven *is* at hand"
(Matthew 3:1–2). We must keep in mind the context in which John made
this pronouncement. The belief of the Jews in the first century was
that when the Messiah would come, he would restore the kingdom to
Israel. If you talked about the Messiah, you automatically were referring
to the restoration of the Davidic kingdom. They were connected.
The Jews had misunderstood the nature and focus of the Messiah,
expecting him to set up an earthly kingdom. Jesus had to continually
challenge this misunderstanding and try to get them to see that the
messianic kingdom was a spiritual one. In his life and ministry, Jesus
was continually confronted with the misconception of the Messiah to an
earthly kingdom. Even now that misunderstanding is still being made
today! Many Jews and some Christians still expect a Christ (Messiah)
who will set up a kingdom on this earth.

After his baptism, Jesus went out to the wilderness where he was
tempted by Satan. One of the temptations the devil tried to entice him
with was to take the easy way out. He tried to offer Jesus the earthly
kingdoms of the world if he would bypass the cross. Without any pain
or any suffering! All Jesus had to do was to bow down and worship
Satan. It was the temptation to trade the heavenly spiritual kingdom for

the glamour of earthly kingdoms. Praise God! Jesus was not willing to do that! If he had, God's plan for saving humanity from sin would have failed.

In Jesus's ministry, he was continually teaching and preaching about the kingdom of God. Over and over again! The kingdom of God was not just one theme among many. It wasn't one theme he would bring up now and then. The kingdom of God was a theme he taught and exemplified. He did this through his parables, in the performing of his miracles, in the casting out of demons, and in his confrontations with the religious leaders. In the gospels, it is clearly apparent that the kingdom of God was a predominant aspect of his life and ministry.

In his very first sermon, found in Matthew 4:13–17, Jesus began preaching saying, "Repent, for the kingdom of God is at hand." Don't you think Jesus's emphasis on the present aspect of the kingdom of God in his first sermon is noteworthy? Shouldn't we seek to understand the kingdom of God being a present reality?

In Matthew 6:33, we read the very familiar words from the Sermon on the Mount in which Jesus tells his followers that we are to "seek first his kingdom and his righteousness, and all these things will be given to you as well."

How many of Jesus's parables began with the words, "The kingdom of heaven is like …"? Then, he used different metaphors and illustrations to help us understand the kingdom of God. It is like a fishing net, a pearl, a sower, a farmer, a master who leaves and delays coming back, and a banquet to be attended. Each one pointing out different aspects of what it means to belong to God's kingdom—not just in the future but beginning in the here and now!

In Matthew 9:35, it says that wherever Jesus went he proclaimed "the gospel of the kingdom." When he sent his disciples out, it says that he gave them the instructions to proclaim the gospel of the kingdom, that the "kingdom of heaven is near" (Matthew 10:7, NIV).

On the cross, they hung a sign over his side that said, "Jesus of Nazareth, the King of the Jews" (John 19:19).

During the forty days after his resurrection, the Book of Acts tells us that Jesus "went about proclaiming the kingdom of God" (Acts 1:3). The kingdom of God was his last message in his earthly ministry! The very same message he had given at the beginning of his ministry. The very same message he gave throughout his ministry! We dare not miss how important the kingdom of God was to Jesus. It should be important to us as well!

Yet, while focusing on the present aspect of the kingdom of heaven, we must not forget the future aspect of the kingdom! We experience the kingdom in the present while we wait for it in its fullness in the future. Jesus taught us to pray, "Your kingdom come, Your will be done on earth as it is in heaven," with *both* aspects of the kingdom in mind!

The kingdom of God is both present *and* future. Unless we belong to and participate in God's kingdom in the here and now, we will not belong to or participate in God's kingdom when Jesus comes again.

The Kingdom of God Is the Heavenly Realm and Reign of God

By the heavenly realm, I am not primarily talking about the location of the kingdom in heaven. I am talking about the universal nature of the kingdom over which God reigns. It is the awareness that His kingdom is not limited to either time or space. He, as the Creator of the universe, rules over the entire universe. There is not a place that does not, ultimately, come under His rule and reign. He, in His omniscience and wisdom, puts into place physical and spiritual laws for the good of His creation, both animate and inanimate. Therefore, His created beings will only find their purpose and fulfillment as they come under His rule and reign.

The reign and rule of God is one of the most obvious aspects of the kingdom. In reality, there are very few explicit texts that refer to His reign and rule. At the same time, His rule and reign are implicit in almost every mention of the kingdom. It is something that is intrinsically true in all of the proclamations regarding the kingdom.

There are only two places in the gospels where I find explicit references to the reign and rule of God. These are in the Sermon on the Mount and also in the answer Jesus gave to Pilate when he asked Jesus if he was King of the Jews.

In the first instance, after stating the Beatitudes, Jesus told his followers that they were to be "salt and light" in the world. Jesus then announced that He had come as the fulfillment of the law and the prophets, meaning as the fulfillment of the entire revelation of God in the Old Testament.

> [17]"Do not think that I have come to abolish the Law or the Prophets; I have not come to abolish them but to fulfill them. [18]For truly, I say to you, until heaven and earth pass away, not an iota, not a dot, will pass from the Law until all is accomplished. [19]Therefore whoever relaxes one of the least of these commandments and teaches others to do the same will be called least in the kingdom of heaven, but whoever does them and teaches them will be called great in the kingdom of heaven." (Matthew 5:17–19)

Jesus's statement clearly indicates that to belong to the kingdom of heaven is to accept the law and authority of the King of the kingdom.

And in the most explicit statement of all, Jesus said to the scribes and Pharisees in Matthew 7:21, "Not everyone who says to me, 'Lord, Lord,' will enter the kingdom of heaven, but the one who does the will of my Father who is in heaven."

In other words, those who enter the kingdom will be those who accept the will or rule of the King.

The second instance occurred when Jesus stood before Pilate. Pilate asked Him, "Are you the king of the Jews?" (John 18:33). After a bit of banter in which Pilate tried to sidestep Jesus's personal appeal to him, Jesus answered him:

> [36]"My kingdom is not of this world. If my kingdom were of this world, my servants would have been fighting, that I might not be delivered over to the Jews. But my kingdom is not from the world." [37]Then Pilate said to him, "So you are a king?" Jesus answered, "You say that I am a king. For this purpose I was born and for this purpose I have come into the world—to bear witness

to the truth. Everyone who is of the truth listens to my voice." (John 18:36–37)

Here Jesus tells Pilate two things about the kingdom of heaven. First, God's kingdom is not just one more earthly kingdom over which He is seeking to regain control. His kingdom is not just of this world but also the kingdom over which his Father reigns and over which He will reign. It is none other than the kingdom ruled over by the Sovereign of the universe. And second, Jesus came to reveal the true characteristics of the King and how they define the qualities and characteristics of the kingdom. Therefore, the kingdom of heaven as the reign and rule of God undergirds all the other aspects of God's kingdom that Jesus reveals. Without this aspect, the others have no purpose, meaning, or standing.

The Kingdom of Heaven Is a Place of Righteousness

History is filled with example after example of kingdoms whose laws and whose citizens reflected the characters of the kings, queens, or leaders. The Roman Empire itself, ruled by hardened, ruthless, immoral Caesars, became known as the Iron Empire. It was known for both the callousness and immorality of both rulers and the people. The interests and views of Queen Victoria and her husband, Prince Albert, who was her trusted advisor, became the characteristics of the Victorian period. Albert's interest in the advances in industry created by the Industrial Revolution did much to promote England's economic growth and worldwide influence. Queen Victoria's interest in peace, the arts, culture and civility, religion, and her concern for sexual propriety all became defining marks of the Victorian period.

The character of the King of the kingdom is that of holiness and righteousness. Therefore, God's kingdom will be a kingdom of righteousness! The kingdom will be a place where righteousness dwells.

This aspect of the kingdom of God is clearly stated in the Sermon on the Mount in the following verses:

[10]"Blessed are those who are persecuted for righteousness' sake, for theirs is the kingdom of heaven." ... [20]"For I

tell you, unless your righteousness exceeds that of the scribes and Pharisees, you will never enter the kingdom of heaven"; … ³³"But seek first the kingdom of God and his righteousness, and all these things will be added to you." (Matthew 5:10, 20; 6:33)

Jesus covered the same concern about the kingdom of heaven being a kingdom where righteousness dwells when he gave the parable of the two sons responding to the father's request to work in the vineyard.

> ²⁸"What do you think? A man had two sons. And he went to the first and said, 'Son, go and work in the vineyard today.' ²⁹And he answered, 'I will not,' but afterward he changed his mind and went. ³⁰And he went to the other son and said the same. And he answered, 'I go, sir,' but did not go. ³¹Which of the two did the will of his father?" They said, "The first." Jesus said to them, "Truly, I say to you, the tax collectors and the prostitutes go into the kingdom of God before you. ³²For John came to you in the way of righteousness, and you did not believe him, but the tax collectors and the prostitutes believed him. And even when you saw it, you did not afterward change your minds and believe him." (Matthew 21:28–32)

Jesus clearly equates doing the will of the Father with the righteousness that John the Baptist called the Jews to accept.

Perhaps the strongest and most striking depiction of righteousness as an important characteristic or quality of the kingdom is the visual parable Jesus gave in Mark 9:47–48. There he said:

> ⁴⁷"And if your eye causes you to sin, tear it out. It is better for you to enter the kingdom of God with one eye than with two eyes to be thrown into hell, ⁴⁸where 'their worm does not die, and the fire is not quenched.' Everyone will be salted with fire."

The startling word picture is that anything that causes sin (unrighteousness) will not be in the kingdom of heaven but will be destroyed in hell.

However, the righteousness that is required in the kingdom is far more than mere outward compliance. George Eldon Ladd hit the nail on the head in describing this aspect of the righteousness that is required in the kingdom. He wrote the following: "The righteousness which the kingdom of God demands is not concerned alone with outward acts of sin. It goes behind the outward act, behind the deed, to the heart, and deals with what a man is in himself before God. Kingdom righteousness says, What you *are* is more important than what you *do* (Ladd's emphasis). 'Except your righteousness exceeds the righteousness of the Scribes and Pharisees, you will not enter the kingdom of God'. ... The righteousness of God's kingdom is the product of God's reign in the human heart. God must reign in our lives now if we are to enter the kingdom tomorrow."[32]

If the kingdom of heaven is a place where righteousness dwells, where righteous people live, where nothing that causes sin is found, and where the kind of righteousness exceeds outward obedience alone, how can we hope to belong to such a kingdom? The next quality of the kingdom gives us the answer and provides us with hope!

The Kingdom of Heaven Is Made Available through Grace

When we read all that Jesus said about the kingdom of heaven, this aspect is perhaps the most profound. While it is true that Jesus never uses the actual word "grace" to describe the kingdom of God, his teachings make it clear that grace is the basis upon which we enter God's kingdom. Jesus describes grace more than he defines it. He does this in two ways.

First, Jesus called his teaching about the kingdom of heaven the gospel of the kingdom. It is important for us to remember what the word gospel means. It simply means "good news." Throughout the New Testament, the good news is the story of the life, death, resurrection,

---

[32] George Ladd, *The Gospel of the Kingdom* (Grand Rapids: Erdman's Publishing, 1959), 83.

ascension, and intercession of Jesus (Romans 1:1–4; 2 Timothy 1:8–10; 2:8). The gospel includes the message of what Jesus has done. He lived a perfect life. He died and rose again. It includes what He is doing. He intercedes and serves as our High Priest. It includes what He will be doing. He is coming back. The good news is that God is able to restore us to Himself, to save us and to receive us blameless before His throne (Jude 24–25). He does this not because we are worthy but because Jesus is worthy. This is grace!

Unfortunately, we have a far too limited view of grace. Grace is usually thought of in terms of forgiveness or being saved. It is much bigger than just forgiveness. A friend and mentor of mine put it this way. We are saved by grace. We live by grace. We serve or minister to others by grace. And we lead by grace.

My understanding of grace is this:

> Grace is God's power
> at work in my life
> to enable me to live,
> both now and in the future,
> as His son (or daughter) in His kingdom.

Theologically this means we are justified by the power of His grace. We are sanctified by the power of His grace. And we are given gifts by the Holy Spirit to minister or serve and to lead others by the power of His grace.

In Luke's version of the Sermon on the Mount, Jesus said, "Fear not, little flock, for it is your Father's good pleasure to give you the kingdom" (Luke 12:32). The word translated as "good pleasure or good will" has the meaning of earnest desire or purpose. According to the online Theological Dictionary of the New Testament, "the word that is translated 'give' is one that signifies a bestowal or gift from God." Putting the two together, what Jesus was saying is those who belong to the kingdom of heaven receive the kingdom as a gift from God. And that is grace!

Second, in his teaching Jesus used a number of parables to teach us that entrance into the kingdom of heaven is based on grace. The parables of the sower (Matthew 13; Luke 8); the leaven (Matthew 13; Luke 8); the mustard seed (Matthew 13); the king and the debtors (Matthew 18); the invitation to the wedding banquet (Matthew 22; Luke 14); and the parable of the lost sheep, the lost coin, and the lost sons (Luke 15) all teach us that the kingdom is available to all by the grace of God.

Perhaps the clearest, and to some the most disturbing, of all the parables on grace is the parable of the laborers, found in Matthew 20. Here is what Jesus taught:

> [1]"For the kingdom of heaven is like a master of a house who went out early in the morning to hire laborers for his vineyard. [2]After agreeing with the laborers for a denarius a day, he sent them into his vineyard. [3]And going out about the third hour he saw others standing idle in the marketplace, [4]and to them he said, 'You go into the vineyard too, and whatever is right I will give you.' [5]So they went. Going out again about the sixth hour and the ninth hour, he did the same. [6]And about the eleventh hour he went out and found others standing. And he said to them, 'Why do you stand here idle all day?' [7]They said to him, 'Because no one has hired us.' He said to them, 'You go into the vineyard too.' [8]And when evening came, the owner of the vineyard said to his foreman, 'Call the laborers and pay them their wages, beginning with the last, up to the first.' [9]And when those hired about the eleventh hour came, each of them received a denarius. [10]Now when those hired first came, they thought they would receive more, but each of them also received a denarius. [11]And on receiving it they grumbled at the master of the house, [12]saying, 'These last worked only one hour, and you have made them equal to us who have borne the burden of the day and the scorching heat.' [13]But he replied to one of them, 'Friend, I am doing you no wrong. Did you not agree with me for a denarius? [14]Take what belongs to you and go. I choose to give to this last worker as I give to

you. [15]Am I not allowed to do what I choose with what belongs to me? Or do you begrudge my generosity?' [16]So the last will be first, and the first last." (Matthew 20:1–16).

This parable was given after Jesus's encounter with the rich young ruler who wanted to know "what good deed must I do to have eternal life?" (Matthew 19:16). In dialogue with the rich young ruler, Jesus first told him that to inherit eternal life he must keep the commandments. The young man thought he was a good commandment keeper, keeping all ten of them. Jesus, pointing to the second half of the law that refers to how we interact with and care for people, was able to show him that his struggle was with greed, a form of stealing and covetousness. His selfishness, the root of all disobedience to God's law, was exposed.

After Jesus finished dialoging with the young ruler, the young man left feeling he could never do what Jesus asked of him. The disciples were aghast! It was the common belief that wealth was a symbol of God's blessing and approval. If this man wasn't good enough for the kingdom, who would be?

The Jews believed and taught that there were two main criteria for a person to be approved by God as worthy of his kingdom (eternal life). The first criterion was to be a Jew, preferably by birth. Although it was possible for a Gentile to become a member of God's chosen people, they would be considered second-class Jews. The second criterion was to obey the law. The results for people who met the criteria were that they would be blessed by God with children, health, and wealth. Jesus had just shown that outward obedience to the law did not qualify anyone to receive eternal life. As a result, you could not determine who God approved of by the amount of blessings they had or had not received.

So the question of the astonished disciples was, "Who then can be saved?" (verse 25). Jesus responded by saying to Peter and the rest of the disciples, "It's impossible for people {to save themselves}, but it's not impossible for God to save them. Everything is possible for God" (Mark 10:27, God's Word Version).

The disciples struggled with trying to make sense of it all. According to Luke's version, it was Peter who then spoke up and tried to show Jesus how he and the rest of the disciples had succeeded where the rich young ruler had failed. He reminded Jesus how *they* had left behind all *their* possessions and even *their* family relationships to follow Jesus. They had met the criteria by what they had done.

It was after this that Jesus gave the parable of the laborers in the vineyard you just read. Let's review the story. The master of the house hires temporary laborers to work in the vineyard. He agrees to pay those who came early in the morning a day's wage. Another group comes three hours later, and he agrees to give them what is right. Another group comes in six more hours after the first group, and the master makes the same arrangements as he made with the second group. He hires another group nine hours after the first group, agreeing to pay them what is right. Then he finds a group of workers standing idle an hour before quitting time, and he tells them to go to work. When he pays them, he gives them all the same wages—one day's wage or a denarius, beginning with those he had hired at the last hour of the day and then dealing with each group until he pays the group that he had hired at the beginning of the day.

Those who had worked hard all day watched as those who had worked so little, in comparison to themselves, received the full day's wage. They began to get excited as they assumed that they would receive more than had been promised them. However, when the master came to them, he gave them exactly what he had promised them—one denarius. The very same wage as he had given the idlers who had worked only one hour! They were incensed! Quickly they complained. It wasn't fair! They had worked longer and under tougher circumstances, in the heat of the midday sun, than the idlers. They deserved to get more. They had earned it!

Let's be honest. We would be upset, too, wouldn't we? Labor unions, labor laws, or denominational policy would never allow such a thing! We would feel as if we had been treated unfairly. Can you imagine if a new employee came into your workplace and immediately received the same wages and benefits that you received? You would feel mistreated and unvalued. Notice Jesus's response.

In essence he told them, "Did not the money with which I paid everyone belong to me? Did I not pay you the wages that you agreed as being fair? I did not mistreat you. Take your wages and go. Don't I have the right to use my money and pay the workers as I choose?" Then he asked one more question that reveals the main point of the whole parable. "Do you begrudge my generosity?" (verse 15). Literally he asked, "Is your eye evil because I am good?" In essence he was asking them if they were jealous that he was treating the latecomers with such generosity. In other words, do you want to deny my grace as the means by which God's people are saved?

Then Jesus prophesied to his disciples about his crucifixion and resurrection (verses 17–19) because those two events would become the basis of his generosity or his grace. It would be those two experiences that enabled God to make His kingdom available to people who did not deserve to belong to His kingdom, "wherein dwells righteousness." Therefore, entrance into His kingdom is extremely fair. *All* enter because of God's generosity, on account of His grace!

In his parables of the kingdom, Jesus revealed God's grace as the key to entrance into the kingdom.

The Kingdom of Heaven Is Available to All

The next aspect of the kingdom of God was proclaimed by Jesus's example in his interactions with Jews, Samaritans, the unclean, and those considered to be under God's curse. Most Jews would avoid interaction with Samaritans by going around Samaria instead of passing through it on their way to or from Galilee. Jesus went through Samaria because he was not only willing but eager to interact with Samaritans. He desired to proclaim the kingdom of God to all. The gospel stories are filled with such social and spiritual interactions.

Jesus proclaimed that the kingdom is available to all through the miracles he performed. He healed lepers, the blind, the lame, people who could not speak, a woman who had a flow of blood for twelve years, and he cast out demons. He not only healed them, but he touched them! He often touched them *before* he healed them, when they were still unclean and viewed by others as under God's curse! Which meant in the eyes of many—especially the religious leaders—*he* would be considered unclean, too!

Jesus also proclaimed that the kingdom is available to all through his teaching, both in his parables and in straightforward statements. Two parables come to mind. The first is the parable of the net.

> [47]Again, the kingdom of heaven is like a net that was thrown into the sea and gathered fish of every kind. [48]When it was full, men drew it ashore and sat down and sorted the good into containers but threw away the bad. [49]So it will be at the close of the age. The angels will come out and separate the evil from the righteous [50]and throw them into the fiery furnace. In that place there will be weeping and gnashing of teeth. [51]"Have you understood all these things?" They said to him, "Yes." (Matthew 13:47–51)

Now the primary message of the parable is that only God will be able to correctly judge between the righteous and the unrighteous at the end of time. However, there is another facet of the parable. It is found in the type of net used in the story.

There were two kinds of nets used for fishing. One was a small circular net that was cast, usually from the shore. The other was a drag net. It was a much larger net used by fisherman from a boat. It was designed to catch all the fish that it would surround. This would include fish that are good to eat and also junk or trash fish. Thus, the message Jesus gave was that the kingdom is available to all, and it is God who decides the "keepers."

The second parable that Jesus gave to show that the kingdom is to be available to all was the parable of the great banquet. Of course, this should not surprise us, since Luke's gospel is primarily devoted to showing that Jesus ministered to the Gentiles as well as the Jews:

> [15]"When one of those who reclined at table with him heard these things, he said to him, 'Blessed is everyone who will eat bread in the kingdom of God!' [16]But he said to him, "A man once gave a great banquet and invited many. [17]And at the time for the banquet he sent

his servant to say to those who had been invited, 'Come, for everything is now ready.' [18]But they all alike began to make excuses. The first said to him, 'I have bought a field, and I must go out and see it. Please have me excused.' [19]And another said, 'I have bought five yoke of oxen, and I go to examine them. Please have me excused.' [20]And another said, 'I have married a wife, and therefore I cannot come.' [21]So the servant came and reported these things to his master. Then the master of the house became angry and said to his servant, 'Go out quickly to the streets and lanes of the city, and bring in the poor and crippled and blind and lame.' [22]And the servant said, 'Sir, what you commanded has been done, and still there is room.' [23]And the master said to the servant, 'Go out to the highways and hedges and compel people to come in, that my house may be filled. [24]For I tell you, none of those men who were invited shall taste my banquet.'" (Luke 14:15–24)

It was common practice at that time to send out an initial invitation to a banquet or wedding. It was very similar to the current practice today of a "save the date" card. Today cards are sent out months in advance of a regular wedding invitation to ask the recipient to mark the date on their calendar. Those who receive them can count on receiving an invitation. It was the same way in the time of Jesus. Just before the banquet or wedding, there would be a final invitation. In the parable, it was obvious that Jesus was referring to religious leaders, and perhaps even the Jews, as those who were refusing to accept the final invitation. They were too busy with their own activities to accept a gracious invitation! So the king then invited the marginalized of Jewish society: "the poor, the crippled, the blind, and the lame. When there was still room, the king sent his servant *out* to the highways and hedges, ..." that is, beyond the king's area of influence. Of course, Jesus was referring to the Gentiles!

Clearly this parable was told by Jesus to proclaim that the kingdom of heaven is to be made available to all! The parable teaches that the invitation to the kingdom is not reserved exclusively for those who are worthy due to their social class, their race, or even their religious beliefs!

Jesus was also very straightforward in stating that the kingdom of heaven is available to all. He did not want this point to be missed! In Luke 13:28–30, Jesus declared:

"In that place (where the wicked are destroyed) there will be weeping and gnashing of teeth, when you see Abraham and Isaac and Jacob and all the prophets in the kingdom of God but you yourselves cast out. And people will come from east and west, and from north and south, and recline at table in the kingdom of God. And behold, some are last who will be first, and some are first who will be last."

How shocking it must have been for the Jews to hear that descendants of Abraham, Isaac, and Jacob would be among those who were cast out. Even more shocking was the thought that people from outside Israel, *Gentiles* coming from the four corners of the earth, would replace the Jews at the table in the kingdom of God! Jesus could not have been clearer. The religious leaders could not have been more offended.

The Kingdom of Heaven Is Entered through Faith

We have seen that grace is the key provided by God that makes entrance into the kingdom possible. We now will look at what Jesus said and did to teach us that we enter into the kingdom through faith. Grace is what God has done to make us worthy to be citizens of the kingdom. Faith is our response in which we accept the invitation to belong to the kingdom. But what is faith?

For most people, faith has two meanings. It means first and foremost the content of what we believe—that is, our doctrines or intellectual beliefs. Therefore, we tend to judge the quality of a person's faith by *what* they believe. Second, it refers to the amount of our belief—that is, we believe firmly enough for a miracle to take place, that Jesus is coming soon, and so on. This is an element of faith that is part emotional and part volitional. We tend to judge this kind of faith by the results we see or don't see. Did a miracle occur? Are they at peace in the midst of trying circumstances? Are there issues in their lifestyle? But is that the basic meaning of faith?

Faith is a gift of the Holy Spirit (1 Corinthians 12:9). How is faith given as a gift? Initially, it comes through God's self-revelation to a rebellious humanity. God revealed Himself to Moses as "... ⁶a God merciful and gracious, slow to anger, and abounding in steadfast love and faithfulness, ⁷keeping steadfast love for thousands, forgiving iniquity and transgression and sin, but who will by no means clear the guilty ..." (Exodus 34:6–7). The gift of faith is nothing less than God revealing Himself to us!

For many Christians, their understanding of faith often centers on us, what *we* believe. How strong is *our* faith? I would like to suggest that a better way to understand faith is by replacing the word faith with the word trust. It is a good translation of the Greek word *pistis*, the common word for faith in the New Testament. Trust centers on whom or what we trust in—the object of our trust. Our trust in God first affects our relationship with Him. It then redefines our interaction with others and our actions toward them in ways that are consistent with the characteristics of the kingdom of God.

A couple that was new to our church came to my office. They have a precious baby girl they wanted to dedicate to God. Since I had not met the family, I was getting acquainted with Dad, Mom, and their baby. I talked with them about the dedication service and gathered information about the family for the church records. This enabled me to get to know them and their needs and gave them the chance to get to know me. At the end of our visit, I reached out my hands to the girl, hoping to hold her. She came to me briefly, took one look at this stranger, and gave a soft cry for her mommy. I didn't take it personally. After all, she didn't know me. She had no reason to *trust* me. You cannot trust someone you do not know!

At the same time, trust does not deny belief. We trust people we believe have the qualities or characteristics that make them trustworthy. We can believe in them! I suggest *what* we believe about God, which is informed by the doctrines we believe, is what makes Him *trustworthy.* Our trust in who He is, in what He is, and in what He does enables us to entrust our lives to Him.

It is possible to believe without trusting, but you cannot trust without believing! The devil and his angels believe in God and tremble. But they do not trust in God. I trust in the Second Coming because I believe Jesus's promise when he said, "I will come again." We enter the kingdom of God through faith because we trust that God has provided a way for us to enter it.

The connection between the kingdom of heaven and faith is more often implied by Jesus rather than plainly stated. The clearest connection is found in the Sermon on the Mount in both Matthew and Luke. Let's look at Matthew.

> [27]And which of you by being anxious can add a single hour to his span of life? [28]And why are you anxious about clothing? Consider the lilies of the field, how they grow: they neither toil nor spin, [29]yet I tell you, even Solomon in all his glory was not arrayed like one of these. [30]But if God so clothes the grass of the field, which today is alive and tomorrow is thrown into the oven, will he not much more clothe you, O you of little faith? [31]Therefore do not be anxious, saying, "What shall we eat?" or "What shall we drink?" or "What shall we wear?" [32]For the Gentiles seek after all these things, and your heavenly Father knows that you need them all. [33]But seek first the kingdom of God and his righteousness, and all these things will be added to you. (Matthew 6:27–33)

Jesus spoke about not being anxious as to whether or not God will supply our physical needs. Being anxious shows a lack of faith, a lack of trust in the God who created us and who sustains our lives. Then he pointed out that we are to seek first the kingdom of God. The implication is that just as we can trust in God for our physical needs, so we can trust Him for our spiritual needs. When we trust Him as we seek His kingdom of righteousness, the material needs become secondary.

In a number of the kingdom parables found in Matthew 13, Jesus implied the role of faith or trust in receiving the kingdom of heaven. When he stated that the kingdom of heaven is like a sower who sowed seed, the sower trusts that in sowing the seed it would grow. In the parable of the mustard seed, it is implied that it takes faith or trust to believe that such a tiny seed could become a tree large enough for birds to perch in its branches. Later he would use the mustard seed as the symbol of faith for performing miracles (see Luke 17:5–60). In the parable of the leaven, the woman had faith in a small measure of leaven to be able to make her dough rise and transform it into bread.

Immediately following the Transfiguration, Jesus came down from the mount with Peter, James, and John to find that the crowd was in turmoil. The rest of the disciples were in a quandary. They had tried to cast a demon out of a boy but had failed (Matthew 17 and Mark 9). After an interchange with the boy's father, Jesus rebuked the disciples for their lack of faith. Then he cast the demon out.

It was in this context that the following interchange between the disciples and Jesus occurred:

> [1]At that time the disciples came to Jesus, saying, "Who is the greatest in the kingdom of heaven?" [2]And calling to him a child, he put him in the midst of them [3]and said, "Truly, I say to you, unless you turn and become like children, you will never enter the kingdom of heaven. [4]Whoever humbles himself like this child is the greatest in the kingdom of heaven. (Matthew 18:1–4)

Jesus did not specify what characteristics children have that are essential to enter into the kingdom of heaven. Commentaries and sermons have suggested several qualities children often possess. These include such things as innocence, their humility, and their ability to forgive without holding grudges. Perhaps their greatest qualifications are their sense of belonging and the trust they have in their parents to love and to care for them.

Ellen White, in commenting on the above passage, made the following observations: "To be great in God's kingdom is to be a little child in humility, in simplicity of faith, and in the purity of love. All pride must perish, all jealousy be overcome, all ambition for supremacy be given up, and the meekness and trust of the child be encouraged. All such will find Christ their rock of defense, their strong tower. In Him they may trust implicitly, and He will never fail them."[33] Notice she uses the words faith and trust interchangeably.

It is often said that we are saved by grace through faith. Sometimes that seems a bit confusing, as if there are two causes for our salvation, God's part in giving grace and mine in accepting it. Perhaps the following will help you see the difference. I am going to write it in the first person for clarification purposes. You can read it in the first person and apply it to yourself.

> *God's grace opens the gates to allow entrance*
> *into the kingdom of heaven. I enter the kingdom*
> *when I trust that the gate is open for me!*

Perhaps the most direct connection between the kingdom of heaven and entering it by faith was made in the question Jesus asked after giving the parable of the persistent widow in Luke 18:8, "Nevertheless, when the Son of Man comes (in his kingdom), will he find faith on earth?" In other words, when Jesus comes in the clouds, he will be looking for those who have faith (trust) that he will gather *them* into his kingdom of glory.

It is quite certain that only those who enter His kingdom in the here and now of their lives will enter His kingdom in the here and hereafter of the kingdom of glory. It requires faith or trust in the King to enter His kingdom, both while on this earth and when He comes again.

Love Is the Compelling Motivation of the Kingdom

The next aspect of the kingdom of heaven that we need to understand is the King of the kingdom and the citizens of the kingdom—His children—are motivated and act out of love. Admittedly there are not many direct statements concerning this characteristic of the kingdom. However, love as the motivation of the kingdom is observed in numerous examples from Jesus's life and ministry.

The first instance where we will observe how Jesus reveals love

---

[33] Ellen White, *Testimonies for the Church, v. 5,* (Mountain View, CA: Pacific Press Publishing, 1948), 130.

as the motivational power of the kingdom was at the conclusion of his discussion with his disciples about the signs of his coming (in his kingdom) and the end of the world. As part of his answer to that question, Jesus gave the parabolic metaphor of the sheep and the goats (Matthew 25:31–40). Jesus told his disciples that the sheep and the goats would be separated on the basis of whether or not they had acted with compassion and kindness. This was seen in the fact that those who were saved fed the hungry, clothed the naked, visited the imprisoned, and gave water to the thirsty. Acts of unconditional love!

At first glance, this seems to be at odds with the fact that the kingdom is made available on the basis of God's grace and not on the basis of our works or behavior. However, there is a subtle aspect of the story that maintains grace as the method by which God's kingdom is made available. The sheep did not know that they were acting out of compassion and love! Their outward acts were done, not to earn favor with God but to express what was in their hearts. The principles of God's kingdom had been internalized in their hearts and minds. They were exhibiting the qualities of the kingdom of heaven because they were *already* living in the kingdom. Their acts of compassion and love were not done to show God how good they were. They were done because they had been inwardly transformed. They were living out the character of Christ. God first overtly declared His character to Moses when He revealed Himself on Mount Sinai as the God of compassion (Exodus 34:6–7). Throughout the gospel record, the ministry of Jesus was referred to as being motivated by compassion, enacted out of love. Therefore, acts of compassion were performed by those who had already entered the kingdom of heaven by grace.

A second instance in the gospels where love was revealed as an aspect of the kingdom is found in Mark 12:28–34, when Jesus was asked the question, "Which is the most important commandment?" Jesus responded by giving his abridged but comprehensive form of the Ten Commandments:

> "[29]The most important (commandment) is, 'Hear, O Israel: The Lord our God, the Lord is one. [30]And you shall love the Lord your God with all your heart and

with all your soul and with all your mind and with all your strength.' (Verses 29–30)

He didn't stop there; He went on to say:

"The second is this: 'You shall love your neighbor as yourself.' There is no other commandment greater than these." (Verse 31)

And the scribe said to him,

[32]"You are right, Teacher. You have truly said that he is one, and there is no other besides him. [33]And to love him with all the heart and with all the understanding and with all the strength, and to love one's neighbor as oneself, is much more than all whole burnt offerings and sacrifices." [34]And when Jesus saw that he answered wisely, he said to him, "You are not far from the kingdom of God." (Verses 32–34)

And after that, no one dared to ask him any more questions.

How could Jesus say that the scribe was not *far* from the kingdom? Hadn't the scribe nailed the truth on the head when he said that love is the fulfilling of the law? That sounds like being in the kingdom, doesn't it? Herein lies the difference. The scribe only understood it theoretically in his mind. He had not embraced it in the actions of his heart and life. He had come to Jesus not to learn from him but to entrap him. Hardly an act of love! He was among those who had questioned Jesus's authority to perform miracles out of compassion. He was among those who had tried to humiliate Jesus on the political/spiritual question of the appropriateness of paying taxes to Caesar. Not only would this be seen as an act of treason, it would also be viewed as a denial of Jesus as the Messiah. For it was believed the Messiah would come to deliver them from the rule and demands of Rome. By paying taxes to Caesar, Jesus would be seen as impotent against Rome. The religious leader was among those who had tried to ensnare him on a thorny theological question of the resurrection and marriage in heaven. The scribe, or teacher of the law, had come to try to get Jesus to deny the law of Moses, which would automatically rule him out for messianic consideration.

It was for this reason Jesus said that although the man understood that love for God and love of man are the fulfilling of all the commandments, he lacked the experience of loving God and man. If he had, he would have recognized Jesus as the Messiah. It is not a coincidence that in the very next incident Mark writes about, Jesus identifies himself as the Messiah. The religious leader's refusal to acknowledge Jesus as the Messiah, the one sent from God, revealed his lack of love for God.

Then Jesus went on to warn those who were there against the teachers of the law. They used rabbinic rules to get around God's law of love in order to foreclose on widows' houses. At the same time they would try to impress others with their outward piety. This revealed their lack of love for their neighbor.

Luke tells us that at that point Jesus looked up and saw the rich ostentatiously depositing their offerings to be seen by others. They wanted others to see how much God had blessed them. Then Jesus pointed out a poor widow giving her last penny. Her poverty would have been evidence of her disfavor with God. He commended her for her heartfelt gift. The widow's sacrificial gift was thus standing in stark contrast to the refusal of the teacher of the law to give from his heart.

The Kingdom of Heaven Involves Sacrifice

When it comes to sacrifice, most people think of it as giving up something we value now for the good of someone else or for something else even better that we might receive at a later time. When it comes to following Christ, people are often called upon or urged to sacrifice or surrender their sins, habits, or cherished possessions in order to truly follow him. Another type of sacrifice that people make in order to follow Christ is when a person gives up a cherished dream, position, personal happiness, or fame for the kingdom of God. The following story is a good example.

Gladys Aylward was a missionary to China during and after World War II.

Gladys' ministry in China was chronicled in the film, *The Inn of the Sixth Happiness.* She suffered terribly during her journey across the mountains of China in order to bring 100 orphans to safety in Sian in Shensi. Ranging in age from 4 to 15 years old, these children were saved because of Gladys' faithful obedience to God.

But it was not without cost.

When Gladys arrived in Sian with the children, she was gravely ill and almost delirious. She suffered internal injuries from a beating by the Japanese invaders in the mission compound at Tsechow. In addition, she suffered from relapsing fever, typhus, pneumonia, malnutrition, shock and fatigue.

Through her ordeal Gladys learned more about obedience to Christ. She learned to choose Christ over anything else life had to offer—so much so that when the man she loved, Colonel Linnan, came to visit her in Sian as she was recovering and asked her to marry him she declined. In her heart she knew she could not marry him and continue the work God had for her among the children of China. Out of her obedience to God, she said goodbye to Linnan at the train station. And they never met again. Gladys continued serving God faithfully in China and England until her death in 1970.[34]

No one can deny that Gladys made huge sacrifices to follow her conviction that God had called her to serve Him in China. She knowingly made a sacrifice that included her health, her personal happiness, and even the possibility of giving her life for the cause of Christ. Many, if not most, people would question her decision to give up so much for the kingdom of God!

It is without question that Jesus taught us that to belong to the kingdom of heaven will require sacrifice! Jesus made that link

---

[34] Gary Preston, *Character Forged from Conflict* (Minneapolis: Bethany House Publishers, 1996), 43–44.

repeatedly both by the example of his life and in his teaching. There are two direct statements made by Jesus in the gospels linking sacrifice and the kingdom of heaven.

The first is found in Matthew 8:19–20. A scribe came to Jesus and said to him, [19]"I will follow you wherever you go." Jesus replied, [20]"Foxes have holes, and birds of the air have nests, but the Son of Man has nowhere to lay his head."

The second one is found in Mark 8:36. Jesus, in speaking about the cost of discipleship, of belonging to the kingdom, said, "For what does it profit a man to gain the whole world and forfeit his soul?" In this teaching, Jesus wants us to realize the sacrifice of worldly gain for eternal life is well worth it! Of course, Jesus himself gave us the ultimate example of sacrifice at Calvary.

In these texts as well as in others, Jesus makes it clear that to belong to God, to follow Jesus and to be a part of the kingdom of heaven includes real sacrifices that may come in a variety of ways. It may include such things as financial sacrifice, or foregoing career advancement, or putting the things of the kingdom ahead of even family relationships. We have already looked at such a passage when we looked at the kingdom of God and grace.

> [28]And Peter said, "See, we have left our homes and followed you." [29]And he said to them, "Truly, I say to you, there is no one who has left house or wife or brothers or parents or children, for the sake of the kingdom of God, [30]who will not receive many times more in this time, and in the age to come eternal life." (Luke 18:28–30)

The context of this interaction between Peter and Christ is important. After the rich young ruler was unwilling to sell his possessions and give it to the poor, the question had been asked, "Who then can be saved?" Jesus had responded that only God has the ability or the possibility of providing salvation or entrance into the kingdom. After telling the story of the laborers in the vineyard, he announced the ultimate sacrifice is that he would give his life to save those who could not save themselves.

The primary claim of Jesus was that it would be his sacrifice that would not only bring us near the kingdom but also bring us into the kingdom. At the same time, we cannot deny what he told Peter in Luke 18. When we make sacrifices for the sake of the kingdom, we will receive rewards far superior to the sacrifices we have made!

We must be careful to make a crucial distinction between the sacrifices we make of our time, possessions, relationships, and/or our reputations and the true Sacrifice of our very selves that make the variety of sacrifices possible and meaningful![35] Jesus had this distinction in mind when He made the following declaration:

> [24]Then Jesus told his disciples, "If anyone would come after me, let him deny himself and take up his cross and follow me. [25]For whoever would save his life will lose it, but whoever loses his life for my sake will find it. [26]For what will it profit a man if he gains the whole world and forfeits his soul? Or what shall a man give in return for his soul? [27]For the Son of Man is going to come with his angels in the glory of his Father, and then he will repay each person according to what he has done. [28]Truly, I say to you, there are some standing here who will not taste death until they see the Son of Man coming in his kingdom." (Matthew 16:24–28)

Certainly Jesus is referring to the fact that following him may indeed lead to the sacrifice of a person's physical life. He is telling his disciples, and that includes us, that they may indeed be called to face a martyr's death. It is important to notice the way in which he said it. Before he talks about giving one's life, Jesus said there is to be a denying of one's self (Verse 24). Taking up our cross involves the same struggle that Jesus faced in taking up his cross. It was the battle that Jesus won in Gethsemane when he said, not once but three times, "Nevertheless, not my will, but Yours be done."

---

[35] For the purposes of clarity in this section, the word sacrifice written with a small *s* will refer to things we give up. The word Sacrifice written with a capital *S* will refer to submitting our wills or selfish ego to Christ.

The Sacrifice that we are required to make for the kingdom of heaven is the yielding of our will to the will of God. Those who belong to the kingdom of God will make the same Sacrifice that the apostle Paul made. While he made many sacrifices in his life, including even being martyred, he described his ultimate Sacrifice when he said:

> "I have been crucified with Christ. It is no longer I who live, but Christ who lives in me…" (Galatians 2:20)

That Sacrifice is the greatest Sacrifice. All other sacrifices pale in comparison!

David Livingston, famous missionary to Africa, made the following observation about the sacrifices people thought he had made and how he viewed them.

> People talk of the sacrifice I have made in spending so much of my life in Africa. Can that be called a sacrifice which is simply acknowledging a great debt we owe to our God, which we can never repay? Is that a sacrifice which brings its own reward in healthful activity, the consciousness of doing good, peace of mind, and a bright hope of a glorious destiny? It is emphatically no sacrifice. Rather it is a privilege. Anxiety, sickness, suffering, danger, foregoing the common conveniences of this life—these may make us pause, and cause the spirit to waver, and the soul to sink; but let this only be for a moment. All these are nothing compared with the glory which shall later be revealed in and through us. I never made a sacrifice. Of this we ought not to talk, when we remember the great sacrifice which He made who left his Father's throne on high to give Himself for us.[36]

---

[36] David Livingstone, Speech to students at Cambridge University (December 4, 1857), http://davidlivingstone2013.blogspot.com/2012/05/cambridge-speech-of-december-1857.html.

Obviously, while not stating it specifically, Livingstone understood that the Sacrifice we make is dependent on the *Sacrifice* the triune God made to make the kingdom of God available to us.

The Kingdom of Heaven Includes God's Power over Evil

At the very outset of his ministry, Jesus linked the message and coming of the kingdom with God's power over evil and the power of evil as evidenced by suffering due to sickness, disease, and demon possession. Nothing could be plainer than the introduction of Jesus's ministry with the following words from Matthew:

> And he went throughout all Galilee, teaching in their synagogues and proclaiming the gospel of the kingdom and healing every disease and every affliction among the people. (Matthew 4:23)

Later, when the scribes and Pharisees were trying to discount his ministry and cast doubt on Jesus as the Messiah, they ascribed his miracles to the power of Satan. Notice how Jesus countered their attacks:

> "But if it is by the Spirit of God that I cast out demons, then the kingdom of God has come upon you." (Matthew 12:28)

We tend to attribute this aspect of the kingdom to the power of Jesus's divinity. We have already seen that Jesus lived his life and performed his ministry only as he depended on his Father and the Holy Spirit. That power over evil—in the form of suffering through sickness, injury, disease, and demonic activity—is available to Christ's disciples, and that includes you and me. This is evident from the fact that when Jesus sent his disciples out to minister to people, he gave them the following command: "And he called the twelve together and gave them power and authority over all demons and to cure disease and he sent them out to proclaim the kingdom of God and to heal" (Luke 9:1–2). And miracles were performed through them.

I can already hear the question being asked, "If that is true, then why don't we see more miracles?" Some will say it is because we lack the faith for miracles to occur. Others will counter that we simply live in a society far too self-dependent on what modern medicine can do and too sophisticated to believe in demonic activity and possession. Others are simply waiting for a future time just before Jesus comes when the Holy Spirit will be poured out again in the Later Rain experience. And the rest may have different reasons for the lack of miracles.

I have to admit that I wish miracles that proclaim the kingdom of heaven and God's power over every kind of suffering, sickness, disease, injury, death, emotional illnesses, addictions, and demon possession would be experienced more often. However, I can honestly say that I have witnessed miracles. I have had the privilege of participating in anointing services where God's power was evident in the service and afterwards. In just about every instance, there has been some kind of miracle. There have been some miracles over physical sufferings, some over emotional suffering, and some over addictions. In almost every situation, a spiritual healing occurred. A greater trust in God's providence! A firmer faith in ultimate healing! A deeper awareness of God's love, grace, and presence!

I will never forget when Doris, a member of the church where I served as pastor in Escondido, California, came to me asking for anointing. She was going deaf. She had gone to the world-famous House Ear Clinic in Los Angeles, California, and had been told that nothing could be done at that time.

A couple of days after the subsequent anointing service, she came by the church for something. Her face was beaming. I asked her if her hearing was better. "No," she said through her smile. "But praise God! He has taken my fear of going deaf away." The emotional healing enabled her to live with her physical limitation. That in turn affected her spiritually as she trusted God's providence and presence in her life.

Finally, we are reminded of what Jesus told his disciples in John 14:12–14:

> [12]"Truly, truly, I say to you, whoever believes in me will also do the works (miracles) that I do; and greater works than these will he do, because I am going to the Father.

¹³Whatever you ask in my name (character), this I will do, that the Father may be glorified in the Son. ¹⁴If you ask me for anything in my name (character), I will do it."

The Kingdom of Heaven Expects Growth

While grace may be the most profound aspect of the kingdom of heaven, the growth of the kingdom is referred to the most times. It is the reason why Jesus came, to seek and to save the lost. It was the reason for his ministry and his sacrifice. It is seen in his expanding the kingdom to include Samaritans, women, the lame, and the pronouncement that he came to free the captives of every result of sin and to make them part of his kingdom.

The kingdom includes growth, both in quality and in quantity. The parables of the kingdom in Matthew 13 clearly reveal both types of growth. The parable that highlights this aspect of the kingdom best is the parable of the talents in Matthew 25:14–30.

¹⁴For it [the kingdom of heaven, see verse 1] will be like a man going on a journey, who called his servants and entrusted to them his property. ¹⁵To one he gave five talents, to another two, to another one, to each according to his ability. Then he went away. ¹⁶He who had received the five talents went at once and traded with them, and he made five talents more. ¹⁷So also he who had the two talents made two talents more. ¹⁸But he who had received the one talent went and dug in the ground and hid his master's money. ¹⁹Now after a long time the master of those servants came and settled accounts with them. ²⁰And he who had received the five talents came forward, bringing five talents more, saying, "Master, you delivered to me five talents; here I have made five talents more." ²¹His master said to him, "Well done, good and faithful servant. You have been faithful over a little; I will set you over much. Enter into the joy of your master." ²²And he also who had the two talents came forward, saying,

"Master, you delivered to me two talents; here I have made two talents more." ²³His master said to him, "Well done, good and faithful servant. You have been faithful over a little; I will set you over much. Enter into the joy of your master." ²⁴He also who had received the one talent came forward, saying, "Master, I knew you to be a hard man, reaping where you did not sow, and gathering where you scattered no seed, ²⁵so I was afraid, and I went and hid your talent in the ground. Here you have what is yours." ²⁶But his master answered him, "You wicked and slothful servant! You knew that I reap where I have not sown and gather where I scattered no seed? ²⁷Then you ought to have invested my money with the bankers, and at my coming I should have received what was my own with interest. ²⁸So take the talent from him and give it to him who has the ten talents. ²⁹For to everyone who has will more be given, and he will have an abundance. But from the one who has not, even what he has will be taken away. ³⁰And cast the worthless servant into the outer darkness. In that place there will be weeping and gnashing of teeth."

Nothing could be clearer! The parable uses servants entrusted with their master's money as a symbol of the gifts and abilities God entrusts to His people. The Master rightly expected them to do more than just play it safe by hiding it away. He expected them to handle his money as he himself would. He would look for opportunities for his money to increase in value in order to enlarge his fortune. God rightly expects you and me to use our talents to enlarge His kingdom.

We do this in two ways. First, we use our talents or gifts to introduce people to the King and His kingdom. Those who trust the King will be added to the kingdom. Second, we enlarge the kingdom when we are continuously being transformed into the character of Christ.

To fail to have a part in enlarging the kingdom is to attempt to hoard the privileges of the kingdom. Hoarding in this life results in clutter and robs the hoarder of their joy. They are miserable! Spiritual hoarding results in cluttering up our spiritual lives as well. It robs us of joy. It leaves us miserable! The kingdom exists for the purpose of offering life to all. Those who belong to the kingdom will seek to enlist new citizens for the kingdom! This is done by introducing them to the King of the kingdom.

The Kingdom of Heaven Is Jesus

This aspect of the kingdom is both an explanation and a summary of all other aspects of the kingdom.

- It is the secret of the kingdom.
- It is the heart of the kingdom.
- It is the life of the kingdom.
- It is the soul of the kingdom!

We first observe the fact that the kingdom is Jesus when Gabriel told Mary that she was going to conceive the Messiah through the power of the Holy Spirit. Notice what Gabriel told her:

> [31]"And behold, you will conceive in your womb and bear a son, and you shall call his name Jesus. [32]He will be great and will be called the Son of the Most High. And the Lord God will give to him the throne of his father David, [33]and he will reign over the house of Jacob forever, and of his kingdom there will be no end." (Luke 1:31–33)

John the Baptist was the first to announce that with the coming of Jesus, his ministry of the kingdom of heaven had also arrived. Notice what he said as he announced his mission to prepare the way for the Lord, the Messiah: "Repent, for the kingdom of heaven is at hand" (Matthew 3:2). John could not be referring to himself, for he would later say, "He must increase and I must decrease" (John 3:30).

For John, the kingdom of heaven was present because Jesus, the Messiah, was present.

When Jesus began his ministry, he repeated John's statement and applied it to himself. "From that time Jesus began to preach, saying, "Repent, for the kingdom of heaven is at hand" (Matthew 4:17).

Toward the end of his ministry, Jesus restated this claim in an exchange with the Pharisees:

> Being asked by the Pharisees when the kingdom of God would come, he answered them, "The kingdom of God is not coming with signs to be observed, nor will they say, 'Look, here it is!' or 'There!' for behold, the kingdom of God is in the midst of you." (Luke 17:20)

This connection between the presence of Jesus and the kingdom was not lost on the apostle Paul. He was in prison awaiting his own martyrdom for proclaiming the gospel of the crucified and risen Savior. Furthermore, Luke records that:

> He (Paul) lived there two whole years at his own expense, and welcomed all who came to him, proclaiming the kingdom of God and teaching about the Lord Jesus Christ with all boldness and without hindrance. (Acts 28:30)

For Paul proclaiming the kingdom and teaching about Jesus went hand in hand. Throughout his writings, he made reference that his ministry was only the fulfilling of God's will and call on his life.

God's Will

To pray for God's kingdom to come, with all its various aspects, is not enough. We must pray that it comes according to God's will. This was true of Jesus's life and ministry.

> [37]"All that the Father gives me will come to me, and whoever comes to me I will never cast out. [38]For I have come down from heaven, not to do my own will but the will of him who sent me. [39]And this is the will of him who sent me, that I should lose nothing of all that he has

given me, but raise it up on the last day. [40]For this is the
will of my Father, that everyone who looks on the Son
and believes in him should have eternal life, and I will
raise him up on the last day." (John 6:37–40)

In Gethsemane when Jesus prayed, "Not my will, but Your will
be done," he was praying about the kingdom, for there is a connection
between the kingdom of God and the will of God as we will soon
discover.

With that in mind, let's look again at the phrase in the Lord's Prayer:

"Your kingdom come, Your will be done ..."

When Jesus used this phrase, he was telling us that we need to make the
kingdom of God a priority in our lives and in our prayers, too.

The Connection between
the Kingdom of God and God's Will

There is an important literary technique that is often used in the
Bible called parallelism. It is frequently used in the psalms as well as
other places. In parallelism, one concept or thought is given, and then
it is restated, using different words in the next phrase or sentence.
Sometimes it is an exact parallelism, sometimes it is a contrasting
parallelism, and other times it is adding additional meaning to the first
thought. The phrase "Your will be done" is given to help us understand
what takes place in our lives when we live as citizens of the kingdom
of heaven. What Jesus was saying is that when we request for God's
kingdom to come, we are at the same time submitting to His will for
our lives. And that will is to be done, not just one day in heaven, but
it is to be done today, on earth, as we are preparing to live in eternity.

I am not saying that we should not pray for the Second Coming to
take place soon. I am not saying that we should not desire to be taken
out of this sinful, sorrowful, sad world. Of course, we should and do
pray for the Second Coming! That is part of the kingdom message. But
it is not the primary message.

As stated above, the primary message is understood when we realize that we experience the kingdom of God the moment we invite Jesus Christ into our lives. This happens when we ask Jesus to be the ruler of our minds, hearts, and bodies. It happens the moment we decide to change our allegiance from the kingdom of this earth to the kingdom of heaven. Moffat translated the beginning of the petition this way: "Thy Reign begin."

I would like to suggest to you that in living the Christian life, we too change allegiance. To change our allegiance from one kingdom to another:

- from an earthly kingdom to a heavenly kingdom
- from the kingdom of darkness to a kingdom of Light
- from a kingdom of sorrow and pain to a kingdom of joy and holy delight

Even though it is easy to see the contrast in those phrases, it doesn't mean that we give up our allegiance to the kingdom of darkness and sorrow easily or all at once. We still have sinful natures. We still sin. Our struggle against selfishness and sin is continuous. That is why Paul wrote about moral and relational issues in the last part of the majority of his letters. In these sections, Paul gave instructions about how we are to live as Christians in a world hostile to God and His ways. He warned against continuing to practice sinful behaviors. And he exhorted Christians to live godly lives. But we must keep in mind these were written *after* he had written about what it means to *be* saved!

Colossians has an enlightening perspective. Speaking of God the Father, it says:

> [13]... he has rescued us from the dominion of darkness and brought us into the kingdom of the Son he loves, [14]in whom we have redemption, the forgiveness of sins. (Colossians 1:13–14 NIV)

First, who is the subject of the verse? It is God, the Father. He is the One who delivered us from the domain of darkness to the kingdom of his beloved Son. We can't deliver ourselves! We *can* accept His offer. We can't make it happen or accomplish it ourselves. We can ask for the transfer; we can agree we need to be transferred. God, through Christ, made it possible for us to be transferred to His kingdom.

The word domain in the English Standard Version is referring to the rule of Satan. The Revised Standard Version and New International Version translate it as dominion. This translation conveys the idea that to be in the domain of darkness is not just to be under the authority and laws of a kingdom or its realm. Those who live in the dominion of darkness are under the power or dictates of the ruler of the kingdom of darkness. The New King James Version and the majority of the dynamic translations use the word power of darkness in place of word domain. Those who belong to the kingdom of darkness are under the power and authority of Satan as the one who rules over them and dominates them.

The transfer of allegiance Paul describes is awesome news! This is the greatest escape that has ever been made! Can you imagine what it would be like living in a country under the rule of an evil, maniacal dictator? Living in fear! Knowing that with one false move you could end up in jail or die! Then, can you imagine waking up to discover that you are now living in a free society whose ruler governs with justice and equality? Whose rules are intended to be the very best for everyone in society. Who acts out of unselfish compassion and genuine care and concern for all. Yet that kind of transfer would be *nothing* in comparison to being transferred from the domination of the realm of darkness to the kingdom of the beloved Son of God, wherein dwells absolute righteousness!

Notice, Paul did not say that God *will* deliver and transfer us from the kingdom of darkness. He says that He *has* transferred us. In God's mind, we were transferred into His kingdom when Jesus died on that cross and rose again. It was his death and resurrection that delivered us from sin and provides us with his righteousness.

Why is this so important? Unless we experience the deliverance from the kingdom of darkness and are transferred into the kingdom of heaven *here on earth*, we won't be part of the kingdom of God when the Second Coming takes place.

Taylor Bunch made an astute observation about this when he wrote:

The kingdom of grace is set up in this rebel world to win subjects for the kingdom of glory that will bear rule over the Redeemed world. The kingdom of heaven is therefore present and future—present in its spiritual aspect and future in its manifestations of power and glory.[37]

He reminds us that it is a kingdom based on grace. He also reminds us that being part of God's kingdom is a journey we are on, and the journey takes us to heaven.

How do we know if we belong to the kingdom of God? I think the identifying marks of the kingdom can help us. The apostle Paul gives us characteristics of those who belong to God's kingdom in Romans.

The kingdom of heaven is not a matter of eating and drinking, but of righteousness, peace and joy in the Holy Spirit. (Romans 14:17)

People on opposite sides of dietary issues often take this passage out of context. On the one hand, there are people who say this passage says it doesn't matter what we eat or drink anymore. On the other hand, there are those who insist that God's righteousness includes what we eat and drink.

In context, Paul tells us in the book of Romans that the righteousness we need comes to us through faith and faith alone. We are justified by faith and made right in God's sight.

- It becomes real in our lives as we are sanctified by God's Spirit.
- It becomes real in our lives as we are changed and transformed by God's grace.
- It becomes real when we are transformed by the renewing of our minds.

That kind of righteousness will affect what we do and what we eat and drink. However, our primary focus will not be on what we do. It will

---

[37] Taylor G. Bunch, *The Perfect Prayer,* 4.

be on what God has done. It will not continually be on what others do or don't do. It will be on what God has done and is doing. It will not be on our behaviors but on His character. For it is in beholding we become changed (2 Corinthians 3:18).

When our trust and focus are on Him, we experience righteousness, peace, and joy in our lives, which are the characteristics of His kingdom. The gifts of His righteousness, peace, and joy remain in spite of circumstances! These characteristics show through in spite of trials, troubles, and even persecution. A righteousness that remains when everything is going wrong! Not because the believer is so strong but because God's kingdom of grace is so pervasive. It provides a peace that remains in the face of chaos. This does not occur because the believer has the ability to remain calm but because the peace God gives passes understanding. It creates a joy that defies description. Not because the believer has experienced events that give joy but because God's eternal promises provide a confident hope that makes joy insurmountable!

What are we asking for when we have this perspective as we pray for God's kingdom to come? We are asking that others will be able to observe these kingdom characteristics in our lives. This will enable our verbal witness to be supported by the louder witness of our lives. It is not just by doing what is right and avoiding what is wrong but in the living out of the principles of God's kingdom, His righteousness.

However, it is imperative that we understand what it means to do the will of God. We must ask the question, "What is involved in allowing God's will to be done in our lives?" The most obvious answer and the one that usually comes to mind at first is that God's will is revealed in the Ten Commandments. An example of one text that conveys this message is Psalm 40:8. It says: "I delight to do your will, O my God; your law is within my heart."

- The Ten Commandments must be written on our hearts. They can only be kept by God's grace and by His power.
- The Ten Commandments are for our benefit and protection.

- The Ten Commandments are a revelation of His character of love.
- The Ten Commandments are summarized by Jesus as having love for God and love for others in our lives.

What is God's will? Jesus gave us the following commandment that we should obey: "This is my commandment, that you should love one another just as I have loved you" (John 15:12). Unconditionally! Nonjudgmentally! Seeing others through the eyes and heart of God! Seeing others for what they can become through His grace. This requires the grace of God and the transforming power of the Holy Spirit!

What is God's will? It is "every word that proceeds from the mouth of God" (Matthew 4:4), which we learn by studying his Word.

What is God's will? It is for us to follow the promptings of the Holy Spirit as we live day by day by His power (Ephesians 1:11–14).

All of these can be summed up in God's one great desire. It is the desire that Peter declared when he wrote that the Lord "is not willing that any should perish but that all shall come to repentance" (2 Peter 3:9 NKJV). God's plan of salvation was to send Jesus to seek and save the lost. This is the ultimate revelation of His will! This is the umbrella under which the previous aspects of doing the will of God must be understood and applied.

Jesus understood and applied the will of God to the plan of salvation through his life, ministry, and teachings. This came as somewhat of a surprise to me. For the predominant example in the gospel accounts of Jesus doing the will of God was in the fulfillment of his ministry to others!

Jesus first alluded to this at the age of twelve. Jesus had gone with his parents to the Passover in Jerusalem. After it was over, Joseph and Mary discovered Jesus was not with the company making their way home. Three days later, they found him teaching the teachers in the temple. Mary and Joseph chided him for causing them to worry. Jesus defended his actions of staying behind in Jerusalem to his parents with the words, "I must be about my Father's business (what He wants me to do)" (Luke 2:49 NKJV).

The second time Jesus referred to ministering to others as doing the will of God was when his brothers and mother came to discourage and dissuade him from continuing his ministry in Galilee (Matthew 12:46–50). They were upset that his ministry was not being accepted by the religious leaders in Jerusalem. Jesus was told that they were outside, wishing to speak to him. He replied, "Who is my mother, and who are my brothers?" And stretching out his hand toward his disciples, he said, "Here are my mother and my brothers! For whoever does the will of my Father in heaven is my brother and sister and mother" (Matthew 12:48–50). His response reveals his decision to let nothing stand in the way of fulfilling his Father's will of making his ministry the top priority of his life.

On two other occasions, people tried to stop Jesus from fulfilling God's will for his life by discrediting and halting his ministry. The first was when the disciples tried to get him to interrupt his ministry to the woman at the well and eat the food they had brought him. What was his response? "My food is to the will of Him who sent me and to accomplish His work" (John 4:34).

The second occasion was after he had healed the man at the pool of Bethsaida on the Sabbath. The religious leaders tried to use that event to damage the reputation of Jesus as the promised Messiah. They had charged him with working on the Sabbath by healing. Furthermore, Jesus had encouraged the man he had healed to work by carrying his mat. Jesus's defense for healing the man on Sabbath and for his ministry and his mission as Messiah was:

> "I can do nothing on my own. As I hear, I judge, and my
> judgment is just, because I seek not my own will but the
> will of him who sent me." (John 5:30)

Jesus refused to allow anyone to disrupt his ministry to others and thus keep him from fulfilling the will of his Father.

Jesus's most explicit statement connecting the concept of doing the will of God with ministering to others was made in the context of the miracle of the feeding of the five thousand. Notice what he said:

[38]"For I have come down from heaven, not to do my own will but the will of him who sent me. [39]And this is the will of him who sent me, that I should lose nothing of all that he has given me, but raise it up on the last day. [40]For this is the will of my Father, that everyone who looks on the Son and believes in him should have eternal life, and I will raise him up on the last day." (John 6:38–40)

Jesus said that the will of the Father was for everyone to look on the Son. And those who would look and believe would have eternal life. He wanted his disciples and the crowd to know that in doing his ministry he was fulfilling the will of the Father to give people the opportunity to believe in Jesus and be saved.

Jesus's greatest example of submitting to the Father's will, of making the kingdom of God available to all, took place in Gethsemane. He wrestled against the temptation to abandon his ministry to save a lost world. Not once but three times he prayed, "Not my will but Yours be done." Jesus's struggle to fulfill the will of God speaks volumes to us. First, it reminds us that doing God's will in ministry may not be expedient, pleasant, or even accepted by those we serve. In fact, it may be painful and lead to being rejected, ridiculed, and yes, even persecuted. Yet we should continue to do so. Second, it again highlights that God's ultimate will is the saving of the lost.

While it is true that God does not ask us to be the savior, it is His desire or will for us to enter into ministry to others in order that the sacrifice of Jesus and God's plan of salvation will be available to those within our sphere of influence. We begin to fulfill His will when we talk or pray about how we can minister to others in the day-to-day living of our lives. I must confess that until studying God's will in this context, I had not considered this fact that when I pray the Lord's Prayer and say,

"Your will be done on earth as it is in heaven ..."

it includes praying about daily involvement in ministry. For pastors, that means it must be on a personal as well as on a professional level.

As disciples of Christ, it means all of us are to pray about our daily involvements in ministry!

Applying to Our Prayer Life

How does all of this affect our prayers? As we pray with the Lord's Prayer in our minds, we will find ourselves talking with God about four ongoing responses we need to make in our relationship with Him.

1. We Admit Our Ongoing Needs

We must admit that we live in a rebellious world that is against God and the things of God. This world doesn't like God's kingdom very much. It makes fun of God's kingdom with its characteristics and principles. In fact, Jesus said that the world hates him and his followers.

> "If the world hates you, know that it has hated me before it hated you. If you were of the world, the world would love you as its own; but because you are not of the world, but I chose you out of the world, therefore the world hates you." (John 15:18–19)

The world seeks to distract us from the characteristics of the kingdom through diversions, majoring in minors, or short-term counterfeits for righteousness, peace, and joy. We need to admit that as residents of this world we have fallen and sinful natures that are attracted to this world that is under the dominion of Satan. Therefore, we need God's ongoing deliverance if we are to belong to His kingdom.

When we say, "Your kingdom come, Your will be done," we must admit that it is not easy to adequately verbalize those words. When we pray those words sincerely with our heart, we recognize that we must give up control of our lives and our desires to God. To be more specific:

- To pray those words means that we recognize that there are areas of our lives that still do not reflect the characteristics of His kingdom.

• To pray these words means that all too often we are like a toddler, tenaciously holding on to a shiny dime while he is being offered a ten-dollar bill.

It is only when we make the admission that it is difficult to pray for His kingdom to come that we are able to take the next step.

2. We Commit Our Lives

We must commit our lives to the King of the kingdom. This may mean coming to recognize you are incapable of living the life God requires in your own strength and power. If this is the case, you too must be willing to allow Him to be your sovereign and rule over your life as you live in the realm where righteousness dwells. You must be willing to say to God: "I am tired of being the ruler in my own life. All too often I mess up. I want You to be the sovereign who rules over my life and transforms me into a new creation."

Or, it may mean coming to the point where you simply recognize the love, mercy, compassion, and grace of God. You are enthralled with His invitation to come and experience what it means to be His son or daughter. You are willing to pray, "Lord, be merciful to me, a sinner."

Are you willing to give God everything, including your life? Have you committed your mind, your body, your emotions, your relationships, your attitudes, and your will to Him?

Of course, this need to surrender our wills requires a daily, ongoing, lifelong submission to the King of Kings and Lord of Lords.

3. We Submit to God's Will

When we begin our prayers talking with God about our lives in His kingdom and about doing His will, our prayer life becomes transformed. It affects how we pray! It changes what we talk about with God! And it will impact why we pray!

We should not think for a moment that this will happen quickly or come easily. In fact, it will require intentionality and even a struggle.

It is easy to say we submit our lives to God. It is more difficult to truly and totally submit our lives to Him. It is easy to say, "Your will

111

be done"; it's another thing to allow Him to be in control of our wills and our lives.

Those who have been involved in the training of children will remember times when you told them to do something, *or else!* And their response was a sigh and a soft-spoken, resigned, "Okay, I'll do it." But their hearts were not in it. It is a *resigned* submission.

There is another kind of submission that is a *defiant* submission. An angry, resentful, punctuated, "Okay, I'll do it!" God is not looking for either a resigned or a defiant submission to His will. He is looking for a third kind of submission. *Willing* submission!

Willing submission is the same kind of submission Jesus revealed when he prayed in Gethsemane, "Not my will, but yours be done." Jesus had to say this prayer at least three times as he struggled with submitting to his Father's will.

The apostle Paul revealed how we should submit to God's will:

> "I have been crucified with Christ. It is no longer I who
> live, but Christ who lives in me. And the life I now live
> in the flesh I live by faith in the Son of God, who loved
> me and gave himself for me." (Galatians 2:20)

Perhaps Ellen White had this verse in mind when she wrote the following words about the importance and effect of yielding our wills to God: "As the will of man co-operates with the will of God, it becomes omnipotent. Whatever is to be done at His command may be accomplished in His strength. All His biddings are enablings."[38] At first glance, that sounds almost blasphemous and offensive to say that our wills may become omnipotent or all powerful. But notice, that *only* takes place as we cooperate with God's desires for us. And that cooperation involves submitting our wills to Him! It is also quite close to what Paul had in mind when he wrote the Philippians the following promise:

> "I can do *all things* through Christ who strengthens me."
> (Philippians 4:13 NKJ, emphasis mine)

---

[38] Ellen White, *Christ's Object Lessons,* 333.

Jesus added the phrase "on earth as it is in heaven" to let us know that God is not looking for mere outward obedience. He is looking for an obedience that comes from transformed minds and hearts. So often on earth we go kicking and screaming to do God's will, as the prophet Jonah did when God commanded him to go to Ninevah (see the book of Jonah). Or we feel like we have to get a stronger backbone to enable us to do God's will. Or we think we need better skills, just like Moses (Exodus 3:10–12; 4:1, 10–ff) or Jeremiah (Jeremiah 1:4–6). What God wants more than anything is to transform us by writing His law on our hearts so that when we obey, we do so willingly. We truly obey when we learn to be. Then out of being flows our doing.

When Jesus said, "May Your will be done on earth as it is in heaven," he was reminding us that angels willingly, adoringly, lovingly, worshipfully, thankfully appear before God's throne to do His bidding in ministering to others. It is not *mere* obedience; it is *pure* obedience. It is the kind of religious experience that leads to joining with God in seeking and saving the lost!

If we are honest about our prayers and the prayers we have heard from others, we will admit that we spend little time in prayer seeking—and struggling—with God's will for us in our ministry to others.

What a challenge it is for us when we recognize we can pray to have the same desire, priority, and commitment to minister to others as Jesus did! Praying "Your will be done" is an acknowledgment that God's will for us is that we are to live in the kingdom now as we prepare to live in the kingdom forever. And it is an acknowledgment that we are to minister or serve others as we seek ways to invite them into God's kingdom, too.

4. We Wait ...

We pray these words or similar words with an awareness that we are waiting for the blessed hope and the glorious appearing of our Lord and Savior Jesus Christ.

We pray for Jesus to come soon, don't we? We long for Jesus to come soon. We are tired of a world filled with violence, sickness, heartache, death, destruction, and pain, aren't we? We are tired of watching the news and seeing pictures of children starving, families losing their homes, victims dying, and people being used and abused by others. I think we are tired of wars and rumors of wars and politicians who promise the moon and deliver a flashlight or no light at all!

The truth is …

- Unless I pray meaningfully to experience God's will in my life today, it doesn't make much sense to pray for Him to come soon.
- Unless I am willing to evaluate my own life and my need for the transforming power of the Spirit, it doesn't make sense to pray for the blessed hope and the glorious appearing of Jesus.
- Unless I am willing to pray and commit my life to Christ and ask him to be Lord of my life, it doesn't make sense to cry out, "Even so, come, Lord Jesus!"

It makes no sense to pray for Jesus to come again in the clouds unless I am willing to pray, "I submit my will to Your will. I want Your will to be done in my life here on earth."

I stated the above in the first person because we can only apply the request for God's will to be done in our own lives and not in the lives of others. We can only submit to His will for ourselves.

It is for this reason that we need to take this phrase in the Lord's Prayer far more seriously than we have in the past. I am convinced that this phrase is the hardest one to say while being honest with ourselves and with God. *Only* when we pray, "Your kingdom come, Your will be done," are we prepared to apply the rest of the Lord's Prayer when we pray. Some may be concerned that applying the pattern of the Lord's Prayer to our personal prayers may become repetitious. Ironically, when we use the Lord's Prayer as an outline or a model on a regular basis, our prayers will be less repetitious and more meaningful.

Implementation

So how do we pray for God's kingdom to come and His will to be done in the here and now of our lives? Allow me to share the following suggestions.

1. Keep a list of the various aspects of the kingdom of God in front of you when you pray. A list with a brief explanation is in an appendix that you can copy.

2. Be honest with yourself in order that you can be honest with God. This may not be as easy as it sounds. For "The heart is deceitful above all things, and desperately sick; who can understand it?" (Jeremiah 17:9). It is being honest with ourselves and God that makes praying this phrase both difficult and effective in allowing God to transform us.

3. Reflect and talk with God about those aspects of His kingdom that His Spirit has placed in your life and that you have been able to share with others. Pause silently and allow Him to communicate with you through His still, small voice, impressions, or reminders of recent interactions in your life with others. Ask Him to bring to your mind their unsolicited affirmations of the aspects of God's kingdom in your life. Thank Him for the Spirit's work in your life.

4. Ask God to reveal to you those aspects of His kingdom that He desires you to experience more fully at the present time. Look up or think about passages of scripture you know that deal with that aspect. Talk with God about those passages. Again, pause silently ...

5. Ask God to reveal any aspects of His kingdom that you are lacking or need to understand more fully. Again, look up passages that deal with that aspect and pause silently ...

6. Ask God to enable you to share the aspects of His kingdom that will connect with the needs of those within your sphere of influence. Again, pause silently ...

7. Ask God to enable you to honestly assess your willingness and ability to yield or submit your life to Him that day and in each situation, temptation, and or relationship of your life.

When we take this phrase seriously and pray it from our hearts, the following happen:

- The characteristics of God's kingdom will be seen in our lives in more powerful ways in our day-to-day living.
- The kingdom characteristics of righteousness, joy, and peace will be seen in deeper and richer ways in our lives. Even if we don't see them ourselves, others will recognize them and see God at work in us.
- The characteristics of God's kingdom will be seen in spite of our failures and the sins we commit and as we confess them to God.
- The characteristics of God's kingdom will be seen in spite of circumstances, in spite of trials, in spite of temptations.

When the characteristics of the kingdom become more and more evident in our lives, they will be evidence that *He* is in our lives.

> Those who take Christ at his word, and surrender their souls to his keeping, their lives to his ordering, will find peace and quietude … As through Jesus we enter into rest, heaven begins here. We respond to his invitation, "Come, learn of Me," and in thus in coming to Jesus we begin life eternal. Heaven is a ceaseless approaching to God through Christ. The longer we are in the heaven of bliss, the more and still more of glory will be opened to us; and the more we know of God, the more intense will be our happiness. As we walk with Jesus in this life, we may be filled with his love, satisfied with his presence. All that human nature can bear we may receive here.[39]

The rest of the Lord's Prayer demands that we pray this phrase first. As we shall see, only as we live in God's kingdom, while submitting to His will, can we learn to depend on Him for the needs of our lives, experience forgiveness for ourselves as we offer it to others, and be delivered from the evil one. May our daily prayers include this phrase!

---

[39] Ellen White, *The Desire of Ages,* 332–333.

Prayer

Our Father in heaven, we come to You as Your children. May we do so with the full realization of Your holiness and a greater understanding and appreciation of Your character of compassion, mercy, love, justice, kindness, goodness, and faithfulness. Father, teach us what it means to live in Your kingdom now as we prepare to live with You in Your kingdom forever. May your Holy Spirit convince us of our need to honestly evaluate the extent to which our lives reflect the characteristics of Your kingdom.

Forgive us for the times we stubbornly cling to our own ways and fail to yield to Your will for our lives. Remind us that it is Your will for us to be engaged in ministry to others. Open our eyes to see the opportunities we have to exhibit the characteristics of Your kingdom that we might extend compelling invitations for others to enter Your kingdom, too. May the prayer of Jesus, "Your will be done," become part and parcel of our every prayer.

In Jesus's name. Amen.

Chapter 5

The Provisions of Prayer:
The Needs of Life

Give us this day our daily bread.
—Matthew 6:11

The book *Coffee Break with God* (David Cook) reports that "A person conducted an informal survey about the prayers of people in his church found that most people pray one of two types of prayers. The first is an SOS—not only 'Save Our Souls.' But, 'Oh God, help us now.' The second was SOP—'Solve Our Problems.' People asked the Lord to eliminate all needs, struggles, trials and temptations. They wanted carefree, perfect lives and fully believed that is what God promised them."[40] This is probably not how Jesus prayed, but it is usually the way we pray. Unfortunately, my personal observations from hearing people pray, and sometimes my own prayers, support the informal survey. However, that is not how Jesus taught us to pray.

Someone made the following observation about prayer: "Many people pray as if God were a big aspirin pill; they come (to Him) only when they are hurting." A friend of mine observed, "Many Christians don't pray. They just whine."

All too often our prayers are mere requests for blessings. We ask for help in emergencies and deliverance from catastrophes. In so doing, we have reduced prayer to seeking the material blessings of life and neglecting the spiritual aspects of life. We reduce God from a sovereign

---

[40] David Cook, *Coffee Break with God* (Tulsa: Honor Books, 1996), 68.

ruler and heavenly Father to a magical Santa Claus or cosmic genie. Prayer, then, becomes meaningful only if we get the answers we are seeking to obtain. For too many of us, prayer becomes necessary only when we are in the midst of a crisis, have a specific need, or are in circumstances beyond our control. Prayers can all too easily become either like the doors over the wings of an airplane, used in an emergency only, or like the frequently used greeting, "How are you?" uttered without really expecting a meaningful answer.

We are looking today at the phrase, the petition, "Give us this day our daily bread." It is the prayer of request for our needs. And if we are going to be honest, all too often this phrase is the focus of our prayers. We spend more time in our prayers making appeals for our physical and emotional needs than we spend focused on our spiritual needs.

We also seem to be more interested in asking for a change in our circumstances or the circumstances of others. Once again, praying for changed situations for ourselves or interceding for others is appropriate. However, if that is the *primary* purpose of our prayers, could it be that we are setting our sights too *low* when we think of the nature and purpose of praying to the God of the universe? Isn't it strange that while praying, we seem to spend less time asking for transformation of character, giving thanks for blessings received, and/or even focusing on God than we do in making requests?

In the prayer Jesus taught us to pray, spiritual needs and concerns are the primary focus. In fact, as we shall see, the petition for daily bread goes beyond praying for the necessities of this life to praying for the necessities of the life to come, the abundant life Jesus says we can have beginning now (John 10:10). The petition for daily bread is a petition to depend on God in *all* areas of our lives. And this is especially true for our spiritual lives! Our spiritual life will shape how we view and deal with the physical, emotional, and social aspects of our lives.

Prayer

Our Father in heaven, we come to You, the compassionate, merciful, and holy God whose love is unconditional and who is just and holy in all that You do. Today we want to experience Your kingdom in our lives. We especially need to learn what it means to have faith in You. Lord, we believe; help our unbelief! May we submit our wills to Yours.

Teach us to trust You to lead and guide us in the paths of righteousness in our relationship with You and with others. As we reflect and focus on the petition for daily bread, may we understand it as Jesus intended when he taught it to the disciples. May the daily bread we seek be the Daily Bread from heaven.

In Jesus's name. Amen.

The request for daily bread is seen by many as a transition point in the Lord's Prayer. Many commentators say that up until now, the focus of the Lord's Prayer has been on God. And this focus prepares us to appropriately say the rest of the prayer, which focuses on us and our needs. There is some truth in this concept. However, it may not be that cut and dried! I have learned, both by study and by experience, that the *entire* prayer maintains a focus on God. This is true even when we are making personal requests. When we recognize this focus of the Lord's Prayer, the importance of the pattern of his prayer becomes more apparent.

Most of the time, the sequence in the Lord's Prayer is appropriate to preserve. It is fitting to acknowledge who God is and His divine qualities and characteristics and the communal nature of the Christian life before we ever ask *anything* of Him in prayer. It is necessary to submit our wills to His will as we seek to live in His kingdom in the here and now *before* making our requests.

Otherwise, this happens:

- We fall too easily into the rut and routine of asking out of our limited knowledge instead of seeking His omniscience.
- We fall too easily into asking from an earthly perspective instead of a heavenly one.
- We fall too easily into asking out of selfish motives instead of selfless ones.

To the point, we ask out of our fallen human perspective instead of God's perfect, divine perspective. N.T. Wright warns against beginning our prayers with requests for those things "I (we) simply must have." He then makes the following thought-provoking observation: "To do this, of course, is to let greed get in the way of grace."[41]

Of course, it is sensible in times of crisis to pray with a focus on our needs. Peter's prayer, "Lord save," as he was sinking in the wave on the Sea of Galilee, were the only words he could get out. A prayer for deliverance in time of danger would be short and concise. But most of the time, we are not in immediate crisis. Most of the time, we can, and should, take the time to follow the sequence of acknowledging the character of God and submitting to His will before we make *any* requests for our needs and wants or even the needs of others.

As already stated, the majority of prayers that are sent up to God are prayers making personal requests, asking for what we want, what we desire, and what we think we should have. Most of these requests are for good things—noble things, honest needs, and helpful things. God has invited us to ask Him to supply all our needs. God has encouraged us to bring our joys and sorrows, our perplexities and weaknesses to Him. However, if prayer is reduced to mere wish lists for an easier, better life, what does that say about our relationship with God?

Imagine if you are at home and the doorbell rings. You open the door, and before you can even say "Hello," the person who rang the bell quickly says "Hi!" and then launches into a laundry list of things he wants you to do for him. Things he expects you to do for him! In the exact manner and time frame as he thinks you should fulfill all of his requests! The tone of voice, the look in his eyes, and his body language—they all tell you that if you don't come through on every request, he will seriously question

---

[41] N.T. Wright, *The Lord and His Prayer,* 36.

your value as a human being, let alone as a friend. Before you can even respond, he says, "Good-bye," and tells you how much he appreciates you and how he is looking forward to being with you soon.

If that were the extent of your communication with your friend, how long would your friendship last? If we are going to be honest, haven't we been guilty of doing the same thing with God? Don't you think prayer should have a little more to it than treating God like a divine vending machine?

Jesus's Life and Ministry
Reveal the Meaning of This Request

As you think of this request, "Give us this day, our daily bread," have you ever thought of how often bread and food come up in the life and ministry of Jesus? It's huge! Bread and food are mentioned multiple times in the gospels. Unfortunately, we see them as incidental parts of the stories. Jesus saw them as much more. At the beginning of his ministry, Jesus was sent out to be tempted in the wilderness. The very first temptation of Jesus was Satan's taunting enticement to "Take these stones and turn them into bread." His earthly ministry concluded with Jesus providing breakfast as He reaffirmed the call of his disciples. This took place just prior to his ascension.

The Temptation in the Wilderness

When Jesus was tempted by the devil to turn stones into bread, He responded by quoting from what God said through Moses: "Man shall not live by bread alone, but by every word that proceeds from the mouth of God" (Deuteronomy 8:3).

Obviously the temptation of Satan was not merely for Jesus to feed himself with bread that was miraculously made out of stones.

- The temptation was to distrust his Father's care and to destroy his relationship as God's Son.
- Satan's desire was for Jesus to depend on himself and his own power rather than submit to his Father's will and his Father's

power. The temptation was to place his material and physical needs *before* his ontological, spiritual needs.

That Jesus put his need for spiritual food "from the mouth of God" ahead of his need for physical food after forty days of fasting is astounding! It should say something to us about what he might have had in mind when he taught us to pray, "Give us our daily bread."

Jesus's response to the temptation is quite interesting. First, what he didn't say is important. He did not even refer to his physical needs. He did not respond by saying anything about either his lack or desperate need for food or that he would trust in his Father to provide his food. His response was: "Man shall not live by bread alone, but by every word that comes from the mouth of God" (Matthew 4:4). We dare not miss the fact that his response was focused not on his need for physical sustenance but on the greater priority of being spiritually sustained. Bread nourishes the body and keeps us temporarily alive. God's Word nourishes the soul. When we assimilate it and apply it to our lives, it will have eternal effects.

Second, we should keep Jesus's attitude toward bread in the first temptation in mind when we read about his ministry. Jesus used miracles, parables, and social occasions that were all connected with food and/or drink for conveying spiritual truths that restored man with God. In his interactions with people, Jesus also used social occasions with food and/or drink to restore people spiritually, emotionally, and socially. By taking a look at these occasions and what they accomplished, we will have a clearer understanding of what it means to ask God to "give us this day, our daily bread."

The Wedding at Cana

The very first miracle Jesus performed was turning water into wine at Cana. This wasn't bread, but it was refreshment. It was dealing with social needs. To run out of wine or food at a wedding celebration in any culture or in any era is an absolute no-no. It would be seen as a huge faux pas and a cause of great shame. This miracle acknowledged the importance of major life events, such as weddings. Jesus also performed the miracle to honor his mother, to set an example of filial love, respect, and deference.

We should take note of what Jesus saw as being important in this issue. At first glance, Mary's focus seemed to be on the lack of wine. But it was more than that, as we shall see. Jesus's focus was on his messianic mission. That is clear from the comment he made to his mother, "Woman, what does this have to do with me? My hour has not yet come" (John 2:4). Jesus's reluctance to miraculously provide wine was not due to a lack of concern for the reputation of the bridegroom's family, who provided the wine, or his own mother's part in the wedding. Nor did his use of the word "woman" signal any disrespect for her! In fact, it was the accepted way of showing honor to a woman in that culture, including one's mother. The hesitancy of Jesus to act was due to his concern of how the miracle might be misinterpreted and that people might insist that he would become an earthly Messiah.

More than likely, this is what was behind Mary's request. Perhaps Gabriel's pronouncement preceding the miraculous conception of Jesus came to her mind when she heard of the baptism of Jesus. His return from the wilderness had raised her hopes that Jesus was about to realize and fulfill his role as Messiah. Certainly Mary was aware of the common beliefs about the Messiah and the messianic age. One of those beliefs was that during the messianic age wine would flow. This belief was anchored in Amos 9:13, which speaks of the mountains flowing with wine. "About the time John's Gospel was written, another work not included in the New Testament, called 2 Baruch, described the messianic age as when there will be plenty, including plenty of wine. In fact, the work says that one of the signs of the messianic age will be that each grape will yield the equivalent of 120 gallons (about 450 liters) of wine. We noticed in the Cana wedding story how much water became wine; at least 120 gallons—without even one grape!"[42] How Mary and those present must have marveled and been in awe when they witnessed Jesus turn the purification water in those large clay jars into wine! Obviously, Jesus was doing more than providing for a physical need. He was introducing himself as the Messiah!

---

[42] Kendra Haloviak Valentine, *Signs to Life, Reading and Responding to John's Gospel,* (Victoria, Australia: Signs Publishing, 2013), 14.

When we compare some of the details from Christ's first miracle at Cana with some of the events that took place at the cross, we will see there are spiritual lessons to be learned from the miracle of the wine. The chart below may help us see some of them:

At Cana	At Calvary
• Jesus said the time had not come.	• Jesus said the time had come.
• Ministry began by supplying wine at a wedding.	• Ministry ends with Jesus giving new meaning to wine at Passover.
• Clay jars contained water for outward purification.	• Wine was used at the Lord's Supper as a symbol for inward purification.
• Water from the jars became wine.	• Blood from his side was mixed with water.
• The miracle occurred on the third day of the feast, when the lack of wine would turn the feast into a failure.	• The apparent failure of Jesus as Messiah would be turned to victory on the third day with the resurrection from the grave.[43]

The miraculous supply of wine would have been seen as evidence that the Messiah had arrived to restore Israel to a place of earthly prominence. In the wedding at Cana, Jesus used some of those symbols on which they had pinned their hopes of the promised Messiah when he turned the water into wine. At Calvary, those same symbols were provided to reveal the spiritual Messiah. The water and wine at Cana solved the immediate problem but only for a short time. The water and blood at Calvary solved humanity's ongoing problem of sin forever!

Further, while the master of the feast is amazed at the quality of the wine being served at the end of the wedding feast, the disciples are amazed at the miracle. They recognized the glory or the character

---

[43] Comparisons between the wedding at Cana story and the cross scene in John's gospel were influenced by the work *Signs to Life: Reading and Responding to John's Gospel* by Kendra Haloviak Valentine, cited above.

of God at work, and they believed in Jesus as the one sent of God, the Messiah. Once again, Jesus's response serves as an indication of the meaning of daily bread and drink in the prayer he taught us. God is the One who sustains our spiritual lives even as we live our daily lives!

Two Miracles of Multiplying Bread and Fish

Two of the biggest miracles of Jesus were the feeding of five thousand and then feeding of the four thousand. The number of people counted in both cases did not include the women and children. Why the duplication? The first miracle of the feeding of the five thousand was done for the benefit of Jewish people. The second miracle of the feeding of the four thousand was performed in ministry to Gentiles. Both were done initially to alleviate the hunger of the crowds. The feeding of the five thousand took place after Jesus had been teaching and healing all day. It was a desolate place. The people had not eaten all day, and food was not readily available for them. The feeding of the four thousand occurred *after three days*. Jesus was supplying their needs for nourishment so they could make the trip home safely. In both cases, Jesus had spent many hours ministering to their spiritual needs before providing them with food. In both cases, Jesus used a miracle of providing food supernaturally to teach the disciples and both crowds important spiritual lessons.

The first lesson from these twin miracles is that we are dependent on God for the provisions of life. God can supply our needs, even in difficult circumstances. He has the power and ability to care for us and sustain our physical lives.

The second lesson is that while God is concerned with our temporal needs, He is more concerned with meeting our spiritual needs. Again, notice that he first taught and healed before providing them with food. While healing them, he also met their physical and emotional needs. In Jesus's ministry, spiritual healing went hand in hand with physical healing. Ellen White makes the following pertinent point: "Christ never worked a miracle except to supply a genuine necessity, and every miracle was of a character to lead the people to the tree of life, whose leaves are for the healing of the nations.'[44] Did you notice that she states the primary purpose of *every* miracle was for spiritual healing? How clear can it be?

The third lesson from the two miraculous feedings of the multitudes tells us that we are to work in the same way, ministering to physical, emotional, and social needs in order that we might bring them to Christ. Again Ellen White speaks to the point: "The work (our work as disciples) is of God, and He will furnish means, and will send helpers, true, earnest disciples, whose hands also will be filled with food for the starving multitude. God is not unmindful of those who labor in love to give the word of life to perishing souls, who in their turn reach forth their hands for *food for other hungry souls*"[45] (emphasis mine).

She also brings out another lesson from this miracle regarding how we are to minister to others: "In Christ's act of supplying the temporal necessities of a hungry multitude is wrapped up a deep spiritual lesson for all His workers. Christ received from the Father; He imparted to the disciples; they imparted to the multitude; and the people to one another. So all who are united to Christ will receive from Him the bread of life, the heavenly food, and impart it to others."[46]

Have you ever thought about the fact that the bread had to multiply *as it was being passed out?* The miracle began as Jesus broke the bread and gave it to the disciples. The miracle had continued as the disciples distributed the bread to the people! Even then, it would have been impossible for the twelve disciples to carry and personally pass out the bread to each person in those large crowds! The bread must have multiplied as the people passed it to one another. And there were twelve baskets leftover after the five thousand were fed and seven baskets after the four thousand were fed! It may be worth considering that in the Bible, the number twelve often is symbolic of the kingdom, and the number seven is symbolic of perfection. Which prepares the way for the fourth lesson.

God is concerned for all people. This may have been the most important lesson from these miracles for the disciples and the Jews

---

[44] Ellen White, *The Desire of Ages*, 366.

[45] Ellen White, *The Desire of Ages*, 370.

[46] Ellen White, *The Desire of Ages*, 369.

of Jesus's day, as well as for us today. As previously noted, Jesus's miraculous feeding of the five thousand was to a largely Jewish audience, and the feeding of the four thousand was largely to Gentiles. When he told the disciples that he did not want to send the crowd of four thousand away hungry, their response was, "Where are we to get bread in such a desolate place?" The miracle of the loaves and fishes in Galilee was still a recent event. They had to know that he was just as capable of miraculously providing food here in the Decapolis as he had been on the shores of Galilee! It seems to me that their objection to the desolate area was more about their perceived desolation of the Gentiles by God than the desolation of the terrain. Jesus simply asked how many loaves of bread they had and repeated the miracle of instant mass food production. Then the food was to be given to Gentiles through them! Gentiles were to be the recipients of the kingdom of God, too! If my consideration of the possible meaning of the two different numbers of leftover baskets is correct, could it be possible that Jesus was preparing the disciples to see that the kingdom is available to all? That while it began with the twelve tribes of Israel, it will reach its perfection in the inclusion of all who will receive the spiritual food provided by Jesus.

This lesson is for us, as well. How often do we treat non-believers, people of other religions, Christians of other denominations, or even members in our own church as if they are in a desolate place, a place too far removed for God's grace to reach? A place too isolated for them to have access to God's compassion! A place too barren for God's mercy to grow faith! Maybe we need to listen to Jesus and bring the loaves of our Christian experience and spiritual gifts to Jesus so that he can feed those we have written off as unworthy. So his spiritual provisions can be multiplied in our hands!

Finally, Jesus also performed the miracle for the five thousand as a sign to point to himself as the Messiah. There is something many Christians do not know about the messianic beliefs in the first century. There was a common teaching about the Messiah that may appear strange but was very vivid. They held that when the Messiah came, and when the golden age dawned, there would be a messianic banquet at which the chosen ones of God would sit down to eat.

At that banquet, the slain bodies of the monsters Behemoth, the largest monster of the earth, and Leviathan, the largest monster of the sea, would provide the meat and the fish courses of the banquet. It would be a kind of reception feast given by God to His own people. In the miracles of the feeding of the five thousand and the four thousand, it was more than a provision of a meal to hungry people. It was an announcement by Jesus that said in effect, "I am the Messiah." And I am the Messiah for *both* Jews and Gentiles.

It was also believed that the Messiah would come as a new prophet in the manner of Moses. This was prophesied in Deuteronomy 18:15 and 18, where it was written, [15]"The LORD your God will raise up for you a prophet like me from among you, from your brothers—it is to him you shall listen ..."

This explains why John recorded the surprised response of the crowd, who, after eating the food miraculously provided them, proclaimed, "This is indeed the Prophet who is to come into the world" (John 6:14).

This was another way of saying Jesus was the expected Messiah. But they wanted a Messiah to deliver the temporal blessings they sought. So when they tried to crown him king, he withdrew to a mountain to be alone and to pray" (John 6:14–15).

The dialogue on this occasion led to Jesus's startling pronouncement:

"I am the bread of life." (John 6:35)

Those who heard it were startled. The Jewish leaders were horrified, accusing Jesus of promoting cannibalism. Jesus then summarized the meaning of both the miracle and his statement when he said:

> [50]"This is the bread which comes down from heaven, that a man may eat of it and not die. [51]I am the living bread which came down from heaven; if any one eats of this bread, he will live forever; and the bread which I shall give for the life of the world is my flesh." (John 6:50–51, RSV)

With this teaching in mind, how can we possibly think that in the phrase Jesus taught us to pray, "give us this day our daily bread," that

Jesus was merely referring to our physical needs? In fact, receiving Jesus as our daily *spiritual* bread is the most important aspect for praying this phrase of the Lord's Prayer! For it is in receiving Jesus as our daily bread that we receive eternal life, the adoption as children, the new birth, and so much more (John 1:12). However, we do not receive Jesus as our daily bread for ourselves only. We receive him so that we can pass on to the others the miracle of salvation we have received.

What is even more startling is the fact that Jesus made the provision to provide daily spiritual bread as well as physical bread to as many people as possible superseded the Jews' rules regarding the Sabbath!

Preparing Food on the Sabbath

On one occasion, Jesus had to defend his disciples against the charges of the scribes and Pharisees that His disciples had broken the Sabbath by working. In plucking the grain as they walked through a wheat field, they were guilty of reaping. When they crushed the wheat in their hands, they were thrashing, and when they blew the chaff away before eating it, they were winnowing. Jesus defended them by reminding the religious leaders of the time David and his men were fleeing from King Saul. They were hungry and ate the shewbread from the table located in the sanctuary, which only the priests were supposed to do.

Then Jesus said, "The Sabbath was made for man, not man for the Sabbath" (Mark 2:27). It was important to Jesus that His disciples remain engaged in ministry. Being refreshed physically enabled them to continue to serve him and to minister and serve others. For Jesus, the purpose of the Sabbath is to restore people physically, emotionally and spiritually. The exact work Jesus came to do! Once again, the spiritual restoration of people, their receiving spiritual nourishment, is the primary goal of Jesus's ministry. But to do ministry requires being sustained physically, too. There are more lessons to be learned from "the daily bread" of Jesus's life and ministry.

Jairus's Daughter

Remember the story of Jairus's daughter? Jairus came to Jesus and pleaded with him to come and heal his daughter who was sick. On the way there, Jesus was delayed by ministering to others in need. By the time he arrived at Jairus's home, his daughter had died. People were already outside the house, wailing and weeping to show their sympathy with Jairus's family. They told Jesus not to bother going inside. He was too late. But Jesus went in anyway. He commanded her to rise up. And she got up! Before anyone could say a word, Jesus commanded those present to give her some food to eat. This detail is often overlooked in this story.

At first glance, it may seem an odd thing to do. Jesus in effect interrupted their joyful celebration and told them to get her some food. Why interrupt the celebration of such an amazing event? I am sure that if it were my daughter, I would simply want to hold on to her and not let her go for a long, long time! Wouldn't you? I can think of three possible reasons. First, perhaps she had been ill for a long time and her body needed immediate nourishment to regain her strength. A second reason might have been that by giving her food, Jesus was showing that she was completely cured. After all, eating a meal immediately after a sickness isn't always the best idea. And a third reason might have been that through this act, he is simply teaching the principle that there is nothing wrong with attending to the practical details in life. Even after a miracle such as the one He had just performed! Or it could be a combination of all those reasons. By telling them to give her food, Jesus was indeed meeting her basic physical needs after he had raised her from the dead—a simultaneous spiritual and physical miracle!

Jesus's miracles weren't the only vehicles he used to teach spiritual lessons from food. Throughout his ministry, social occasions provided opportunities for him to teach and interact with people for the purposes of revealing the character of the Father and of promoting the gospel of the kingdom.

Jesus's Ministry at Meals

How often did Jesus's ministry take place around a table? One day, while walking through Jericho, Jesus stopped, looked up in a tree, saw Zacchaeus, and invited himself to dinner at Zacchaeus's house. While they were feasting on food—both physical and spiritual—Jesus observed the miracles of repentance and transformation in Zacchaeus's life.

There were so many banquets and dinners where Jesus was the honored guest. These included the banquet at Simon's house, meals at the home of Lazarus, Martha, and Mary, and then the meal at Emmaus. It was at that meal when he was recognized as the risen Christ as he broke and blessed the bread. These meals were important because at each of them Jesus taught, healed, forgave, and restored people to God! It was at these meals that He taught the importance of sitting at Jesus's feet and responding to Jesus as the saving Messiah. Over and over again in his ministry, Jesus used the provision of daily bread as the opportunity to introduce his provision of restoration to God and his provision for eternal life.

It was after the Passover meal that Jesus instituted the Lord's Supper. It was there that he broke bread and offered the cup of wine to be a continual reminder of his sacrificial death and resurrection to the believers of all ages. The Communion Service would provide sustenance to their spiritual lives, just as food provides sustenance for their physical lives. It was there that Jesus told them all to eat and drink, both as a way to remember what his sacrifice would accomplish and as a way to proclaim their trust in what he had done in their behalf.

Every Communion Service provides us with the opportunity to gain new insights from the bread that is an emblem of his body given for us and the wine, that is an emblem of his blood shed for us. While we call this the Last Supper, it was not the last meal at which Jesus would teach his disciples—of all ages—spiritual lessons and truths before he would ascend to heaven.

Jesus on the Beach

The last recorded incident in which Jesus and food were connected took place on a beach (John 21). The disciples were in a quandary. They were still struggling with what the death and resurrection of Jesus meant to their hopes and dreams of him being the Messiah. They were still unsure of their status, if any, as his disciples. On top of that, they had all abandoned him. Most had quietly abandoned him by staying away from his trial and death. Peter had outright denied him—three times. They were unsure if Jesus even wanted them to continue to be his disciples. If he did, what would that mean? The majority of them decided that they needed to make ends meet, so what else could they do but go back to fishing? After all, this was the original profession of Peter, Andrew, James, and John.

How well we remember the story! The disciples had worked all night and had caught nothing. Then a man on the beach told them to cast their net on the other side. They obeyed the man's command, and their net was filled to overflowing. John recognized Jesus. All the other disciples remembered. They remembered a similar miracle (Luke 5:1–11). A miracle that had sealed their calling to become disciples of Jesus! They had hoped Jesus was the long-awaited-for Messiah. It was after that first miraculous catch of fish that they had left all to follow Jesus (verse 11). In speaking of that miracle and its results, Ellen White wrote, "Until this time none of the disciples had fully united as co-laborers with Jesus. They had witnessed many of his miracles, and had listened to his teaching; but they had not entirely forsaken their former employment."[47]

This duplicated miracle was in effect a renewed call to *all* the disciples. All were guilty of abandoning Jesus after his arrest and during the crucifixion, except John. All, including John, were unsure of what was expected of them from now on. Jesus's death and resurrection had changed everything. Not one of them had any idea of what it would mean to continue to be a disciple of Jesus. If they could continue to be one at all!

Jesus repeated the miracle of the fish for two reasons. First, it was to

---

[47] Ellen White, *The Desire of Ages*, 248.

let them know that they were forgiven for their tacit denial of him and their lack of faith. Second, it was to reaffirm their call and commission to be disciples and minister to others in his kingdom of grace.

As the disciples were bringing in the haul of fish, Peter left the rest of the disciples and scrambled to the shore to worship his Lord. Only this time Peter did not ask Jesus to leave him alone because he was a sinner, as he had done previously. This time, being with Jesus was the only place he felt safe!

When the disciples came ashore, Jesus had a surprise in store. He had cooked some fish over a fire—a charcoal fire. The word for charcoal fire in the original language is found just twice in the gospels. It is found here and in the story of Peter's denial. In the presence of all the disciples, Jesus changed the charcoal fire from being a reminder of Peter's failure into a reminder of Jesus's love, forgiveness, grace, acceptance, and fellowship. Jesus wanted Peter to know that he was still called to be Jesus's disciple. He wanted the others to know it, too. Jesus had redeemed Peter's failure!

By the time the meal was over, every disciple who was there had been offered the chance to sign a lifelong discipleship contract. To make sure that Peter got the message from the miraculous catch of fish and the heavenly breakfast Jesus had fed him, Jesus and Peter took a walk on the beach. While on the walk, Jesus reinstated him as His disciple. Not once but three times! Once for each public denial he had made in the courtyard on the eve of Jesus's crucifixion.

Was it important for the disciples to have food after working all night? Of course it was. Did Jesus provide their daily bread that morning? Absolutely! However, he did much more than that:

- He forgave them.
- He reestablished them as his disciples.
- He reminded them of his command to love one another as they served others.
- He reaffirmed that God would provide for them what they couldn't provide for themselves.

That breakfast satisfied their hunger and provided the energy their bodies needed. The heavenly food would give their lives meaning and purpose. The same Jesus who had provided them physical food for their daily lives would be the one to provide them the spiritual necessities in their ministry as his disciples to others.

Why did food play such a big role in the ministry of Jesus? He knew that at meals or at meetings with refreshments or at parties and celebrations people have a chance to develop emotional, social, as well as interpersonal ties. Jesus understood that these ultimately provide us with the opportunity to build mutual trust and confidence with others. Jesus was mindful that when people eat together, they are provided moments of togetherness—moments of intimacy—moments of shared laughter, shared concerns, shared ideas and philosophies of life, shared hurts, and so much more. Because these things are true, Jesus used occasions when food was shared to overcome the gaps of social, emotional, and spiritual barriers in his ministry to others. They provided Jesus the opportunities to gain insights into the lives of others and assess their needs. At the same time, it gave people the chance to entrust their lives to him. Food keeps us alive. Jesus was aware of the basic necessities that give our lives meaning.

Jesus's use of food as a vehicle for ministry should not surprise us. We should not forget that when he first taught the Lord's Prayer, he did so to teach people how to pray in keeping with the spirituality described in the Sermon on the Mount. The second time he taught the Lord's Prayer was when the disciples asked him to teach them how to pray *because they wanted to learn the secret of his life and of his ministry.* Both times Jesus taught the Lord's Prayer were in the context of teaching people how to depend on God. First for their spiritual needs and then for their physical needs.

Jesus was aware that just as God gave us the desire for food through hunger, so God gives us the desire for spiritual food when we hunger and thirst for righteousness. We must remember that in the Sermon of the Mount, Jesus quickly moved from addressing the concerns regarding spiritual needs in Matthew 5:12–6:24 to addressing the concerns for physical needs briefly in Matthew 6:25–34. Jesus addresses such issues as food, clothing, and shelter, the basic needs of life. His point is that God is a compassionate God. He not only cares about our spiritual lives,

He is also concerned about our physical, emotional, and social needs. He even invites us to ask Him to meet the real and necessary needs of our lives. He then concluded the Sermon on the Mount in Matthew 7 with a return to addressing spiritual concerns and the need to have God as the foundation of our lives. To sum it up, Jesus wants us to understand that we need to depend on him in all areas of our lives.

We Can Ask God to Meet Our Needs

In teaching us to ask for bread, it is almost as if Jesus had Psalm 23 in mind:

"The Lord is my Shepherd, I shall not want.

He makes me lie down in green pasture.

He leads me beside the still waters." (Verses 1–2)

One translation reads: "The LORD is my shepherd; I have everything I need" (New Living Translation). Another translation puts it this way: "the Lord is my Shepherd, I lack nothing" (Today's New International Version).

To pray for God to provide us with our daily need for food is for us to be reminded that it is God who provides everything that keeps us alive. We depend on Him to continue to live. He provides the nutrients in and on the earth:

- the sun's rays
- the air we breathe
- the rain and snow
    the miracle of photosynthesis
- the life in the seed of every plant and much more

Every person alive, whether he acknowledges it or not, is dependent on God for his daily bread. So why should believers ask God for what He provides to everyone?

Let's go back and address the question again—what did Jesus have in mind when he told us to ask for our daily bread? Have you ever wondered why he taught us to ask for just bread? I have heard it said that the reason Jesus told us to ask for bread was because it is a basic staple food just about worldwide. Many people believe the request for bread is a request for God to supply our basic need for food. Some have even gone so far as suggesting that Jesus taught us to request bread to keep us from becoming selfish and asking for more than what we need, thus enabling us to keep our priorities straight.

However, isn't that giving God a bad rap? A God who says ask for the basics and no more? Didn't Jesus himself say, right after giving the Lord's Prayer the second time, that "if our earthly parents want to give their children good gifts, how much more does our Father in heaven want to give good things to His children?" I am aware that Jesus's main point was that it is our Father's desire to give the Holy Spirit to us. At the same time, let's not forget the metaphor and the principle Jesus used. If earthly parents desire to give their children those things that provide for them, give them things that bring them satisfaction and joy, and even give them things they don't deserve, wouldn't our heavenly Father have an even greater desire to do the same for His children? And this includes you and me!

So, is it wrong to ask for more than just bread? To ask for more than mere basics? Jesus was not telling us that we can only ask for the bare minimum necessities for life or for the kind of food that only poor people can afford to eat. He wanted us to know that God is interested in both the little things of life as well as the big things. He is interested in all aspects of our lives, not just in the spiritual part of it. His interest goes far beyond the basics of our lives!

There is something we don't think about in our culture that was an extremely important part of everyday life in Jesus's day. It is essential to be reminded of why it was important to receive bread daily. Remember, they did not have knives, forks, and spoons to eat with. They didn't use chopsticks. And they didn't eat with their fingers. The eating and serving utensils of the Middle East in Jesus's day was bread! They would take a piece of bread and break it off from the loaf, dip it in the food that was prepared, and then put it in their mouth and eat the bread and whatever liquid or type of food it had been dipped in or whatever kind of food it was used to pick up off the common plate. So when

Jesus said, "give us this day our daily bread," he wasn't just talking about bread alone. The bread included almost everything else in the meal that provided their sustenance. They had to use the bread to eat their vegetables, honey, lamb, fish, or whatever else they were eating! If we apply that to our physical needs, what Jesus was saying is that since He is our daily bread, everything in our lives will be touched and transformed for his purposes.

Therefore, to ask for bread was to ask for *all* their needs to be met. It included all the food they ate. It also was a symbol for all the necessities of life. It included:

- shelter
- clothing
- our physical and emotional health
- dealing with the varied difficulties, circumstances, and problems we face in our lives

After all, almost immediately after giving the Lord's Prayer in the Sermon on the Mount, Jesus said the following:

> 25"That is why I tell you not to worry about everyday life—whether you have enough food and drink, or enough clothes to wear. Isn't life more than food, and your body more than clothing? 26Look at the birds. They don't plant or harvest or store food in barns, for your heavenly Father feeds them. And aren't you far more valuable to him than they are? 27Can all your worries add a single moment to your life? 28And why worry about your clothing? Look at the lilies of the field and how they grow. They don't work or make their clothing, 29yet Solomon in all his glory was not dressed as beautifully as they are. 30And if God cares so wonderfully for wildflowers that are here today and thrown into the fire tomorrow, he will certainly care for you. Why do you have so little faith? 31"So don't worry about these things, saying, 'What will we eat? What will we drink? What

will we wear?' ³²These things dominate the thoughts of unbelievers, but your heavenly Father already knows all your needs. ³³Seek the Kingdom of God above all else, and live righteously, and he will give you everything you need. ³⁴"So don't worry about tomorrow, for tomorrow will bring its own worries. Today's trouble is enough for today." (Matthew 6:25–34 NLT)

Certainly, the connection between our need for the necessities of life and asking for daily bread in our prayers is obvious.

Our Daily Bread

Since the petition for bread includes all areas of life, why did Jesus ask us to pray for our *daily* bread? The petition literally reads in the Greek, "The bread of us daily give to us today" or "each day" in Matthew's version. In the original, the emphasis is on "today." Why not ask for a weekly or even a monthly supply? In fact, in the largely agricultural society of Jesus's day, and throughout much of this world's history, people depended on their crops for a yearly supply. Why then should we ask for our *daily* bread?

This is another indication that the petition for bread is focused on asking God to meet both our spiritual and our physical needs on a daily basis. Remember the story of the provision of manna in the wilderness? The Israelites were instructed to gather just enough manna on Sunday through Thursday for each day's supply. However, on the preparation day, Friday, the Israelites were to gather enough for that day and their portion for Sabbath, too.

The manna was a reminder of their need to depend on God. It was also a reminder to rest in Him spiritually. We must depend on God each and every day to supply us with the spiritual nourishment through daily Bible study, prayer, meditation, and sharing with others what we have seen, felt, and experienced in our journey with God.

The manna would spoil and become inedible if left to the next day. In the same way, our spiritual life becomes stale and stagnant if not replenished daily. It then becomes unappealing when we try to share with others. Just as the manna could not be selfishly hoarded for the next day, neither can we hoard the spiritual blessings we receive from God and expect that which we receive today will be sufficient for tomorrow. We cannot rest on our spiritual past to see us through our present circumstances. To do so leads to spiritual stagnation!

Dependent on God for Necessities of Life

Ultimately, this petition is to serve as a reminder that in every area of our lives we are dependent on God. Period!

- Every single heart beat!
- Every inhalation and exhalation of breath!
- Rain and sunshine!
- Love of family and friends!

Everything necessary to provide and sustain life comes to us as a gift from God.

A farmer may grow the food. A truck driver or train engineer may haul it to a bakery or a food processing plant. A baker or cook may bake or cook the food. A clerk may put it on the shelf and then sell it to us. And we may prepare the food. However, the bread came from a kernel of wheat. Only God can grow a kernel of wheat. Every seed contains the miracle of life. Scientists still cannot completely explain the life that is found in the seeds of every plant!

In our self-sufficient society, we pause briefly to thank God from whom all blessings flow, and then we continue as if He hadn't been there at all. I think Taylor Bunch's observation about our food and all provisions for our lives is spot-on. "Man cannot make his food. Food must be given life before it can impart life. Since God is the Life Giver and the only one source of life, food is a gift from God."[48]

Most Christians usually say grace before they eat their meals. Here, I may step on some toes, including my own. How many times do we say grace, our prayers for meals, in the same way, using the same words, over and over and over again?

---

[48] Taylor Bunch, *The Perfect Prayer*, 77.

How often do we use phrases such as, "Thank you for the food. Please bless the hands that prepared it"? Sometimes we even ask Him to bless the hands that prepared it before we thank the One who created that which was prepared! Do we pause to think about what it means to be eating the food that has been provided to us as a gift by a compassionate, caring, and generous God? For this reason, I have personally found that thanking God for the food He graciously provides me is far more meaningful than to ask Him to bless it. It already comes blessed with the nutrients I need to supply my body's physical needs (assuming I am eating good food). By thanking Him, I am reminded of the blessings He has already given.

There is a surprising statement made in the chapter on the Lord's Supper in the book *The Desire of Ages* that will create in us a new attitude toward every meal we eat and every provision we receive from God's hand. It may change the prayers you say before you eat. Here it is:

> To the death of Christ we owe even this earthly life. The bread we eat is the purchase of His broken body. The water we drink is bought by His spilled blood. Never one, saint or sinner, eats his daily food, but he is nourished by the body and the blood of Christ. The cross of Calvary is stamped on every loaf. It is reflected in every water spring. All this Christ has taught in appointing the emblems of His great sacrifice. The light shining from that Communion Service in the upper chamber makes sacred the provisions for our daily life. The family board becomes as the table of the Lord, and every meal a sacrament.[49]

How incredible! Have you ever thought of that? Every meal a sacrament! Every meal an avenue of God's grace! Every meal purchased by the blood of Christ! When we view God's provisions for daily bread in this light, it dispels the practice of separating life into isolated areas of the sacred and the secular. We begin to see that the petition for daily bread reminds us that we are asking God's blessing on *every* aspect of our lives. We are more aware that what takes place in the secular areas

---

[49] Ellen White, *The Desire of Ages,* 660.

of our lives affects us spiritually. What takes place in the spiritual areas of our lives will determine the choices we make for the secular areas of our lives. The Lord's Prayer merges them into one arena—our journey with God as we live with others.

Our Responsibility

While this petition reminds us that every good and perfect gift is given to us ultimately by God, we must keep something else in mind. The Bible is perfectly clear in stating that we are expected to work to receive our daily bread. Go back to Genesis 3, and you discover that one of the consequences of sin is that man would have to work by the sweat of his brow for his food, sustenance, and the necessities of life. Paul says in 2 Thessalonians 3:6–12 that everyone should work for their food, and if someone is not willing to work, they shouldn't eat. The book of Proverbs has much to say about the importance of work and the dangers of idleness and laziness.

While God says we should ask, He doesn't promise that the answer will always come. Just as rain falls on the just and the unjust, famines fall on the just and the unjust! Recessions fall on the just and the unjust. Sickness and bad health fall on the just and the unjust. We live in a world of sin, and the consequences of sin affect both God's people as well as those who choose to live apart from him.

There is an often-overlooked aspect to this prayer. Did you notice that Jesus did not teach us to pray, "Give *me* this day *my* daily bread"? Instead he taught us to pray, "Give *us* this day *our* daily bread." In so doing, Jesus reminds us that our relationship with God is not merely an individual one. It is to be a communal prayer. Is it possible that Jesus taught the disciples to request our heavenly Father to give us *our* daily bread, because in so doing it reminds us of the importance of caring for one another? The widows, orphans, and poor among us are not to be overlooked by us in our prayers and in our actions!

While we need to live responsibly to meet our own needs as best we can, we are commanded to meet the needs of others as situations arise and as God impresses us through the convictions we receive from His Spirit. But with so many needs to meet, how can we help when our resources are insufficient and/or our wisdom in knowing how to help is challenged? Could it be that Jesus taught us to include the needs of others in our prayers to keep us from just focusing on our own personal needs and wants? And how often are the needs of others greater than our own? Could it be that one of the reasons Jesus taught us to include the needs of others in our prayers was to provide a safeguard against the selfishness of the human heart? To remind us that we have an obligation to share what God has given us with others? And more importantly, could it be that he recognized that we need the wisdom and heart of God to know how and when to help others?

We are currently living in a time that has created difficulties for people. Over the past few years, we have experienced a recession that has affected so many. People are trying their best to find jobs so they can provide food for their families and pay their mortgages or rent. They feel guilt and shame. Their self-esteem takes a beating when they don't have a job. Often they are embarrassed to ask others to help. We must recognize that our prayer for daily bread must include an intercessory prayer for others to receive their daily necessities, too. Perhaps, more than we do, we need to see ourselves as God's answer to that prayer, both individually and as the body of Christ.

The following poem says this so succinctly:

> You cannot pray the Lord's Prayer
> and even once say I.
> You cannot pray the Lord's Prayer
> and even once say My.
> Nor can you pray the Lord's Prayer
> and not pray for one another,
> And when you ask for daily bread,
> you must include your brother.
> For others are included
> … in each and every plea,
> From the beginning to the end of it,
> it does not once say Me.
> (Anonymous)

Reflection and Application

Please keep in mind the following as you reflect upon the questions below:

- Jesus and Jesus alone can satisfy the longings of *our* hearts and lives. Every real need we have, physical and spiritual, He can supply.
- Jesus and Jesus alone can provide us with that which will cause us to flourish, prosper, and grow into the likeness of His character.
- Jesus and Jesus alone can provide that which we need to live the life He has called us to live.

Take some time to reflect on what it means to ask God for our daily bread:

1. What has this phrase meant to you in the past?

2. How has this chapter changed your understanding of what it means to request daily bread from God?

3. How can you follow the example of Jesus's life in using food in ministry to others?

4. What insights, thoughts, or questions have come to you as you read this chapter?

5. How do you think praying about the various aspects of God's kingdom and His will might change the requests you make and the way you make them?

6. How will your prayers be affected by this phrase of the Lord's Prayer? How can you apply this phrase in your prayers?

Prayer

Our Father in heaven, we come to You as Your children. We so long to have people recognize Your holy character as they see You in us. Father, we long to see the principles and effects of Your kingdom in place in our lives as we continue to submit to Your will. Sometimes it is so hard to surrender our wills to Yours and to give up our cherished desires and ways. Soften our hearts and wills so that we will be willing to do so.

Father, all too often we have viewed the prayer for bread as merely requesting what we need—and the things we want. Forgive us …

Give us the hunger for the spiritual provisions You offer. Your Word, Your Spirit, Your character of love and compassion! For only as we receive them can we begin to be transformed into the people You have called us to be!

Bless each reader! I pray that each one will seek to incorporate the Lord's Prayer on a regular basis,

In Jesus's name. Amen.

Chapter 6

The Pardon of Prayer:
Experiencing and Expressing Forgiveness

And make us free of our debts, as we have
made those free who are in debt to us.
—MATTHEW 6:12, BIBLE IN BASIC ENGLISH

On December 11, 2008, Bernie Madoff was arrested for defrauding thousands of investors of what was initially estimated between $17.5 and 20 billion! The victims he betrayed included many faceless people who had entrusted him with their life savings or with their retirement funds. It also included business associates, friends, and even his family! All victims! Many were left with anger and bitterness and a desire for revenge. His family experienced embarrassment, shame, humiliation, and deep grief as well.

Madoff pleaded guilty and was sentenced to 150 years in prison. A virtual death sentence! Many of his victims would not be placated by his plea or his sentence. The press and victims assumed that his wife, Ruth, and their sons, Mark and Andrew, were in on the largest Ponzi scheme in history, along with him. They denied it, but the attacks kept coming. Madoff's son, Mark, came to the point where he had all he could take. Finally, with his own young son in a nearby room, on the second anniversary of his father's arrest, he hung himself.

In an interview with *60 Minutes* reporter Morley Safer, which aired on October 30, 2011, Madoff's other son, Andrew, acknowledged that he had not spoken to his father since the arrest. Then, with his jaw appearing to be clenched, in a calm voice that sounded hollow and hopeless, Andrew declared, "What he (his father) did was unforgivable, and I will never speak to him again." He said it more than once in the interview.

When Andrew paused, Morley Safer asked a question that seemed to be more of an observation than a quest for more information. "So in your mind your father is dead."

Andrew responded, "He died three years ago."[50]

Admittedly, I do not know all the details of the story. A British judge in 2013 rejected the trustee's case in Britain against Madoff's sons because there was no evidence that they were involved in the Ponzi scheme. To what extent, if any, did Bernie Madoff feel remorse? Was he sorry for the pain, suffering, and heartache he had caused his clients, friends, and family, or was he sorry for the consequences of his actions, including the suicide of his son? Did his stated and written words of regret contain repentance or were they uttered in necessity like a child caught with his hand in the proverbial cookie jar? Only Mr. Madoff knows for sure, and only God can truly judge him.

I couldn't help but think, as I watched and listened to that interview, how I wish I could have told Andrew that no one is unforgivable! If the cast of characters found in Hebrews chapter 11, such as David, Samson, Rahab, Jacob, and others could receive forgiveness, so can his father.

How I wish I could have told Andrew that he needed to forgive his father! Not because his father deserved his forgiveness—he did not! Andrew needed to forgive his father because he needed to be released from his own hurt, anger, shame, and bitterness that seemed to surround him in that interview, like the dirt cloud that enveloped and followed the cartoon figure Pigpen drawn by Charles Shultz in his Snoopy comic strips.

While Andrew's father was in prison for his crimes, Andrew seemed to be imprisoned by hurt, betrayal, and bitterness. Both Andrew and his father needed the hope and healing that true forgiveness can bring.

Don't misunderstand me. Forgiveness for such a repulsive betrayal does not come easily. Nor should it! Forgiveness for such hardhearted dealings is difficult, as it should be! Forgiveness for such unspeakable

---

[50] CBS News: *60 Minutes* interview with Morley Safer, October 2011.

selfishness is costly. However, the cost is cheap when compared to the alternative of living with hurt, anger, bitterness, and/or resentment without any relief! These negative emotions often destroy relationships, shatter lives, and rob people of peace and fulfillment and can affect other relationships as well.

It seems that Andrew chose to view his father as dead, denying his existence rather than dealing with all the various emotional pain and heartache caused by his father's betrayal. To continue denying his father's existence in his life was a form of escapism. It solved nothing and created new, equally difficult problems! Andrew may have appeared to escape his father on the surface, but he could never escape his father within his heart: the hurt and shame were always with him. What could Andrew do? Would it have been possible for Andrew to forgive with his father without condoning what he had done?

Let's keep this story in mind as we focus on the next phrase of the Lord's Prayer.

> "… and forgive us our sins, as we forgive those
> who sin against us." (Luke 11:4, NLT)

This aspect of the Lord's Prayer is so essential for maintaining healthy spiritual and emotional well-being. And it is necessary for maintaining meaningful, loving, and healthy relationships with others. This phrase is perhaps the most complicated part of the Lord's Prayer for us to comprehend and to say:

- not because we don't know the words
- not because we can't pronounce them
- not because we aren't sure if we should say, "Forgive us our debts," or "Forgive us our trespasses"

But because to truly say those words, either verbatim or in our own words, means that we must admit that we are debtors incapable of paying our own debts.

- We must acknowledge that we are offenders unable to undo or clean up our own messes.
- We must confess that we are sinners unworthy of forgiveness.
- We must admit we have offended others and do not deserve to be forgiven by them.

We are all sinners in need of a Savior. We have all offended God, family, friends, and neighbors. All but God have offended us. Therefore, the prayer for pardon is not an option. It is *essential*!

To truly say those words means that we must also be willing to forgive those who have offended, hurt, or mistreated us! Even when they don't deserve to be forgiven! We must admit we all receive forgiveness as an act of grace!

- We must acknowledge the difficulty of forgiving others.
- We must forgive others at all costs—to us!

Therefore, forgiving others is not an option. It is indispensable! But how can we possibly find a way to truly forgive when it is the last thing we feel like doing?

To accomplish that which is essential, to ask to be forgiven our debts that we cannot repay, requires the work of the Holy Spirit on our conscience. To accomplish that which is indispensable, to forgive others, demands the work of the Holy Spirit on our hearts. Both will genuinely become a reality only as we make prayer a priority in our lives.

Prayer

> *Our Father in heaven! Before we begin to look at the prayer of pardon, we acknowledge that You are the God of all grace, comfort, and hope. It is Your holy character that provides grace for us to be forgiven. It is Your divine mercy that enables us to be merciful.*
>
> *As we reflect on the prayer for pardon, may we see forgiveness as one of the key characteristics of Your kingdom and our forgiving others as one of the main means through which Your will is done on earth. Prepare each reader's mind, heart, and will to be receptive to the work of the Spirit in their lives.*
>
> *May each reader receive new insight into the life of Jesus in the area of forgiveness. May that insight enable them to receive the spiritual bread they need to enable them to live for You.*
>
> *Thank you for the power of Your grace that provides pardon for us and enables us to forgive others. In Jesus's name. Amen.*

Debts or Trespasses

The God of the universe created us in His image, but sin shattered His character of love in humanity. Therefore, we sin and offend God and one another frequently. Most of the time, it is unintentional, but all too often we sin and hurt God and others knowing full well what we are doing. While that image of God in us is marred, it is still present in varying degrees. But we deny it when we refuse to receive His forgiveness that restores us to Him or when we refuse to forgive others. That is why this phrase of the Lord's Prayer is so important. Without it, we remain alienated from God and from others.

Before we discover the meaning of this phrase and how to apply it in our prayer life, let's take a moment to address the dilemma we often face when we recite it in public. Is it "forgive us our debts as we forgive our debtors," or is it "forgive us our trespasses as we forgive those who trespass against us"? Which one is *right?*

It is an awkward moment we have all experienced. Perhaps it is at an event that is sponsored by a local ministerial association for the community. Or maybe it occurs at a worship service, at a wedding, at a funeral, or at a church of a different denomination. The pastor or person leading out invites the congregation to join in saying the Lord's Prayer together. All join in as they begin to recite the familiar words in one voice. Then, there comes the awkward moment. The moment when the congregation seems to pause, and then in a quieter, more uncertain tone, they either mumble the words they are used to saying or try to quickly figure out which word rendering they should use, "debts" or "trespasses." Quickly the audience recovers by the time they get to the next phrase, and the prayer ends with the same certainty and volume with which it was begun.

For many years, I thought that "debts and debtors" was the *right* way to say the Lord's Prayer. I have discovered I am not alone. The pastoral staff of our church takes turns conducting a Sunday morning worship service at an assisted-living facility just up the street from us. The dear people who attend each Sunday come from a variety of denominations. Most of them are from the more traditional churches like Presbyterian, Lutheran, and Methodist. We had been meeting with them for some time. One day as I was reading a book on the Lord's Prayer, I was reminded that worshipers of many churches recite the Lord's Prayer every week in worship. Therefore, most of those who attend were used to reciting the Lord's Prayer every Sunday.

The next time I led their worship service, I asked them if they would like us to include the Lord's Prayer in their services, and they said, "Yes! Of course!" And so we did! Taking into consideration that most of them were from the more liturgical churches, I decided to use the word "trespasses." After a couple of times doing so, Betty, one of the faithful worshipers, said to me before the start of a service, "I was brought up saying the words debts and debtors. I always thought that was the right way to say the Lord's Prayer!"

Betty is not the only person who raises this question. People who are used to reciting the Lord's Prayer using the word trespass often view their way as the *right* way. So which is it? Roman Catholics, Anglicans, Lutherans, and Methodists, among a few others use "trespasses." Presbyterians, nondenominational evangelicals, and Seventh-day Adventists are among those who use "debtors."

I had thought that "trespasses and trespass against us" was the King James Version found in Luke. I was wrong. Matthew uses debts and debtors, while Luke uses sins and debtors. So how did trespasses come in, and does it change the meaning? It is interesting that it was Tyndale who appears to have translated the word debts in Matthew 6:12 as trespasses in 1526. It was written that way in the *Book of Common Prayer* in 1549. It seems to have become the more common way to repeat the Lord's Prayer at that time. But does it make a difference which form of the Lord's Prayer is used? I don't believe it does.

Matthew seems to use the terms interchangeably when he uses the word for trespasses in verses 14–15. In fact, it seems as if he wanted us to know that our sins must be seen as a missing of the mark that creates a debt we cannot repay, and it also causes an offense against others we cannot make right. Both terms reveal the extent to which we need to receive forgiveness from God and how imperative it is for us then to forgive others.

However, it is also important to note here that:

- The word "debts" puts the focus on the *results* of the offensive, sinful behavior.
- The word "trespasses" or "sins" puts the focus on the offensive, sinful *behavior.*

I have personally found that it helps me to keep my sins and my need for forgiveness in proper focus when I vary my use of these terms.

The difference will become clearer as we look at the two contexts in which the Lord's Prayer was taught.

Before we go any further into applying this part of the Lord's Prayer to our lives, let's look at how the prayer for forgiveness was revealed in the life and ministry of Jesus.

Jesus's Ministry of Forgiveness

Some may wonder how this phrase could apply to Jesus's life. After all, he was sinless. Let us keep in mind that the Lord's Prayer was revealed in his life and in *his ministry.* Certainly Jesus did not need forgiveness for himself. Certainly Jesus was "without sin." That is without question, for Satan himself could find "nothing in him" (John 14:30 KJV) to accuse or attack. And oh how Satan tried!

Throughout his ministry, Jesus dealt with forgiveness. Throughout his ministry Jesus pronounced that those who were in bondage (debtors) were to be set free. At the very beginning of his ministry, Jesus entered the synagogue in Nazareth on the Sabbath. He took a scroll and began to read from Isaiah, what is now referred to as chapter 61. Remember, the Jews were looking for a messiah to come and free them from Roman rule. Furthermore, the last part of Isaiah was read through messianic lenses: the promises of restoration to a place of national prominence, the promises of peace, the promises of prosperity, and the promises of blessing.

The Messiah was going to come and bring to fulfillment the promises that God had made to Moses of God's people receiving and ruling over the entire land He had promised them. Just as Moses had led them out of captivity and bondage from Egypt, so would the Messiah lead them out of captivity and bondage from Rome. But this time it would be permanent. This time it would last. This time all the enemies of God's people would be defeated and destroyed, and God's people would live in the land of milk and honey as they had been promised.

Jesus began to read this messianic passage:

> [18]"The Spirit of the Lord is upon me, because he has anointed me to proclaim good news to the poor. He has sent me to proclaim liberty to the captives and recovering of sight to the blind, to set at liberty those who are oppressed, [19]to proclaim the year of the Lord's favor." (Luke 4:18–19)

Jesus had come to set the captives free! We read in Matthew

that Jesus taught us to pray, "forgive us our debts as we forgive our debtors" (Matthew 6:12, KJV).

We immediately translate that into forgiveness from sin. That is appropriate, as we shall soon see. However, when we do, we miss an important part of Jesus's ministry and message! Jesus used words that were not generally spoken when talking about sin. He used the words debts and debtors when he first gave the Lord's Prayer. Why did he use *debts* the first time he taught the prayer and *trespasses or sins* the second time?

Jesus was addressing an issue of the people that was all too familiar in his day. In that society, when debtors needed to pay their debts, they usually had only one recourse. They could sell whatever they had of value to pay the debt. It began with divesting themselves of their possessions and quickly moved to divesting themselves of their freedom. They would sell their families and then themselves as slaves. Most often there was very little opportunity or ability to repay the debt! While God had given the Year of Jubilee in the Torah to provide debtors with their freedom every fifty years, it seems as if it was seldom applied!

In his ministry, Jesus proclaimed release from the chains of suffering, inhumanity, and degradation that bound social outcasts of all kinds—women, children, the lepers, the blind, the lame, the demon-possessed, and of course, Samaritans! At the same time, he often pronounced that they were forgiven from sin. He did this for two reasons.

- First, it was commonly understood that such situations were the result of a person's sin.
- Second, and more importantly, such circumstances were caused by the consequences of living in a world of sin.

Either way, through his miracles or through his offer of forgiveness, Jesus was releasing the captives—those imprisoned by their lot in life and by their sins.

From Debts to Trespasses

Jesus taught His disciples to pray about forgiveness within the context of the Sermon on the Mount. There, he said that it is just as wrong to hate as to murder. It is just as wrong to minimize the value and worth of others through lust as through immorality, through not following the spirit of the law while following the letter of the law. It is just as wrong to be greedy as to steal. He takes on such common practices as being judgmental, prejudiced, and hypocritical and declares them in violation of God's righteousness. In so doing, Jesus was announcing that the messianic kingdom was primarily a spiritual one and not an earthly one.

Jesus used the term "debts" and "debtors" for the following reasons:

- He did it to show that just as debtors who had become slaves could not possibly repay the debt they owed, so those who are debtors to God could not possibly free themselves from sin. They were as spiritually enslaved to sin and its final consequences as financial debtors were to their owners in that culture!
- He did it to show that debtors who have been forgiven of their debts should be forgiving of those who are in debt to them. Jesus wanted to show that since we have been forgiven for our sins, which we cannot repay, we should forgive others. God is more concerned with how we treat others than with the keeping of religious rules, rites, and traditions.
- He did it to show that just as a debtor could be set from his debt due to the compassion and generosity of their owners, it is only because of the love, mercy, and grace of God that forgiveness is experienced *and* expressed. God alone is the source of forgiveness.

Forgive Us Our Trespasses

Jesus did not just teach forgiveness; he embodied it. He epitomized it! When he was falsely accused of being possessed by Beelzebul (another name for Satan, the prince of demons), he warned his accusers of the dangers of attributing the work of the Spirit to Satan (Matthew

12:22–32). He did not want them to close the door on the Spirit's work. Rather than seeking revenge for their libelous accusations, he offered help. When they tried to belittle him in the eyes of others, Jesus sought to lift them up in the eyes of God.

The best example Jesus gave of the power and effectiveness of forgiveness is found in the story of his crucifixion. Speaking of those who had betrayed him, those who unfairly arrested him, followers who abandoned him, witnesses who had lied about him, those who had tried him, convicted him, spat on him, beaten him, scorned him, taunted him, ridiculed him, and nailed him to the cross, he said:

> "Father, forgive them, for they do not know
> what they are doing." (Luke 23:34)

It is noteworthy that in the original language, it reads, Jesus *kept on saying,* "Father, forgive them."

He said it repeatedly.

Exactly when he began to say it, the Bible does not tell us. Perhaps he began to pray those words:

- When Judas betrayed him.
- When his disciples abandoned him.
- When the fickle Jerusalem crowd changed their chant. Just five days before they had joyously proclaimed Jesus their Messiah when they had shouted, "Hosanna to the Son of David." On the preparation day before the Passover Sabbath, they had proclaimed him worthy of death when they shouted, "Crucify him, crucify him."
- When the religious leaders had twisted his words, had bribed others to lie, and had sought to impeach his character.
- When Pilate washed his hands.
- When Jesus was beaten and mockingly installed as king with a cheap purple robe and a crown of thorns.
- When the wad of shame-filled spit struck and stuck on his body.

- When he staggered under the weight of the cross beam on the road to Calvary.
- When he was taunted!

Certainly those words rang out with each clang of the hammer pounding the nails through the flesh of his hands and feet as he was being nailed to the cross. Most likely he continued repeating them when words of rejection and ridicule cut his heart deeper than the gashes caused by the whip. Words more painful than the nails pounded into his flesh! Most likely he kept repeating them as he noticed that only one of his disciples, John, had come to be there with him. The rest of the disciples had fled out of fear for their lives and remained in hiding. He kept on repeating them as he heard the continued taunts from the crowd and from his two companions in crucifixion (Matthew 27:38–44).

He kept on repeating them as he bore the sins of the world, which became the barrier between him and his Father's presence and approval. For the sins he bore had become the avenue of his Father's disapproval and wrath against sin.

Jesus offered forgiveness to *people who didn't deserve it.*

- He offered forgiveness when it would have been easier to get revenge by calling down ten thousand angels to free him and destroy his accusers.
- He offered forgiveness out of love for the unlovable!
  o Out of tender compassion for the hardhearted!
  o Out of mercy for the merciless.
  o Out of kindness for the cruel!
- He offered forgiveness for debtors by paying the debt they could not pay.
- He provided forgiveness for a world that treated him as a criminal instead of worshipping him as the Creator.

Regardless of when Jesus uttered those words of forgiveness, "Father, forgive them," he said them with every sinner who has ever lived on his heart and mind! That plea for pardon included you and me!

And it still does!

Keeping this in mind, let's go back to our opening illustration. Perhaps, as you read about Bernie Madoff, you saw him as one of the lowlifes of human history. Out of greed for money and power, he took advantage of thousands of people—not just rich people but also many common, average people. He defrauded them! He robbed them of their future security. He destroyed their hard work, hopes, and dreams. Perhaps you put him on the disgraceful pedestal of one of those who are unforgivable, as his son Andrew did.

May I remind you that:

* Jesus forgave a thief who was hanging next to him.
* He forgave Peter who had denied him.
* He forgave a woman who had been caught in adultery.
* He forgave Zacchaeus, who overcharged common and poor people for their taxes and was considered a traitor.
* He forgave murderers, gossipers, idolaters, and many more.

You name the sin, big or little, and Jesus's plea for pardon, "Father forgive them," covered *every* one of them. His plea embraced every sin you and I have ever committed. This includes the wrong acts, the hurtful and offensive behaviors we have committed, and the good deeds we have failed to do.

The plea for pardon Jesus repeatedly uttered overwhelms us. Because of His plea for pardon:

* We have an awareness of the forgiveness Jesus came to this world to provide for all.
* We are amazed at the depth and breadth of the forgiveness Jesus gives.
* We have humility due to the undeserved forgiveness Jesus offers.
* We become the recipients of the mercy, grace, and forgiveness of God when we confess our sins and accept his amazing gift of

forgiveness. For only those who accept his offer of forgiveness are forgiven.

Whatever sin we have committed, Jesus offers us forgiveness. When we accept the forgiveness he has provided, we then experience the peace, hope, and joy of being restored as a son or daughter of God!

However, the two thieves who hung on the crosses on both sides of him remind us of something very important. While forgiveness was provided for both men, offered to both men and available to both men, only one accepted the pardon. Only one received the grace lavished upon him. Only one received the assurance of eternal life from the lips of the Savior. He not only received forgiveness from the Savior, he brought the Savior's forgiveness to the attention of the criminal on the other side of Jesus. Through his attitudes, actions, and words, Jesus revealed that God's grace had opened the gates to allow *both* criminals entrance into the kingdom of heaven. One refused the gift. The other believed and trusted it was open for him. Those two choices are available to everyone!

God's grace opens the gates to allow entrance
into the kingdom of heaven.
You enter the kingdom when you trust
that God opened the gate for you!

As We Forgive

However, this phrase of the Lord's Prayer does not end with the petitioner receiving forgiveness for his or her own personal sins or failures. It goes on and gives a condition for receiving continued forgiveness. That condition is found in the second part of the phrase:

"as we forgive our debtors/
those who trespass against us."

This is a part of the prayer that can be the most difficult to pray, especially when *we* have been hurt or wronged or rejected or abandoned or mistreated or betrayed or marginalized or any combination of the above. When the person who has offended us is someone we have trusted or someone who should have been trustworthy or someone who should have protected us instead of hurting us, praying to forgive them becomes extremely painful and difficult. This includes such people as parents, teachers, pastors, or close friends.

Invariably, a number of questions are often asked. There are four that come up most frequently. And they are questions that deserve an answer. Perhaps the most frequently asked question is the following: "But Jesus was the Son of God. It was easier for him to forgive, wasn't it?"

Of course it was easier for Jesus to forgive as the Son of God, with His divine nature. We must remember, however, that Jesus did not suffer and die on the cross in His divinity. He experienced all the emotional and physical abuse, cruelty, and torture in his humanity. It was in his *humanity* he made the pleas for pardon! I believe Jesus was able to plead with his Father to forgive those who had mistreated and offended him because he had daily prayed, "Your Kingdom come, Your will be done." Reread the paragraphs above that describe the types of offenses for which Jesus asked his Father to forgive those who offended and sinned against him. Can anyone say that they have been offended or hurt worse than Jesus had been? If anything, Jesus's desire for his followers, friends, and enemies to be forgiven reveals the fact that to forgive others for the most unforgivable acts and actions is not only possible, it can be done!

Before answering the second question, we need to see that Jesus taught what he meant and meant what he taught when he gave us the second half of the plea for pardon. We dare not minimize the last part of this phrase! Right after he finished giving the Lord's Prayer in the Sermon on the Mount, he made the following statement:

> [14]"For if you forgive others their trespasses, your heavenly Father will also forgive you, [15]but if you do not forgive others their trespasses, neither will your Father forgive your trespasses." (Matthew 6:14–15)

Jesus does not give us an opt-out clause. There is no fine print to be found for this phrase of the prayer. There is not a single exemption at the end of the prayer or anywhere in the Sermon on the Mount to release us from the requirement to forgive.

This leads to the second question: if *my* forgiveness is dependent on my willingness to forgive others, what happened to God's unconditional love and forgiveness?

Perhaps the best answer was given by Jesus when Peter asked him, "Lord, how often will my brother sin against me, and I forgive him? As many as seven times?" (Matthew 18:21). Apparently Peter thought he was being very gracious when he offered seven as the perfect number of times to forgive someone. The real issue for Peter was not the number of times he must forgive. The real issue was how many times he had to forgive in order to fulfill his obligation!

He must have been astonished when Jesus said to him, "I do not say to you seven times, but seventy-seven times" (Matthew 18:22). Jesus wanted Peter to understand that forgiveness is unconditional. He gave a number so high that it would seem unreachable. And it is unreachable when forgiveness is offered merely to fulfill a requirement. In essence, Jesus was telling Peter, you truly forgive others when you stop counting up their sins and holding them against the offender (2 Corinthians 13:5, NASB). It was for that reason that Jesus gave the parable of the unforgiving servant.

Here is a contemporary, abridged version I found:

> A certain man owed his king two million dollars. He couldn't pay so the king ordered the man, his wife, his children and his property sold to pay the debt. The man, face in the dust, pleaded with the king, "Oh sir, be patient. I will pay it all."
>
> "Two million dollars! Impossible!" said the king. But then in pity, he forgave him all his debt.
>
> The man overjoyed left the king. Outside, he met a neighbor who owed him twenty dollars.
>
> "Pay up," he demanded.
>
> "Just be patient, and I'll have it for you next week," the neighbor said.

"Nothing doing," said the man, and had him thrown into the debtor's prison.

The king got wind of it all and summoned the man. "You ungrateful, evil wretch," he said. "Here I cancelled that tremendous debt for you, and you have the colossal gall to be unforgiving of a few dollars? You have sentenced yourself! Jail until you pay the 2 million you owe."

Then Jesus said to his listeners, "God can do no other unless each of you forgives your brother from your heart."[51]

In essence, the parable teaches that to deny forgiveness to others is to deny the forgiveness you have received from God. God does not base His forgiveness on what we have done to deserve it, since we cannot repay our debt to Him. He gives it out of love and grace. Then He expects us to do the same. Willimon and Hauerwas put it this way:

The one who has experienced forgiveness is the one best able to forgive ... Our forgiveness (of others) begins as a response to our being forgiven. It is not so much an act of generosity toward our fellow offending human beings as an act of gratitude toward our forgiving God.[52]

They are correct! Our motive for forgiving others is rooted in the loving forgiveness given us by God. The forgiveness He offers us is the springboard for our ability to forgive others. At the same time, we must confess that forgiveness can be difficult.

There is a third question that is often raised over the last part of the plea for pardon. It is stated in a variety of ways. But in essence, this is at the heart of the concern: If I have to *do something* to receive

---

[51] David Augsburger, *The New Freedom of Forgiveness* (Chicago: Moody Press, third edition, 2000), 21.

[52] William H. Willimon and Stanley Hauerwas, *Lord, Teach Us: The Lord's Prayer and the Christian Life* (Abingdon Press, Nashville, 1966), 83.

forgiveness, doesn't that deny grace? Doesn't that make God's forgiveness conditional?

Admittedly, the second phrase, "as we have forgiven others," can be understood as meaning our forgiveness of others must be accomplished before we can receive forgiveness. If that is true, it would indeed negate grace. However, there are three explanations to be considered.

First, Jesus spoke in the Aramaic language. There is a past tense used in Aramaic that can also be translated as a present tense. Matthew wrote this phrase in the past tense in the Greek. Luke wrote it in the present tense. Thus the phrase in Matthew reads, "forgive us our debts as we have forgiven our debtors." Luke wrote, "forgive us our debts as we continue to forgive our debtors." Thus our ability to receive forgiveness from God is not dependent on our past ability to forgive. It is affected by our present willingness to forgive others.

The second solution to this dilemma is found in a basic cause and effect that occurs in our physical, emotional, and spiritual lives. Muscles that are not exercised become weaker and will eventually become atrophied if they are never used. People who cannot identify or state their emotions cannot usually empathize with others. And those who refuse to forgive have a hard time receiving forgiveness. Perhaps a simple illustration will help. A lake receives water from a river or streams. It is a lake because it receives and contains fresh water. It can't make itself into a lake! As long as it receives fresh water from a flowing source, it will remain a fresh water lake. But it also needs an outlet to let the fresh water flow out. If there is not an outflow of water, it soon becomes what we call a salt sea or a dead sea. The water can no longer remain fresh.

That is why Jesus taught us to ask for forgiveness as we forgive. It is not because we earn our forgiveness. There is a difference between earning forgiveness and adopting an attitude that makes forgiveness possible! If we think about forgiveness in light of our lake analogy, God's grace and forgiveness flow into our lives. And as long as we receive fresh supplies from Him, we will experience forgiveness. But if we dam up our lives by refusing to forgive others, the bitterness, resentment, and desire for revenge remove from our lives the peace and joy that are the results of His forgiveness.

The last solution to be considered for this question is that if we have been forgiven, we are already living in God's kingdom. Thus we are the recipients of God's mercy, grace, and forgiveness. It is part of His very character! We have discovered His kingdom is a place where righteousness dwells. His grace opens the gates of the kingdom for us to enter. We enter when we trust that we belong to His kingdom. A kingdom whose laws are motivated by love and obeyed out of love! A kingdom where trespasses are forgiven because of His great love and mercy!

But that still does not mean that forgiveness will come easily! I have heard people say that they must "feel like forgiving" before they can forgive. If that is how forgiveness is given, then forgiveness would never take place when we are deeply hurt or offended! Jesus's struggles in the wilderness, in Gethsemane, and on Calvary demonstrate that we do not wait to forgive until we feel like it! The apostle Paul understood this. That is why his ultimate description of love in 1 Corinthians 13 deals more with actions than feelings. It is described in terms of behaviors and not emotions. And in that description of love, forgiveness is included when Paul wrote: "it (love) keeps no record of wrongs" (verse 5, NIV). Paul's description of love is an expansion of Jesus's statement in the Sermon on the Mount that we call the Golden Rule: "In everything, therefore, treat people the same way you want them to treat you, for this is the Law and the Prophets" (Matthew 7:12 NASB).

With this in mind, we come to the awareness that forgiveness is the ultimate expression of love! It is something we choose to do, even though it may be a difficult choice. It is something we do even though it often involves a struggle to offer forgiveness to someone who has offended or hurt us. It is something we do because it is God's way of expressing His love for us. John 3:16–17 is the greatest manifestation of the love that chooses and prefers to offer forgiveness. He is not eager to condemn.

There is a fourth question that is often raised regarding the mandate for us to forgive. It is often asked, "But doesn't the offender have to *ask* to be forgiven before I forgive them?" The answer is no! Remember, forgiveness is the ultimate expression of love. When children misbehave, most parents forgive them long before the child says, "I am sorry," don't they? The Bible is filled with statements and examples of God's plan and offer of pardon before there was ever a plea for forgiveness.

"Before"[53]

Before there was a problem in Paradise,
    there was a plan in Heaven;[54]
Before man had free will to choose,
    God had a free gift to offer;[55]

Before there was a snake in the tree,
    there was a Savior on the cross;[56]
Before there was a desire by man to be like God,
    there was a decision by God to become a man;[57]

Before there was rebellion in the heart of man,
    there was reconciliation in the heart of God;[58]
Before there was fear to cause man to hide from God,
    there was love to cause God to search for man;[59]

Before there were fig leaves to hide man's shame,
    there was a robe to reveal God's glory;[60]
Before there were fingers pointing blame,
    there were outstretched arms providing forgiveness;[61]

Before there was the curse of sin,
    there was the blessing of salvation;[62]

---

[53] Author, Gary Taber.
[54] Revelation 13:8.
[55] Romans 5:15.
[56] Genesis 3:13–15; Galatians 3:13.
[57] Genesis 3:4–6; Philippians 2:5–8.
[58] Romans 5:10.
[59] Genesis 3:8–10.
[60] Genesis 3:7; Isaiah 61:10.
[61] Genesis 3:11–13; Deuteronomy 11:2; Colossians 1:21–22.
[62] Proverbs 3:33.

Before there was the toil of man's labor,
    there was the peace of God's rest;[63]

Before there were angels to keep sinners from the tree of life on earth,
    there were angels to prepare saints for the tree of life in heaven;[64]
Before there was the disgrace of man's wickedness,
    there was the grace of God's righteousness;[65]

Before there was the unfaithfulness of man,
    there was the faithfulness of God;[66]

And there still is!

Aren't you glad God didn't wait for Adam and Eve to ask for forgiveness before He created the plan of salvation to provide and offer forgiveness? Aren't you grateful God didn't wait for *you* to ask for forgiveness before He forgave you? So often it is the heart that forgives before the forgiveness is requested that enables and inspires the requests for forgiveness!

And yet that does not mean we automatically have the desire to forgive, the willingness to forgive, or even the hope to be able to forgive. True forgiveness does not always come easy. The deeper the offense, the harder it is to forgive. The deeper the hurt we experience, the longer the struggle to find it in our hearts to forgive. The more egregious the offense made against us or our loved ones, the more difficult it is see the possibility to forgive. The path to forgiveness can be a difficult one, indeed.

The Difficulty of Forgiving

It is one thing to say and recognize the need to be forgiving, but it is another to put into practice. It is much harder to truly forgive! It is one thing to recognize the importance of forgiving. It is much harder to

---

[63] Matthew 11:28–29.
[64] Genesis 3:24; Revelation 22:1–2.
[65] Psalm 45:6–7.
[66] Psalm 31:2–5.

respond with forgiveness. For the natural reaction to being deeply hurt, rejected, humiliated, and so on is to seek revenge, to treat the offenders with resentment, to hold a grudge against them, or to hate them. Another form of revenge is to give them the silent treatment while often making sure others know what they have done to you.

Jesus knew that the failure to forgive boomerangs on those who refuse to forgive. They can often become bitter. Or they are filled with an anger, resentment, hatred, and distrust that often spills over into their relationships with others. It always affects their relationship with the God who has already forgiven them. In short, they become imprisoned in the walls of unforgiveness they have built, while the offender most often goes free.

Having identified the importance and necessity of forgiveness for those who are followers of Christ, I must acknowledge that there are times when forgiving others is extremely difficult and painful. Lewis Smedes wrote the following about forgiveness:

> Forgiving is love's toughest work and love's biggest risk ... Forgiveness is God's invention for coming to terms with a world in which, despite their best intentions, people are unfair to each other and hurt each other deeply. He began by forgiving us. And He invites us all to forgive each other.[67]

We dare not ignore or seek to find excuses for failing to pray the second part of the prayer for pardon that Jesus gave in the prayer he taught his disciples—and us—to pray. For if we do not forgive others, we will fail to continue to receive the pardon we may receive—and which we do not deserve, either! Our failure to give grace to others will dam up the flow of God's grace to us. Not because God is not willing to continue to forgive us but because we will have sealed off our hearts to receive it. As Kent Crockett put it:

---

[67] Lewis B. Smedes, *Forgive and Forget: Healing the Hurts We Don't Deserve* (New York: Pocket Books, 1984), 12.

> The longer you allow the root of bitterness to grow in
> the soil of your heart, the more love it will devour. [68]

Only the grace of God can enable a person to offer this kind of forgiveness. This is true even when the person offering it knows very little, if anything, about the God of grace. Grace is an attribute of God that man cannot create. Sometimes it shows up as a vestige of the image of God with which man was created. Most often grace is expressed only after a struggle against our natural reactions for vindication, revenge, and/or restitution.

The problem we have is that the grace of forgiveness does not usually flow out from us naturally.

Therefore, we must struggle with the process of forgiving those who have deeply hurt us. This can be especially true of those we have trusted or who we should be able to trust. This would include people who were supposed to love, care, and protect us, such as our family, teachers, friends, church members, and yes, pastors. Instead of supporting and encouraging us, they wounded us deeply. And that is what can make forgiving so very difficult!

It is also very difficult to forgive strangers who have hurt us or our loved ones in the worst ways, such as theft, rape, and/or murder. We must struggle to the point of being able to forgive those who do not deserve our forgiveness or who have done what seems to be unforgiveable.

Every now and then, we come across amazing stories of people who find a way to forgive the unforgiveable. I want to share one with you. This is a story about a mother whose own child was murdered and her struggle with the resulting painful emotions she experienced. David Collins in the Vintage Voice Newsletter reported:

> In the early 1980's in Southern California a young girl
> was abducted, molested and murdered. The murderer
> was arrested, convicted and sentenced to life in prison,
> but this process brought no healing or consolation to the
> mother. Unable to shake the rage that flooded her each

---

[68] Kent Crockett, *I Once Was Blind But Now I Squint* (Chattanooga, TN: AMG Publishers, 2004), 94.

day, she quit her job and, and with her family, moved to a new location to start again. Then, she moved again. And then, again! Nothing changed except the deepening of the pain.

One day a new acquaintance invited her to go along with them to church. Her response was indifferent, but the friend persisted, and gradually something triggered the beginning of a journey of change. In part, it was the warmth of the circle of new friends, then the support of a prayer group, then the beginnings of exploring the Bible. Slowly, painfully, over a period of three to four years, she discovered that the memories of her daughter were taking on a different color and tone. The recollections of happy days with her daughter began to offer peace rather than remorse and resentment. Forgotten memories appeared to awaken gratitude and surprising joy in recalling her daughter's life. And her feelings toward the murderer began to grow less cold as the monster began to take on human dimensions. In astonishment, she heard herself, as from a distance, use words about forgiving what had been emotionally outside any consideration of forgiveness. She began to talk about this with friends, in a small group, and once in a church service.

Once the transformation began, it accelerated as she accepted an invitation to talk to parents of murdered children, then to several groups of prisoners. Through a chaplain of a nearby state penitentiary she was invited to share her experience in a prison Chapel Service. She clung to the pulpit as her story of years of torment and slow, inexplicable recovery came out with deep emotion.

"I am here to tell you that one person on the outside is seeking to forgive the man who crushed the life out of her cherished daughter, and, in the name of Christ, wants him to feel loved and prized as a human being."

Her words, her tears, her transparency were shattering. In the silence that followed her address, a man stood, identified himself by name, and said,

"I am the man you are waiting to forgive."

She gasped, totally taken aback by this surprise. Tears filled her eyes ... and slowly she opened her arms. The man at last came to the platform. They embraced. Her journey of offering forgiveness was nearing its end. His journey of finding it was just begun.[69]

Let's compare and contrast the story of this mother and the story of Andrew Madoff! One story tells the positive results of forgiving. The other displays the disastrous results of his refusal to forgive. What a difference forgiving others makes in our lives.

Unfortunately, Andrew Madoff's story does not seem to have ended well. In a variety of interviews, he repeatedly stated that he could not forgive his father. In December 2012, the cancer he had fought off in 2003 returned. In an article written in *People* magazine in April 2013, the following statement by the author of the article and a quote by Andrew is telling: "Andrew believes the stress of the last few years at least partially opened the door for his cancer. 'One way to think of this is the scandal and everything that happened killed my brother very quickly,' he says. 'And it's killing me slowly.'"[70]

Andrew Madoff died without ever visiting his father. I wish Andrew had come to recognize his need to forgive his father. I can't help but wonder if the stress that was "killing me slowly" was the added stress caused by the negative emotions of anger, bitterness, and unresolved conflict of refusing to forgive.

So, how do we work through the process of forgiving what to us seems to be unforgivable? If you have been deeply hurt and are struggling with how to forgive someone, there is not enough space in this book to address the vital and important issues of forgiveness. These

---

[69] David Augsburger, *The Freedom of Forgiveness,* 32–33, adapted from David Collins, *The Vintage Voice,* Newsletter, Church Pension Fund, (1991): 1.
[70] Nicole Weisensee Egan, "Andrew Madoff: I'll Never Forgive My Father," *People* (April 22, 2013): 98.

include such issues as what it means to forgive and forget, forgiving yourself, to what extent you have to be reconciled to the offender, and how you know if you have truly forgiven someone.

I have four recommendations for you.

1. Once again look at Jesus and the forgiveness he repeatedly gave to those who were crucifying him. Let his example of divine love and grace soften your heart and give you the will, desire, and ability to forgive. Read and reflect on passages such as Hebrews 12:1–3:

    ¹THEREFORE THEN, since we are surrounded by so great a cloud of witnesses [who have borne testimony to the Truth], let us strip off *and* throw aside every encumbrance (unnecessary weight) and that sin which so readily (deftly and cleverly) clings to *and* entangles us, and let us run with patient endurance *and* steady *and* active persistence the appointed course of the race that is set before us, ²Looking away [from all that will distract] to Jesus, Who is the Leader *and* the Source of our faith [giving the first incentive for our belief] and is also its Finisher [bringing it to maturity and perfection]. He, for the joy [of obtaining the prize] that was set before Him, endured the cross, despising *and* ignoring the shame, and is now seated at the right hand of the throne of God. ³Just think of Him Who endured from sinners such grievous opposition *and* bitter hostility against Himself [reckon up and consider it all in comparison with your trials], so that you may not grow weary *or* exhausted, losing heart *and* relaxing *and* fainting in your minds. (AMP)

2. Begin to pray for that person, asking God to enable you to see them with His heart and eyes.
3. Seek counsel and advice from a pastor or Christian counselor.

4. Read some books on forgiveness. I highly recommend the following:
    *   Lewis B. Smedes's classic books on forgiveness, *Forgive and Forget* and *The Art of Forgiving*
    *   David Augsburger's books, *The New Freedom of Forgiveness* and *Caring Enough to Forgive.*

You may ask your pastor, a counselor, or friend if they have a book on forgiveness they would recommend.

The Power of Grace

We must ever keep in mind that forgiveness requires grace. The grace of God to forgive is not just an act of erasing the sin or offense. Perhaps the graphic below will help you see and better grasp what I am trying to convey.

God's Grace
Is Power

Power to forgive the undeserving.
Power to forgive the unforgivable.
Power to heal the pain
of both the offender and the one offended.
And power to offer reconciliation and restoration
for impossible situations and circumstances.

Lewis Smedes sums up the power of forgiveness in this way: "When we forgive we ride the crest of love's cosmic wave; we walk in stride with God. And we heal the hurt we never deserved."[71]

---

[71] Lewis B. Smedes, *Forgive and Forget: Healing the Hurts We Don't Deserve,* 192.

Reflection and Application

Perhaps you could ask yourself the following questions:

- Is there anyone in your life that you need to forgive?
- Are you struggling with the pain and heartache of being mistreated, offended, or deeply hurt?
- Are you carrying the burden of unresolved anger, bitterness, and/ or hate as the result of what has taken place?
- Are you trapped in the emotional prison of unforgiveness?

Why not take the first step of praying for the ability to forgive as you have been forgiven. Then, seek to take the necessary steps that God impresses you to take.

Prayer

Our Father in heaven, as we think of forgiving others, Jesus's pattern for prayer reminds us that we are Your children and the undeserving recipients of Your love and grace. Remind us that we are not Your only child. That others who call You Father, and others who You see as Your children, receive the same love and grace. Remind us that we need to see them through Your eyes and with Your heart.

Father, Your kingdom of grace includes the call for us to be citizens of Your kingdom who express Your grace to one another as we live together, as we seek Your righteousness. It includes Your will that we forgive others as we have been forgiven. We recognize that we can only truly forgive as we receive the life of Christ by faith as our daily bread. His continued plea for forgiveness for those who crucified him amazes, confounds, and humbles us. We are grateful for the forgiveness we so readily receive from him. We admit the reluctance we too often have to forgive others. Give me, and each reader, the desire, ability, and determination to forgive those who offend, hurt, or violate us.

When we are unwilling to forgive, soften our hearts and remove our reluctance to forgive. Soften our wills and release our resistance to forgive. Give us wisdom to seek the help we need from pastors, counselors, or books that will enable us to truly forgive with the same depth of forgiveness that Jesus had for those who crucified him. Free us from the prisons we have erected in our lives. And may Your loving grace be the power that heals and transforms us and those we forgive.

In Jesus's character. Amen.

Chapter 7

Prayer for Protection:
We Need to Be Delivered

And do not lead us into temptation, but deliver us from the evil one.
—MATTHEW 6:13 (NKJV)

No one is a firmer believer in the power of prayer
than the devil;
not that he practices it, but he suffers from it.
—GUY H. KING[72]

It was November 2006. James Kim, his wife, and their two daughters were going to Seattle, Washington, from San Francisco to celebrate with family the Thanksgiving holiday. On the way back home, they were going to take a little extra time for a vacation on the southwest coast of Oregon.

They left Seattle on Saturday, November 25, and travelled south to Portland. Then they were to head west on the main road from Portland that would take them over to the coast and the resort where they had their reservations. That night it was raining. Somehow they had been delayed, their attention had been diverted, and they missed the turnoff that would lead them to the coast. It was a while before they noticed their mistake. They stopped to get a bite to eat, got out the map, and discovered there was a road that was near them that went straight across

---

[72] Guy H. King, *Prayer Secrets* (Vinton, VA: Christ Life Publications, 1997), 50.

Oregon to the coast. They made the decision to take the road closer to them rather than turn around and retrace their steps.

They were already late, so they called the resort to let them know they would still be coming that night, although they would be very late.

They loaded up in their car and headed down the road, not knowing that local drivers would never travel Bear Camp Road in wintertime if it were raining. The rain soon turned to snow. The longer they travelled, the more inclement the weather became.

It puzzled them that they were the only ones on the road, but they were determined to get to their destination.

The snow was falling so heavily, without any tracks from any other cars. They did not notice when they inadvertently left the main road to follow a logging road.

The first decision to take Bear Camp Road was a bad one. The mistake of taking the logger's road was a disaster. Sometime earlier, someone else had made a major mistake. At the onset of winter, the agents for the Bureau of Land Management were supposed to lock the gate to that road. They knew there were some hunters in the area, and they decided to leave it open for them, fearing they might be trapped behind it. The open gate allowed the Kims to take the wrong road down into a ravine.

By this time they were so tired and exhausted, and it was snowing so much that they decided to sleep in their car for the night. They would leave the next morning, if the weather cleared.

In the morning, they discovered that they were stuck in the snow. They had just a few snacks to share with their two young daughters. They decided that since they did not know how long it would take to either get out or be found, they should eat as little as possible. They rationed the food and gave their two girls a little bigger share. They used the snow for water.

One day passed. Every now and then, they would start the car to get some warmth. But it would last for only a short time. It didn't take very long for the car to run out of gas. They gathered up the few magazines in their car and small pieces of paper. James went out and got as much dry wood as he could find, and he made a fire. Not only was he hoping to provide his family some warmth, he also hoped it would provide a signal so that somebody, *anybody,* would spot them. There was only one huge problem. No one knew they were on this road!

They couldn't get a signal on their cell phones because they were down in the ravine. But they tried sending text messages, just in case.

Another day passed ... and another. Apparently, James had heard or learned that there is a greater chance of surviving if you stay where you are and wait for people to find you. So he and his wife did everything they could to survive the cold and care for the needs of the children. James got out of the car. He got out the car jack and took one tire off and burned it. He was hoping someone would see the black smoke from the tire. Certainly! Someone! Even an animal could bark at the black smoke! Not a single response! At intervals, he burned each tire, until they were all burned up. Unfortunately, no one saw the black smoke.

Finally, on the sixth day, December 2, James told his wife, "I am going to walk out and find help." He looked at his map. He decided they were probably within four miles of the next town. Surely he could find someone to help them! He knew that unless he did something, his family was doomed to die. More than likely, he also knew the risk he was taking for himself. He was willing to risk his own life to save the lives of his family, because he knew that they could not save themselves. So James set out on his own for help. Since he did not know he had taken the logger's road, he chose to go in the wrong direction. That evening, he didn't come back. Nor did he return the next day.

During all this time, search parties and planes had been looking for them, but they were searching in the wrong areas. A man, who was a techie, broke the law and was able to retrieve their text messages. But it still didn't pinpoint the exact location. Because no one would ever expect them to take the logger's trail, they had not searched that area.

Two days later, on December 4, a local helicopter operator, searching on his own, spotted James's wife and two daughters trying to follow James's footprints in the snow. The pilot was able to get help, and they were rescued. They later found James, but he had died of hypothermia. He died a hero who gave his life so his family could live.[73]

Adam and Eve took a wrong turn in the Garden of Eden, and when

---

[73] Details taken from ABC *20/20* broadcast, "Kati Kim Tells Her Family's Harrowing Ordeal," February 11, 2011.

they did, mankind became doomed to death, too. Lost! Unable to save themselves! Mankind would need a deliverer!

- Only when we come to the realization that there is absolutely no way we can save ourselves!
- Only when we come to the realization that there is nothing we can do to win the victory over the devil!
- Only when we admit that we are impotent in the battle with the devil!
- Only *then* will we be able to repeat, either word for word or in our own words, the next petition of the Lord's Prayer, "Lead us not into temptation, but deliver us from evil."

Hopefully, you are now recognizing the importance of what we discovered in the second chapter. The pattern of the Lord's Prayer *is* important! It gives us a new paradigm when we pray. Taking time to reflect on our relationship with our Father in the heavens prepares us for reflecting on what it means to belong to His kingdom. It reminds us that only as we yield to His will can we fulfill His purpose for our lives. This gives us insight into the requests we make for our daily physical, emotional, and spiritual needs. Only then can we know the various ways we have offended God and others. Which will enable us to ask for forgiveness and to offer forgiveness to others. It is then that we are prepared to pray about what it means to be delivered from evil!

Prayer

Our Father in heaven, today we are grateful that we know that You are omniscient, all-powerful. We are in awe that Your love motivates and directs all that You do. We are aware that You are the supreme Sovereign of the universe. And we are amazed that You still long to—and do—dwell within us through Your Spirit. May others see Jesus in us.

Father, thank You for Your plan, which implants the principles of Your kingdom in our hearts and lives today. May others see Your righteousness, grace, and love in our interactions with our family, friends, those with whom we work, and those You bring into contact with us. Give us the desire to fulfill Your will as we serve others. Give us insight into their lives and the needs they have. May we serve them with compassion and love!

Father, Your Word invites us to "taste and see that the Lord is good!" Today we acknowledge our spiritual need of Jesus as the source of our lives, the sustainer of our lives, and the aspiration of our lives.

Father, Jesus told us that Your Spirit will convict us of sin, because we do not trust in Jesus. Forgive us for our failure to entrust our lives to Jesus as our Shepherd who cares, guides, and keeps us. May we forgive others as we recognize your desire to free them from guilt and free us from the emotions created when we have an unforgiving spirit.

As we consider the phrase about temptation and evil in Jesus's prayer, open our minds and hearts to understand and apply the principles of this phrase in our lives. Thank you for the deliverance we have found in You.

In the character of Jesus. Amen.

Three Key Words

Before we go any further, we need to make sure we understand what it is Jesus was referring to when he taught his followers to pray ...

"Lead us not into temptation, but deliver us from evil."

There are three key words that we think we know, but do we? It may surprise you to learn that they have meanings we often have not considered when we recite the Lord's Prayer.

The first key word is the word "temptation." First we need to acknowledge the sources of temptation. Sometimes we are tempted by other people to do something we know to be wrong. The temptation can come in the form of manipulation, peer pressure, fear, flattery, deceit, or a misuse of power.

Other times we experience temptations from within, from ourselves, because we are selfish by nature. These would include our passions, our lusts, our temptation to lie to protect ourselves in some way, our desire to save face, our problems with greed, jealousy, and self-esteem. The list goes on and on of things that create temptations to go against God's Word, either by doing things we are prohibited from doing or failing to do things we have been commanded to do. These kinds of temptations we can't blame on anyone else, if we are being honest. If we are not honest, we will yield to the inner temptation to blame someone else!

And then there are those that come to us from the dark side, from the devil and his angels. He often tries to downplay sin as if it is not a big deal. Then when we fall prey to his temptations, he reminds us how deplorable our sins are to God. How often does the devil tempt us by attacking our spiritual Achilles' heel, those areas of personal weakness that we inherited or into which we have repeatedly fallen (i.e., sinned) and developed "a bad habit" that causes us great pain.

With this in mind, perhaps the question we need to ask is, what does it mean when we pray, "Lead us not into temptation, but deliver us from evil"?

It may surprise you that Jesus had something else in mind than asking God not to lead us into or experience temptation to commit sin(s). By that I mean praying that we are not tempted to commit such acts as lying, gossiping, and swearing. After all, why should we have to ask God not to lead us into temptation, to do that which he has revealed as sinful acts?

Even when I was a young boy, I wondered about this phrase in the Lord's Prayer. Why should we pray for God not to lead us into temptation when it is the devil or wickedness that leads us there? After all, under inspiration, James wrote:

> Let no one say when he is tempted, "I am being tempted by God," for God cannot be tempted with evil, and he himself tempts no one. (James 1:13)

So what did Jesus have in mind? According to the *Theological Dictionary of the New Testament* (TDNT), the main point of the word used here for "temptation" in the original language is not the word for tempting someone to commit a specific sin. It is really a word that refers to the times of testing we face. "What is at issue in temptation is being tempted by ungodly powers, both in the last day tribulation and in all afflictions *(which can include specific temptations)*."[74]

That is why in Gethsemane Jesus told his disciples to watch so that they would not enter into *temptation*. Jesus wasn't warning them about a specific temptation they were to face. He was warning them about a test of their faith and trust in him as Messiah. He wanted them to watch in prayer because in themselves they would be defenseless against the temptations of the devil to distrust God. He wanted them to know that in themselves they had no power to withstand the devil's assault on them.

I want you to notice what is primarily at issue in the phrase, "lead us not into temptation." It is asking God to keep us from those types of spiritual crises when we are making decisions to either follow God or follow Satan. It is not about a temptation to have a moral lapse. It is about a time of testing in which we are deciding who will be in charge of our lives. The Good News Translation captures this nuance very well: "Do not bring us to hard testing, but keep us safe from the Evil One."

The Bible includes numerous examples of times of testing. Daniel

---

[74] Gerhard Kittel and Gerhard Friedrich, eds., Geoffrey W. Bromiley, trans., *Theological Dictionary of the New Testament, v. 6* (Grand Rapids, MI: William B. Eerdmans, 1979), 823.

and his friends experienced such testing when they were required by King Nebuchadnezzar to eat the food that had been offered to idols. To do so would have been considered an act of worshipping the gods of Babylon (Daniel 1). Another example is when Peter and John were ordered by the religious leaders in Jerusalem not to teach and proclaim Christ under threat of imprisonment (Acts 4). Times of testing occur when the devil is working to destroy our faith in God, as he tried to do with Job.

Understanding the above concept adds weight to the meaning of the second key word as given by various manuscripts. They thus translate the word evil as the words "Evil One." To ask God not to lead us into times of testing and to deliver us from the "Evil One" go together, don't they?

Besides, the evil one is the source of evil of every kind. The *Theological Dictionary of the New Testament* describes evil as being "things or people that are bad, or worthless, or ill-natured or unfavorable or sorrowful, or unhappy or are hurtful or who are futile or who are malicious."[75] In other words, it is sin as revealed in various and assorted forms of behaviors or activities that wreak havoc on this world and in your life and in mine.

The third word we want to look at is "deliver." It means for someone to deliver you when you are going downstream and you are caught in the current that is too strong for you to swim to the side. It is the idea of someone who is locked in chains, and they need someone to come and free them from the chains because they cannot free themselves. Furthermore, in Greek, the actions described are being done by someone else. Deliver us from the "evil one" reminds us that we must be delivered, because we *cannot* deliver ourselves.

---

[75] Gerhard Kittel and Gerhard Friedrich, eds., Geoffrey W. Bromily, trans., *Theological Dictionary of the New Testament: Abridged in One Volume,* WORD*search* CROSS e-book.

Jesus's Greatest Temptations

Keeping the meanings of these three words—temptation, evil one, and deliver—in mind, let us look again at the life and ministry of Jesus and see how this phrase was revealed in his life and ministry.

It is not hard to apply this phrase to the life of Jesus, is it? Immediately we remember that at the very beginning of his ministry Jesus was led by the Spirit to the wilderness to be *tempted* by the devil. This was not a casual temptation. This was not a temptation to say a bad word, to spread a juicy piece of gossip, to lie to save face, and so on. This was a temptation to give up his ministry—to distrust God's love, care, and concern for him—to doubt and disbelieve his relationship with his Father. In other words, he was tempted to depend upon himself and not upon his Father.

In fact, the temptation of Jesus in the wilderness did not begin with the temptation to turn the stones into bread by his own power apart from God. The first temptation the devil hurled at Jesus was Satan's sarcastic insinuation, "*if* you are the Son of God." The devil was in effect saying to Jesus, "If God is your Father, why would He leave you out here in this desolate place without food and water? What kind of Father treats His son that way?"

The greatest test Jesus continually faced was the temptation to doubt his relationship with his Father. It was the testing that would determine his success or failure as the Messiah throughout his ministry.

In the wilderness, the devil sought to deceive Jesus. He attempted to get Jesus to forego the plan of salvation. First came the temptation for Jesus to alleviate his hunger by using his own power as the Son of God and turn the stones into bread. The second temptation was for Jesus to jump off the cliff and force God to protect him. The devil's final temptation of Jesus took place at the top of the temple. In effect, Satan offered Jesus the position of being the earthly Messiah the Jews were expecting. He told Jesus that he would give Jesus the kingdoms of the earth to rule over. Without having to go to the cross! Without having to face the separation from his Father caused by sin! All Jesus had to do was to worship Satan!

All three temptations of Jesus in the wilderness by the evil one were, at their very core, tests to get Jesus to distrust God and to rely on himself. Jesus answered every temptation with a quotation from scripture, saying, "It is written." Why? Because he wanted the devil to know that he was trusting in what God said and not what the devil said.

That was not the only time Jesus was tempted. He was tempted over and over again by the scribes and Pharisees. His mothers, his brothers, and even his disciples tempted him to change his mission from being a suffering Messiah to being a kingly Messiah.

In John 6, after Jesus had fed the multitude, the people wanted to recognize him as the Messiah and crown him king. They wanted him to reign over Israel and to drive out the Romans. Jesus refused because that was not the mission his Father had given him. The people for whom He had performed a divine miracle provided the temptation to rule over an earthly kingdom of power. Again, it was a time of testing. It was a temptation for Jesus to take the easy way out

In the Garden of Gethsemane, Jesus faced yet another time of testing. His plea of "not my will, but Your will be done" to his Father was repeated three times. The devil was tempting him to give up the plan of salvation. He was tempting him by telling him the pain he was already suffering, on account of the sins of people, wasn't worth it. He wasn't even to Calvary, yet the temptation and weight of sin were so great that Jesus had sweated drops of blood from the undue stress. It was testing time!

Jesus was submitting his will to the will of the Father. After Jesus made his decision to drink the cup of suffering, God sent angels to encourage and strengthen him. But his anguish remained.

Of course, there was the ultimate time of testing on the cross. Repeatedly he was tested. He was taunted with the words of the mocking crowd, "Save yourself! If you are the Christ, come down from the cross." The chief priests, scribes, and elders mocked him, saying, "He saved others; he cannot save himself." At the beginning, both criminals on either side of him ridiculed him (Matthew 27:37–44). It was a test to doubt the efficacy of his death!

Little did they realize that if he saved himself, he could save no one else. Only if he was obedient to his Father's will and experienced the death on the cross would he be able to save himself and the universe from the ravages and wickedness of the evil one. When he arose from the grave, not only was Jesus delivered from the evil one, but you and I were, too!

Jesus can teach us to pray:

> "Do not bring us to hard testing,
> but keep us safe from the Evil One."
> (Matthew 6:13 GNT)

Because he had been led into temptation and had been delivered from the evil one!

Applying to Our Lives

Having observed how Jesus's life and ministry embodied this aspect of the Lord's Prayer, how are we to include this phrase in our prayers?

You are probably asking the same question I asked when I first understood that this petition means we are asking God not to lead us into times of testing. That question was, "But, God, won't we all face times of testing when we have to face a choice between following God, depending on God, or following Satan and depending on myself? So why should we ask God to deliver us from times of testing when inevitably we know we will experience them anyway?"

The key is in a little word in Matthew's version that is translated as "but" in most translations. It can also be translated as "nevertheless."

> "Lead us not into times of testing;
> *Nevertheless* deliver us from the evil one."
> (my translation)

In other words, Jesus knows that *we will* face times of testing. We don't want to experience them, but we will. When we do face times of testing, if we are trusting in Christ, *nevertheless*, whatever we face, God will deliver us from evil or the evil one. The Bible is filled with examples of people who faced times of testing and were delivered. Esther, Daniel, and Paul and Silas in the prison in Phillipi are just a few. Christian history abounds with stories of God's deliverance during times of testing. Martin Luther experienced God's deliverance when he opposed the papacy. C. S. Lewis was delivered from the evil one. His faith was tested when his wife became ill with cancer and died. The lyrics to the well-known hymn, "It Is Well with My Soul," also known as "When Peace Like a River," were written by Horatio Spafford while on a ship heading to England to be with his grieving wife. Their four daughters had drowned when the ship they were on crashed with another ship. His wife had survived. This tragedy had been preceded first by the sudden death of their son and then by the loss of the family fortune in the Chicago fire just two years earlier. The words of this popular hymn are testimony to God's power to deliver from the evil one in the darkest of circumstances. These are just a few examples of people who were delivered from the evil one.

We are not to look for times of testing. We are not to bring on times of testing by acting inappropriately or by provoking others by the way we convey our beliefs and our relationship with God. Nevertheless, when times of testing come, we can ask God to deliver us from the evil one.

The Bible tells us that ultimately God will do that for every one of us. Jesus won the times of testing in his life and in his ministry. On the cross, he cried out, "It is finished," winning the victory over the evil one for you and me. In the garden, after the resurrection, he told Mary He was going to see his Father to receive the acceptance of his victory on behalf of fallen humanity.

At the end of time, he will shout out:

> "The evildoer must continue to do evil, and the one who
> is morally filthy must continue to be filthy. The one
> who is righteous must continue to act righteously, and
> the one who is holy must continue to be holy."
> (Revelation 22:11, NET)

The times of testing will be over. We will be delivered from the evil one—forever!

In the meantime, while we are waiting for that day, how do we apply this part of the Lord's Prayer to our lives and to our ministry for others?

N.T. Wright has summarized very succinctly what it indicates. "First it means 'let us escape the great tribulation, the great time of testing that is coming on all the world'. "[76] That is part of it. No one wants to go through that awful time. Some of us have had nightmares thinking about it.

Many Christians now believe they get to bypass it through the secret rapture. Why would Jesus teach us to pray asking to be delivered from the time of testing during the tribulation or time of trouble at the end, if he was going to whisk the church away before the tribulation would occur? To pray this part of the prayer serves as a reminder of God's ability to protect, guard, and keep us!

But we can also pray this part of the prayer when we ask God not to allow us to be tempted beyond what we can withstand—temptation that we can't handle. Paul believed that to be true. In Corinthians 10:13, he said that God would not allow us to suffer temptations more than we can bear. I have known more than a handful of people who have suffered much in this world. They suffered so much that they questioned if they were being asked to handle more than they could bear. However, Paul knew what he was talking about. Look at all that he faced:

> [23]I have worked harder, been put in prison more often, whipped times without number, and faced death again and again. [24]Five different times the Jewish leaders gave me thirty-nine lashes. Three times I was beaten with rods. Once I was stoned. [25]Three times I was shipwrecked. Once I spent a whole night and a day adrift at sea. [26]I have traveled on many long journeys. I have faced danger from rivers and from robbers. I have faced danger from my own people, the Jews, as well as from the Gentiles. I have faced danger in the cities, in the deserts, and on the seas. And I have faced danger from men who claim to be believers but are not. [27]I have worked hard and long, enduring many sleepless

---

[76] N.T. Wright, *The Lord and His Prayer*, 73.

nights. I have been hungry and thirsty and have often gone without food. I have shivered in the cold, without enough clothing to keep me warm. (2 Corinthians 11:23b–27, NLT)

Paul spoke from the reality of his own life! He shared his experiences in suffering in order to encourage believers when they would face times of testing.

When we pray "lead us not into times of testing," above all it means we believe our God will enable us to pass safely through the times and events that will tempt us to lose our trust in God. This will include the following types of crises:

- job or career loss
- loss of the family home due to a fire or foreclosure
- sickness, suffering or death of a loved one
- being mistreated, falsely accused or rejected by others, especially those close to us
- mistreatment or persecution at work because of your faith
- experiencing various difficult, tough times that can create doubt and may result in asking "God, why is this happening to me or someone we love?"
- when these things get us to the point of asking, "Has God forsaken me? Am I still his son or daughter?"
- when we are tested for our faith in God

Four Ways to Respond to Evil

In order to pray the second part of this phrase, "Deliver us from evil," we must understand what evil is and how we are delivered from it. There are several ways people have explained how we are to be delivered from evil. These explanations have been around for a long time. I have enlarged upon what one author[77] has observed about four ways people deal with evil:

---

[77] I have expanded on N.T. Wright's treatment of the four ways to respond to evil found on pages 69–71.

There is the ignorance is bliss view of evil. Evil doesn't exist. Can you think of people who try to take that approach to evil? That was the way the Sadducees in the time of Jesus approached evil. They did not believe in the devil. Evil was *dismissed.* Today this approach is becoming more and more the popular way of looking, or should I say, of not looking at evil. This understanding is held at the same time when evil's head is getting uglier and uglier.

There are those who approach evil by focusing on it in order to *avoid evil.* Evil is everywhere. That was the position of the Essenes in Jesus's day. Because of the fear that evil will triumph, they sought to escape it by living out in the desert. They lived more in fear of evil than in the assurance of the love of God. They tried to follow God by *avoiding evil.* Again, there are people today who are more concerned with the devil's ability to deceive us than Jesus's ability to be the "way, the truth and the life" (John 14:6) who takes us to the Father. They are motivated and motivate others more by fear of becoming lost than through love of being redeemed.

Another way to deal with evil is to become self-righteous, to focus on one's goodness and one's spiritual superiority over others. In Jesus's day, those were the Pharisees. They saw themselves as having it all together. They were the ones God favored. They were the ones who were good enough for God. They proved they belonged to God by pointing out other people's sins, failures, and imperfections. They lived by rules and were quick to point out the failures of others. They loved debating the finer points of the law. They believed it was up to them to *defeat evil.* And unfortunately, there are those in the church who focus more on what they—and others—must do instead of on what God has done in Christ. And on what He will do in our lives through the Holy Spirit!

The only way to truly deal with evil is to admit it exists. To acknowledge that only Jesus can deliver us from it. N.T. Wright emphasized this when he wrote, "(We need to recognize) the reality and power of evil and confront it with the reality and power of the kingdom announcement. The result (for Jesus) is Gethsemane and Calvary. His way for his followers is that they, too, recognize evil for what it is, and that they learn to pray, 'Deliver us from evil' ... Jesus intends his followers to recognize not only the reality of evil but the reality of his victory over it."[78]

This phrase differs from the previous one for pardon. The plea for pardon leads to justification, which results in reconciliation. It is about righteousness imputed to us. This part of the prayer, deliver us from evil, is about sanctification, righteousness imparted or given us to transform and change us through God's grace. In essence, we are asking that we become empowered by grace to live for God, as his sons and daughters.

Only when we view the two parts of this petition together do we get what Jesus is really teaching us about, the necessity for us to pray, "lead us not into temptation." Evil is powerful, and the evil one is so determined to defeat us. At the same time, we are weak, sinful, and impotent to handle it by ourselves. In our own strength, we are no match for the evil one. We will—and do—fall! At the same time, Jesus wants us to know that there is a way out. We must be delivered! That is why Jesus taught us to pray, "Lead us not into temptation, but deliver us from the evil one." That deliverance has been provided for us in the death, resurrection, and intercession of Christ. And through the indwelling of the Holy Spirit in our lives!

I think it is important to notice what Jesus did *not* teach us to say:

- Lord, give us the strength to overcome and pass the time of testing.
- Lord, help us to overcome.
- I'll do my part; you do the rest.

Jesus taught us to pray, "Lord, (You) deliver us from evil and the evil one," because he knew we cannot deliver ourselves.

Is it possible that the greatest temptation that we face is when we try to deliver ourselves from evil and the sin in our lives? Of course, it is! I think one of the most difficult temptations the devil uses is to get us to think that we must overcome through our own strength and our own power. Even though deep down we know we can't, we try to deliver ourselves in subtle and not so subtle ways.

---

[78] N.T. Wright, *The Lord and His Prayer,* 70–71.

- We try to deliver ourselves when we regularly neglect both Bible study and prayer for the purpose of knowing God. Then we attempt to live the Christian life by using our own human resources.
- We try to deliver ourselves when we focus more on what we have to do than on what Christ has done or is doing for us.
- We try to deliver ourselves when we say, "I believe in grace, but ..."
- We try to deliver ourselves when our assurance of salvation is tied to "how well we are doing."
- We try to deliver ourselves when our obedience consists of lists of rules that seem to grow in number.
- We try to deliver ourselves when we play the comparison game, comparing ourselves and how "good" we are against others and their failures to measure up, in our eyes at least.

In teaching us to pray this part of the prayer, Jesus was teaching us one of the hardest lessons of the Christian life. It is always, always, always about learning to depend on God rather than depending upon ourselves. We need to be delivered. We cannot deliver ourselves.

Reflection and Meditation

1. Take time to talk with God about the ways in which you depend on Him and the ways in which you depend on yourself.

2. Share with Him the fears you have about being tempted beyond what you can bear.

3. To what extent do you know that you are the beloved son or daughter of God, not based on your performance or lack of performance but based on what He has done for you?

Prayer

Our Father in heaven, what a comfort to know that we can rely on Your fatherly love and care for us! What a relief to know that You have accomplished Your plan to deliver us from evil and the evil one! We long to belong to Your kingdom and to do Your will but know that we are incapable of living up to our commitments to do Your will on our own. We are grateful that Your kingdom is a kingdom of grace in which Your power and love are given to us to transform our lives. We ask You to change our desires and motives. Only when this occurs will our actions truly reflect Your character of love.

We know that times of testing will occur in our lives. Give us wisdom to recognize the true nature of those tests. Give us faith to enable us to trust You to deliver us. Give us hope in the certainty of Your victory that has been won and in Your faithfulness to the promise that nothing can separate us from Your love, thus making us more than conquerors.

In the character of Christ, I pray. Amen.

Chapter 8

Praise and the Results of Prayer:
God Receives the Glory

For Yours is the kingdom, the power
and the glory forever. Amen.
—Matthew 6:13, NKJV

I wish I could put into words the impact that the Lord's Prayer has had on me as I have studied it and included it in my own prayer life. It has enriched my relationship with God. It has added to my worship of God in both personal and communal worship. It has made my prayer life more meaningful as it has provided me with new perspectives. I relate to God more intimately and understand Him, as best I can, on a deeper level. My prayers have a different purpose and focus. And I have been challenged as I seek to live as a follower of Christ. It has served as a constant reminder that God is the Father of all by creation and desires to be the Father of all by redemption, too.

Therefore, in my interactions with others and in my prayers for them, it is important for me to see them in that light and treat them as my brothers and sisters. Thus, having the Lord's Prayer as a guide enables me to intercede for others in a more meaningful way. This is true even if I do not know the person or persons very well, if at all. This is true even if our relationship is strained or we do not see eye to eye.

Beginning my prayer by addressing God as "our Father" compels me to pray with an awareness that I belong to Him along with millions of other people. This enables me to pray for others with a mindfulness and an assurance of His love for them. It enables me to intercede on their behalf with a boldness and confidence of His care for them. It also softens my heart and increases my concern for them. Addressing God as *our* Father motivates me to pray for others, including those with whom I disagree or do not get along, through the crystal lenses of God's love and grace.

When I pray to our Father in *heaven,* I am speaking with the Almighty God of the universe. His compassion, love, wisdom, omnipotence, omniscience, holiness, and righteousness demand my awe, praise, adoration, worship, honor, and exaltation.

When I pray with the pattern of the Lord's Prayer as an outline to be filled in, I cannot avoid examining my life in the light of what it means to live in God's kingdom. I meditate on the various characteristics of His kingdom and reflect on the ways my life does or does not reveal them. I ask for insight into what aspects of the kingdom I need to yield my stubborn, human will to His sovereign, divine will for my life.

Praying with the paradigm of the Lord's Prayer constantly reminds me of my daily need to depend on God to supply all my needs, especially my need of Jesus, who is the Bread of Life.

Applying the Lord's Prayer as a pattern for my prayers creates the opportunity for me to experience a greater appreciation for the depth of God's forgiveness of my sin. And at the same time, there is an increased thoughtfulness for the necessity to forgive others, even when it is difficult to do so!

To pray with the organized flow of the Lord's Prayer prompts me to rely on the Lord when going through difficult times or struggles in the areas of my spiritual, physical, emotional, and/or social life.

Utilizing the Lord's Prayer as a guided process has kept me from praying in a rut: from using the same words, clichés, and thoughts. It has enabled me to express the deepest longings and desires of my heart. At the same time, I am enabled to focus more on God in my prayers and less on myself. I have become less concerned about getting answers to my prayers and more concerned about allowing God to have more access to my life. Thus my prayers have more substance, my prayers are more varied, and my time with God is far richer and precious.

You may ask why I am sharing this review of the Lord's Prayer at this point before we consider the last phrase in the Lord's Prayer. It is because there are concerns whether this last phrase is really a part of the Lord's Prayer as taught by Jesus. It is to show that the pattern of the Lord's Prayer, even in the shorter version, without the final phrase, can and will make a difference. Not just in how you pray but in how you live and interact with others. With that in mind, let's ask God to prepare our minds, hearts, and wills to understand and apply the phrase that gives God glory for what takes place in our lives.

Prayer

Our Father in heaven, what a privilege to accept Your invitation to come boldly before Your throne of grace. What an honor it is to acknowledge You, the God of the universe, as our Father.

Father, we struggle with what it means to live in Your kingdom. We long to allow Your will to be fulfilled in and through us.

May we live as citizens of Your kingdom who have been transformed by Your grace as we await the final establishment of Your heavenly kingdom.

Father, we need a daily revelation of Jesus in our lives. Give us a deeper desire to sit at the feet of Jesus. May we see this as the one thing that is needed and necessary for following Jesus.

We do not know how we would live without Your love that provides forgiveness for our sins and failures. Your grace amazes us! Remind us how much our forgiveness cost You.

May we always remember that we can only do all things when we do it through Christ who strengthens us. We trust and rely on You to accomplish Your purpose for our lives.

In the character of Your Son. Amen.

A Disputed Phrase

Some people have been perplexed when they discovered the phrase, "For Yours is the Kingdom, the power and the glory forever," missing from their Bible. There are those who use this as proof of the need to use only the King James Version of the Bible, as it is one of the very few translations that includes it as part of verse 13. Most translations, if they include it, put an explanation in a footnote explaining that it is left out of the oldest manuscripts. (If the reader is interested in further explanation, see the footnote below.)[79]

Only the translations that are dated prior to the early 1900s include the phrase in their translations, without a footnote. The American Revised Version and the English Revised Version, which were printed right around the turn of the twentieth century, did *not* include them.[80]

In my study, I discovered that there were three approaches to this phrase taken by those who wrote about the Lord's Prayer in books or commentaries. Some authors did not even mention this phrase or even explain why the phrase is omitted. Other authors wrote about the concerns regarding its authenticity and chose not to write about this phrase. And there were authors who decided to write about it and viewed it as part of the Lord's Prayer.

Of those who chose to include this phrase in their book or commentary on the Lord's Prayer, the primary reason they gave was that it just doesn't seem right to leave it out. They gave a number of reasons why they think it belongs in his prayer. Among them was the argument that many Jewish prayers end with words of doxology. These are similar to the phrase that is omitted.

Another reason given by those who believe this phrase belongs in the Lord's Prayer is that there are other prayers or psalms in the

---

[79] Francis D. Nichol, *Seventh-day Adventist Bible Commentary, v. 5.*

[80] The Seventh-day Adventist Biblical Research Institute has an article with in-depth treatment of the view that the King James Version is the best Bible translation. You can access it through the following link:
https://adventistbiblicalresearch.org/materials/bible-canon-and-versions/modern-versions-and-king-james-version.

scripture that end in a similar way. I found ten[81] that did so. Let me give you three examples, one from the Old Testament and two from the New Testament.

The first example is found in 1 Chronicles 29:10–11. The background to this passage is that this is the last recorded prayer of King David. It was given after he had announced that his son, Solomon, would succeed him as king. Solomon would have the responsibility to build a temple for God. David told them everything that he himself was going to do to get the project underway: all the building materials he was gathering, the treaties or contracts he had made with other kings for their building supplies. Then the following words are recorded:

> [10]Therefore David blessed the LORD in the presence of all the assembly. And David said: "Blessed are you, O LORD, the God of Israel our father, forever and ever. [11]Yours, O LORD, is the greatness and the power and the glory and the victory and the majesty, for all that is in the heavens and in the earth is yours. Yours is the kingdom, O LORD, and you are exalted as head above all." (1 Chronicles 29:10–11)

Doesn't that sound very similar to the last phrase of the Lord's Prayer in the King James Version? Of course, it does!

Now! let's look at some New Testament passages:

> "The Lord will rescue me from every evil deed and bring me safely into his heavenly kingdom. To him be the glory forever and ever. Amen." (2 Timothy 4:18)

One could say it is almost as if Paul took this from the Matthew version of the Lord's Prayer.

Here's one more example. It is found in the benediction at the end of Jude:

---

[81] In addition to the three that are cited see the following: Psalms 63:1-4; 145:8-13; Ephesians 3:14-16; Revelation 4:11; 5:12; 7:12 and 19:1.

"... to the only God, our Savior, through Jesus Christ our Lord, be glory, majesty, dominion, and authority, before all time and now and forever. Amen." (Jude, verse 25)

Even while acknowledging the similarities with the ending of these prayers in mind, a definite answer may not be given as to whether or not this phrase came from our Lord's lips when he taught the Lord's Prayer in the Sermon on the Mount. I have wavered back and forth between thinking it did and thinking it didn't. Before I share my personal opinion, let me tell you what I do know.

Nothing is added to the meaning of the Lord's Prayer if it is included. And nothing is lost from the meaning of the Lord's Prayer if it is excluded. Every aspect of the last phrase, as written in the KJV, is already contained in the phrases we have already examined. God's kingdom—his power and glory or character—is already presented in the prayer!

It seems to me that it is more *likely* that the phrase was not given by Jesus in his prayer as he taught it in the Sermon on the Mount as recorded in Matthew 6. In Luke 11, when His disciples asked him to teach them to pray, Jesus did not use this phrase. If the Lord's Prayer needed this final phrase to complete it when Jesus taught it the first time, it would seem it should have been included when he taught it the second time.

Furthermore, immediately following the Lord's Prayer in the Sermon on the Mount, Jesus made a serious pronouncement. He told the multitude, "For if you forgive others their trespasses, your heavenly Father will also forgive you, but if you do not forgive others their trespasses, neither will your Father forgive your trespasses" (Matthew 6:14–15). It is obvious that this statement is a further explanation of the phrase asking for forgiveness. More importantly, Jesus was indicating that the primary purpose of prayer is to change and transform us. Prayer is to be a channel of God's grace that flows to us that it might flow through us. The doxology of the last phrase as found in the KJV seems to interrupt that flow.

However, I have chosen to include this chapter on this phrase for the following reasons:

1. Most Christians have learned the Lord's Prayer and recite it with this phrase included.
2. It enables us to end our prayers in thanksgiving to God. It serves as a reminder that we are under the rule of His kingdom. It acknowledges that any credit that is to be given for any answers to our prayers, including the changes in our lives and the effects of any ministry to others, are to go to Him. He receives the glory.
3. As stated above, there are enough respected scholars who believe it belongs, and therefore, including it as part of our prayers is consistent with what the Bible teaches about God and the prayers offered by God's servants in both the Old and New Testament and since then.

Therefore, there is value in retaining this phrase as part of our prayer.

Now, let's treat this phrase as we have all the other phrases or petitions in the Lord's Prayer. Let's explore its meaning by looking at how it was revealed in the life and ministry of Jesus.

Applied to the Life and Ministry of Jesus

Immediately before teaching His disciples the prayer that was to serve as their model for prayer, Jesus told them how their prayers would affect their lives. Notice what he taught just a few verses earlier:

> [13]"You are the salt of the earth, but if salt has lost its taste, how shall its saltiness be restored? It is no longer good for anything except to be thrown out and trampled under people's feet. [14]You are the light of the world. A city set on a hill cannot be hidden. [15]Nor do people light a lamp and put it under a basket, but on a stand, and it gives light to all in the house. [16]In the same way, let your light shine before others, so that they may see your good

works and give glory to your Father who is in heaven."
(Matthew 5:13–16)

By using the metaphor of salt and light, Jesus taught many lessons. Living as salt and light in God's kingdom and yielding to His will makes a difference in our lives that others will notice. Jesus taught us that the impact of receiving daily supplies of spiritual life from Jesus will attract others to Him.

Through the images of salt and light, Jesus taught us that when our lives are free of anxiety as we face the world that will test our loyalty to God, people will be stirred to trust in Him, too.

Forgiveness, when we receive it from God and when we give it to others, becomes an agent of salt and light in our lives. When we are forgiven by God, our lives are free from guilt and shame. When we forgive those who offend or hurt us, we are free of resentment, anger, and bitterness. Thus people will want to experience such mercy and grace for themselves.

Through a life of prayer, the principles of God's kingdom permeates our lives. We become as salt that gives our lives an appealing flavor to others. Salt that preserves the qualities of the kingdom in a world that is opposed to those qualities. Salt that works in subtle and yet powerful ways to accomplish His purposes in our lives.

Through a life of prayer, we become light to dispel the darkness of evil. Evil inevitably causes pain and results in sin, guilt, and shame that envelop and ensnare society, including those we love. The light that shines through us will lovingly point out sin and point the sinner to the Savior.

Our good works that are the result of our life of prayer will give God glory because they will reveal the perfection of His character. Jesus taught the same principle when He said, "But whoever does what is true comes to the light, so that it may be clearly seen that his works have been carried out in God" (John 3:21). Notice again what Jesus taught us: whatever good works we do are the result of God working in and through us. When that happens, we will give Him the credit. Not because God can't live without receiving earthly accolades but because we can't receive only earthly accolades and truly live. It is almost as if Jesus is setting up a litmus test for trust. Those who truly trust God will give Him glory. Those who depend on themselves will seek glory from others.

Jesus did not just teach the importance of giving glory to God for what occurs as a result of living in His kingdom. He exemplified giving God the glory or credit. Notice what he said: "If I glorify myself, my glory is nothing. It is my Father who glorifies me, of whom you say, He is our God" (John 8:54). Jesus was talking about giving his Father glory or the credit for what he, as the human/divine Son of God, accomplished in his ministry. While living as a man he refused to take credit for the miracles, incredible teaching, and transformational changes he produced in the lives of others. Instead he gave credit where credit was due, to his Father.

Please notice what Jesus said about the importance of who received credit.

> ¹⁵The Jews therefore marveled, saying, "How is it that this man has learning, when he has never studied?" ¹⁶So Jesus answered them, "My teaching is not mine, but his who sent me. ¹⁷If anyone's will is to do God's will, he will know whether the teaching is from God or whether I am speaking on my own authority. ¹⁸The one who speaks on his own authority seeks his own glory; but the one who seeks the glory of him who sent him is true, and in him there is no falsehood." (John 7:15–18)

Jesus's words give a very important reason for giving God the glory. This is the very reason why we should not take the credit for ourselves. When we take glory for ourselves, Jesus says we are lying. Only God can perform the miracles of spiritual transformation, physical healing, and reconciliation with God and one another. Therefore, *He* deserves the credit.

But above all, Jesus lived the principle in his prayer life. Nothing depicts this more than the words of John, the beloved disciple of Jesus, recorded the high priestly prayer of Jesus that he prayed just prior to entering the Garden of Gethsemane. Read this prayer. He prayed it just before his arrest, trial, and crucifixion. Yet much of his prayer was focused on his Father and on his disciples of all ages.

> [4]"I glorified you on earth, having accomplished the work that you gave me to do. [5]And now, Father, glorify me in your own presence with the glory that I had with you before the world existed. [6]"I have manifested your name to the people whom you gave me out of the world. Yours they were, and you gave them to me, and they have kept your word. [7]Now they know that everything that you have given me is from you. [8]For I have given them the words that you gave me, and they have received them and have come to know in truth that I came from you; and they have believed that you sent me. …
>
> [21]That they may all be one, just as you, Father, are in me, and I in you, that they also may be in us, so that the world may believe that you have sent me. [22]The glory that you have given me I have given to them, that they may be one even as we are one, [23]I in them and you in me, that they may become perfectly one, so that the world may know that you sent me and loved them even as you loved me. [24]Father, I desire that they also, whom you have given me, may be with me where I am, to see my glory that you have given me because you loved me before the foundation of the world. [25]O righteous Father, even though the world does not know you, I know you, and these know that you have sent me. [26]I made known to them your name, and I will continue to make it known, that the love with which you have loved me may be in them, and I in them." (John 17:4–8; 21–26)

Did you notice that the shared glory, giving credit to the Father, is in reality an expression of how the Trinity relates to one another and how we are to relate to one another? Is it possible that a result of praying the Lord's Prayer and giving glory or credit to God for what happens in our lives is that we are enabled to relate in a more "Trinitarian" way of deferring to others and being content within ourselves?

If Jesus, who never sinned, could give God the glory for his life and ministry, how much more should we as sinners give God glory for what He has done in our lives? If Jesus, who was human *and* divine, found it necessary to give God glory for what he had done in his life and ministry, why don't we? If Jesus did, who made the ultimate sacrifice in order that God's love could be revealed and experienced in and through his followers, then why can't we help others see that what we accomplish in our lives is for God's glory? His love will be seen through us!

The reason it is essential for us to give God the glory or credit is twofold. First, it keeps us from trying to take credit for ourselves. It keeps us from talking about what we have accomplished instead of what God has accomplished in and through us. Second, and perhaps more importantly, it gives others hope and faith because they can receive the same grace from God that can empower and enable them to live and serve in harmony with His kingdom, too.

Apply the Pattern to Our Lives

As we look at this phrase, "Yours is the kingdom, the power and the glory forever," it reminds us of the phrase at the beginning of the prayer, "Your kingdom come." We can ask for the kingdom to become a reality in our life today because of the promised presence of Christ in our lives through his Spirit. Notice the tense of the verb, "Yours *is* the kingdom."

Jesus has taught us to pray—that is, to talk and communicate with our heavenly Father. We do so with the awareness that the One who loves us unconditionally is also the One who is omnipotent, omniscient, and omnipresent. He is our holy God. When we talk to our Father in the manner Jesus taught us, the following happens:

- We recognize that we are seeking to live in His kingdom under His rule and authority.
- We recognize that He alone sustains us by providing our physical, emotional, social needs and more importantly our spiritual needs.

- We recognize that it is His mercy and grace that provide forgiveness to us and enable us to forgive others.
- We recognize that He and He alone can, in His wisdom and providence, deliver us from times of testing, but nevertheless, when we are tested, He and He alone can keep us from the evil one.

All of this, as we have seen, describes the life and ministry of Jesus. It also describes the kingdom we have been transferred into and the principles of God's kingdom that shape and guide how we live.

To pray "Yours" at the end of our prayer reminds us that we belong to God, our Father. There is something about the concept of *belonging* that is vitally essential in human relationships. It is extremely important in our relationship with God. If you don't know you belong to Him, you will try various ways to make sure you do belong to Him.

It is fascinating to see the lengths that people go to in order to know they belong to people to whom they should belong. It is not uncommon for a child who feels emotionally neglected or even physically or sexually abused to feel uncertain of the love and acceptance of their parent/parents. They often go to one extreme or the other to gain that love and acceptance. This is especially true of those mistreated by their fathers. One extreme is referred to as "acting out." A child acts out by misbehaving and disobeying in obvious and sometimes harmful ways in an attempt to get their parents' attention. It can include such activities as drug abuse, immorality, alienation of affection, and rejection of the parents' morals and/or religion. The other extreme is to become extremely compliant. This is referred to as "acting in." A child who acts in is always trying to please their parents to win the approval they so desperately desire. They often blame themselves for their parents' failures and maltreatment. They are trying to be the perfect child in hopes of attaining the love they have never received. And yet they never know if they are good enough to belong.

So Many Christians Struggle to Belong to God

It is frustrating to hear Christians talk about their relationship with God and their salvation in tentative terms. It is not uncommon to hear people who have been Christians for many years speak of their relationship with God using conditional words to describe it. It is even more common to hear them say the following when they speak of their salvation: "I hope I am saved. I want to be saved." Or "I am not sure I am saved." They struggle with belonging to God:

- not because God has not told them they belong but because the devil tells them they don't belong
- not because God has not revealed His unconditional love to them but because they have yet to accept it
- not because God's divine character of mercy isn't revealed but because their own sins, failures, and mistakes block their view

As a result, God's children also go to extremes to try to feel like they belong. They either *act out* and live defiant lives (antinomianism) denying God's claim and will for their lives or attempting to see if His love is truly unconditional. Or, they *act in,* going to great lengths to win God's love and approval by their strict adherence to both His commands and their additions to His commands (legalism), which also denies God's claims on their lives and denies His unconditional love.

The answer to both extremes is found in God's grace and in giving God the glory or credit for being a God whose unconditional love provides for our every need, pardons our sins and failures, and restores us to Himself as His beloved son or daughter. He then dwells within us through His Spirit as He transforms our lives.

The story of the prodigal son (Luke 15) is a great example of children trying to gain their father's love either by acting out or acting in as a result of not knowing they belong to their father. The younger brother acted out, trying to gain his father's attention. He went to the ultimate extreme of punishing his father by leaving home, demanding his inheritance before his father died, and living a life of debauchery. When he demanded the early inheritance, he was in effect saying that his father was already dead as far as he was concerned. How his father's heart must have been broken!

The older brother stayed at home. He was working as hard as he could for his father. Yet he was still living apart from his father, too. He was acting in. Putting in his time! Trying to gain the father's love by trying to be "good enough!" At the same time, he was keeping track of his brother's indulgent offenses in order to compare them to his fastidious obedience. He was looking for the opportunity to prove to his father that he belonged by comparing his accomplishments to his brother's failures. His faithfulness to his brother's abandonment! His goodness to his brother's vices! Proving he belonged by proving his brother didn't!

The sad reality is that the elder brother was just as removed from his father's presence as the younger brother.

- He may have been living with his father in the father's house, but he was dwelling in the far country of emotional distance. Emotional distances are often further apart and more difficult to overcome than physical distances!
- He may have been eating at the same table with his father, but he was dining alone.
- He may have had the same roof over his head as his father had for protection from the external elements, yet he had nothing over his heart for protection from the internal elements of jealousy, self-pity, self-righteousness, and other negative emotions.

These were the result of trying to earn the love he had already received but had failed to accept.

The older brother was so caught up in self-thoughts that he scorned the party and the fatted calf given in honor of his younger brother by their father. He simply refused to acknowledge his brother. And at the same time, he was unable to acknowledge the times the father had daily lavished his love and care on him. The daily meals shared! The daily protection received! Inclusion in the family activities! Daily interaction with myriad tokens of love and concern for him! He even forgot that the father had given him his portion of the inheritance early, too, so that he would be treated with fairness and honor.

What does all this have to do with the phrase, "Yours is the kingdom, power and glory"? Everything! Including this concept in our prayers regularly will serve as a constant reminder that "every good and perfect gift comes down from the Father" (James 1:17). Including this concept in our prayers serves as a spiritual safety check whenever we struggle to belong by acting out or acting in.

You cannot pray, "Yours is the kingdom, power and glory," when you live in either the far country of selfish disobedience or the far country of selfish obedience. The far country of living apart from the Father by rejecting the Father or of living at home in the far country of isolation from the Father!

Acknowledging that the kingdom, power, and glory belong to Him leaves our own glory in the dust. Acknowledging that the kingdom, power, and glory belong to Him should always remind us that we belong to Him because of what He has done for us, what He does in us, and what He accomplishes through us!

When we pray, "Yours is the kingdom," we are reminded that we belong to God, not because of what we do but because of what He has done through Christ. As the song says, "Not because of what I am but because of who You are," my Savior and Lord. We are saying we want to remain in the kingdom of grace.

In recognizing that the kingdom belongs to Him, we acknowledge and trust in the power of the kingdom of grace. If our prayers are going to be answered, they will be answered through the power of God and not through the effort of man. If the answers to our prayers and the transformed longings of our hearts are going to be realized, they will come about not because we make sure it happens but because we trust in God to accomplish His purposes—in His ways and in His time.

We cannot enter God's kingdom by bashing down the divine walls of holiness in our robes of filthy rags. We cannot provide the elements of God's character that sustain our spiritual lives any more than we can provide the elements of nature that give us food. In ourselves, we do not have the mercy and grace to forgive others or ourselves. We are impotent to deliver ourselves. It is His power, and His power alone, that provides *every* answer to the requests Jesus taught us to make when he gave us the pattern of the Lord's Prayer. Therefore, He deserves the honor and the credit for what takes place in our lives and through our lives.

The Depth of God's Glory

When we think of glory, we usually think of an intense brightness that surrounds God due to his holiness. I do not deny that scripture repeatedly gives that picture of God and his glory. However, that is not the only way to understand the meaning of God's glory as it is used in this setting. It is also used in two additional ways.

First, as we have already seen, it is a reminder of who gets the credit. When we pray, "Yours is the glory," we are saying that God receives the credit for what is happening in our lives as a result of our relationship with Him. As we saw in John 17, Jesus gave God the glory or credit for what occurred in his life on this earth. Jesus acknowledged the role of the Father in his life and in his ministry. He said that God's glory was the result.

Whenever we, in any way, take credit for our spiritual growth, spiritual victories, or spiritual gifts and abilities, we rob God of his glory. We deny His power and grace. We become our own god.

Keeping this aspect of glory in mind allows us to end our prayers with thanksgiving, with an attitude of gratitude. Our adoration of God increases when we intentionally look for the ways God is transforming us and working in and through us to enlarge His kingdom of grace. This keeps us from being like nine of the ten lepers Jesus healed. They were the recipients of God's mercy and grace when Jesus healed them. Only one came back to express gratitude for the gift of grace he had received. In so doing, he was acknowledging Jesus as the one who had healed him. And his gratitude became the focus of what had taken place that day.

Second, it is a reminder of God's character. Throughout the Bible, God's glory is a synonym of his character. That was first seen when Moses was on Mount Sinai receiving the Ten Commandments. Moses asked God to reveal his name (character). Instead of introducing himself as Yahweh again, it says God's *glory* passed before Moses, and then God revealed his character (Exodus 34:6–7).

When our prayers are patterned after the Lord's Prayer, we will always be focused on the character of God. That is as it should be! The ultimate purpose of prayer is to bring us into the presence of God. For it is only when we focus on Him that we begin to understand who He is. It is when we focus on Him that we are transformed and thus reflect His character in our lives. It is when we focus on Him that we receive a desire to minister to others. It is only when we focus on God that we are enabled to introduce others to the God we worship, adore, and serve. And at the same time, we see ourselves as He sees us. We are His beloved children who depend on Him.

When we end the prayer with, "Yours is the Kingdom, the power and glory," we are praising Him, because he is the God who is compassionately in charge of our lives as we live here on this earth. He is the God who has brought us into His kingdom while we await the coming kingdom that will be forever. Then it will be seen that the results of belonging to Him and allowing Him to transform our lives will be forever. Eternal! We will sing the song of Moses and the Lamb throughout the ceaseless ages of eternity because He rescued us and made us part of His kingdom. Forever! Amen! So be it!

Challenge and Application

My desire, dear readers, is not to merely give you a better understanding of the Lord's Prayer. It is to enable you to incorporate it into your prayers and in your journey with God. This is not about learning to say the perfect prayer. This is not about praying the right prayer in order to get the results we want. It is about a life of prayer that will enable you to experience more fully, more deeply, and more completely the life God has in mind for you.

Therefore, I want to challenge you to pray with the Lord's Prayer as your guide. Keep a journal, if it helps. When you do, you will discover that the focus of your prayers will change. You will discover that the requests you make will be different. You will use fewer clichés. You will be surprised at what you include in your prayers. Your prayers will become more inclusive as you pray on behalf of others. You will pray in the awareness that we have the same heavenly Father as our family members, our fellow church members, and other believers. This will include those who don't always understand God and His Word the way we do! Thus, you will see them in new and different ways as you realize that belonging to His kingdom means we belong to one another and need one another!

We need one another:

- if we are to have a balanced understanding and appreciation of the character of God
- if we are to express the principles of the kingdom of God and fulfill His will or mission for our lives
- if we are to be sustained by Jesus, the Bread of Life
- if we are to experience and express forgiveness
- if we are to be delivered from times of testing and from evil and the evil one
- to remind us that in the end the Glory will belong to God forever

Prayer

Our Father in heaven, thank You for the gift of one another. Thank You that we are not an only child as we try to live in Your family. You are our Father. May we have a greater appreciation of what it means to belong to Your family.

Thank you that Your character of love, compassion, mercy, justice, and holiness enables us to trust You completely to do that which is right and good for each one of us. In every circumstance of life! The more we understand Your character, the more we long to live in Your kingdom of grace wherein righteousness not only dwells but where it reigns. We want to submit our lives to the Holy Spirit that we might reveal the aspects of Your kingdom to others.

May we live each day dependent on Jesus as the One who provides every need we have in the spiritual realm. May we trust in His ability to give us every blessing we need and to appreciate every blessing we have received.

Father, thank You for the forgiveness we have received from You. And thank You for the mercy and grace that enable us to forgive others. Thank You for the reconciliation we have with You and the resultant "peace that passes understanding" that we have with You. And for the opportunity we have to be reconciled with others as we forgive those who have deeply wounded us.

We know that there are times of testing ahead. Prepare us for them. Deliver us when we face them. May we think of future events with peace rather than with fear! Peace that is available because of Your desire to deliver us, Your promise to deliver us, and Your power to deliver us

Whatever blessing we receive, however You choose to answer our prayers, may we always give You the credit and the praise for what You have done in us and through us. Your glorious character deserves our praise and our gratitude.

In the character of Jesus. Amen.

Chapter 9

Persistence in Prayer:
It's Not What You Think

If you then, who are evil, know how to give good gifts
to your children, how much more will the heavenly
Father give the Holy Spirit to those who ask him!
—LUKE 11:13

The value of consistent prayer is not that He
will hear us, but that we will hear Him.
—WILLIAM MCGILL

Paul Harvey, well-known radio broadcaster, gave a daily news update for many years. Later he added a daily human interest story about a famous person or event. He did it by telling an unknown part of the story about the person's life. Then he would reveal the person's name or the event and would end with his signature saying, in his rich baritone voice, pausing between each word. "And ... now ... you ... know ... the ... rest of ... the ... story!"

This chapter is the "rest of the story" for the Lord's Prayer. It is Jesus's own concluding remarks given to his disciples after teaching them how to pray. In fact, I believe it was part of his instruction on prayer. At this point, Jesus was not teaching them what they should include in their prayers. He was teaching them about what it means to persist or persevere in prayer.

Prayer

Our Father in heaven, we are grateful for the invitation to come boldly before Your throne of grace. To have an audience with the King of the universe is a privilege that amazes us. To enter into the presence of the holy, compassionate, omniscient, and omnipotent God of the universe humbles us. May every prayer we say reflect the honor and awe we have for You.

Father, as we look into the parable that teaches Jesus's conclusion to how to pray, give us open minds to understand what he said. Give us open hearts to trust his words, his appeal, and his promise. And soften our wills to determine to apply this parable in our life of prayer.

Thank you for Your invitation to come regularly into Your presence. I ask this in keeping with the character of Jesus. Amen.

Two Primary Characteristics for a Life of Prayer

In chapter 2, we saw that Jesus gave the Lord's Prayer as part of the Sermon on the Mount. He did it because prayer for the majority of people, and especially the religious leaders, had become more of a show-and-tell to win the praise and approval of men rather than an honest and open communication with God.

In the Sermon on the Mount, Jesus was trying to get people to see that God's kingdom was concerned with spiritual principles and not with earthly power. He wanted them to understand that it was about the character of God and seeking Him and His righteousness and not seeking power and authority and their own righteousness. He wanted them, and us, to understand that God's kingdom is a kingdom of:

grace and not of force,

humility and not of pride,
　　serving and not being served.

Above all, what Jesus wanted them to understand is that God's kingdom was based on divine forgiveness that enables those forgiven by God to forgive others, as we saw in the chapter on pardon. Jesus, after teaching them the Lord's Prayer, gave a brief and startling statement about forgiveness. He said, "For if you forgive others their trespasses, your heavenly Father will forgive you, but if you do not forgive others their trespasses, neither will your Father forgive your trespasses" (Matthew 6:14).

This statement, which follows the Lord's Prayer in Matthew, was given as the central theme for what it means to live in the kingdom of God. It was Jesus's paraphrased repetition of the request for pardon. It was intended to give additional emphasis on the priority of forgiveness in the kingdom of grace.

As we have already discovered in chapter 1, the second time Jesus gave the Lord's Prayer was when the disciples asked him to teach them to pray. This probably occurred shortly after the feeding of the five thousand men (about 15–20,000 when counting the women and children) and over halfway through his ministry. The disciples had made the connection between Jesus's prayer life and the divine power evident in his life and ministry. They wanted the connection with God that Jesus had so they could perform miracles, too. So they asked Jesus to teach them to pray.

It was almost as if they were skeptical that the prayer that Jesus had taught the multitude in the Sermon on the Mount could be connected with the results of his ministry.

- How could the words of that prayer account for the miracles of loaves and fishes?
- How could the words of that prayer explain the blind having their sight restored, the lame walking, lepers being healed, and the dead being raised?
- How could the words of that prayer provide Jesus with wisdom and the authority of his preaching?

217

- How could the words of that prayer sustain his peace in the midst of turmoil?
- How could the words of that prayer create within him calm in the midst of the storms?
- How could the words of that prayer bestow goodness in response to evil and wickedness?

It was for this reason they asked to be taught how to pray.

It was almost as if they asked it in this way:

"Jesus, teach us the prayer you really pray!"

Jesus reiterated the Lord's Prayer, with a few minor changes in the wording of the prayer but not in the thoughts being stated. Nothing new! No new concepts! Nothing secretive! No secret talisman! No secret mantra! No secret manner of standing, sitting, or kneeling! No magic number of prayers that must be prayed or pray-ers who must pray before God will hear and answer. However, Jesus did give a change in perspective, even though the words were basically the same.

Until he gets to the end!

Until he gives the postscript!

Until he tells the rest ... of ... the ... story of the "secret" of his life of prayer!

A Misunderstood Parable

The "secret" of the power of Jesus's prayers is found in the parable that immediately follows Jesus teaching his disciples how to pray in Luke 11. Verse 5 of Luke 11 begins with a word that can be translated as either "and" or "then", as it is in the NIV, NLT, and the NET. The main purpose of the word, whether it is translated as "and" or "then", was to connect the parable he was about to teach with the prayer he had just taught. After teaching them the prayer, "then" Jesus tells a parable. We call it the parable of the persistent neighbor. It is found in Luke 11:5–13. The parable is about a man who has unexpected guests that arrive at midnight. He has no bread to serve the food. So even though it is midnight, he goes to his neighbor's house and awakens his neighbor to ask for bread.

The neighbor at first says no. It is late, and he does not want to awaken his children (it is more than likely a one- or two-room home). But the neighbor persists because it would be considered extremely rude to ignore the needs of a guest. He would be violating a cultural law of hospitality.

So, the neighbor caves in! He gets up and gives the neighbor what he asked for. He did not do this because the request came from a friend. He did it to rid himself of his persistent neighbor so he and his family could get back to sleep. He was more concerned with his own comfort than his friend's needs!

Jesus then gives the lesson of the parable. The lesson given is in answer to the disciples' real but unstated question, "Why is it that your prayers are so effective and ours are not?" The lesson Jesus taught them is often overlooked or, worse, misinterpreted.

The answer to the disciples' unstated question is not found in praying with the exact right words. The answer is not found in getting enough people to pray. The answer is not even found in praying morning, noon, and night. Every day! Every single day! Although all those things are good to do!

The answer is found when we recognize this is a parable that teaches its lesson by contrast. Ellen White makes this clear. "But the selfish neighbor in the parable does not represent the character of God. The lesson is drawn, not by comparison, but by contrast. A selfish man will grant an urgent request, in order to rid himself of one who disturbs his rest. But God delights to give. He is full of compassion, and He longs to grant the requests of those who come unto Him in faith. He gives to us that we may minister to others and thus become like Himself."[82]

Most of the time when this parable is used, it is used to teach the importance of being persistent in prayer in order to receive the answer to our prayer that *we* desire. For most people, this means we must keep on asking God until He caves in. You must get nine thousand other people to pray with you before God will answer. You've seen the e-mails. Pass

---

[82] Ellen White, *Christ's Object Lessons*, 141.

this e-mail to ten friends with a request for God to heal a child. Don't break the chain of e-mails or God won't heal the child.

I do not discount the importance of intercessory prayer. I do not minimize the impact of a number of people praying together. At the same time, I do not discredit the power of an individual praying. Consider the following:

> How many people were praying to God on Mt. Carmel when Elijah asked God to burn up his sacrifice? Just one that we know of!

> How many people were praying for Lazarus to be raised from the dead? One!

> How many people does James say it takes to accomplish much? The prayers of many righteous people? No, the prayer of one (James 1:16).

I cannot imagine God sitting up in heaven with a counter in one hand and saying, "When they get 250 more people praying about this, *then* I'll do something." Can you? When people demand that no one break the prayer chain or God won't answer, they misrepresent the character of God! They deny Him as a faithful, loving, compassionate Father. They make the answer to prayer dependent on humanity and not on divinity!

Too often our understanding of persistence is in the number of times we pray or in the number of people we get to pray with us. What a difference it makes when we are persistent because we know we are praying to our compassionate, merciful, omniscient, omnipresent Father who can "do exceedingly abundantly above all that we can ask or even imagine" (Ephesians 3:20, NKJV).

The parable is not designed to teach about the virtues of a pesky kind of persistence:

- to keep on asking until God caves in and gives us what we ask of Him (or should I say demand of Him?)

- to continuously plead until we become obnoxious
- to plan for a flash mob of prayer before the throne of grace

It is designed to teach us about the willingness of God to answer our prayers:

- not out of resignation
- not to get rid of us like a pesky fly or mosquito
- but with an eagerness to fulfill our requests
- like a friend responding to a friend in need
- like a father responding to a child's necessities and concerns
- more importantly, with the wisdom, generosity, and grace of a loving God responding to His children whom He created and redeemed

And that is especially true when we ask for the sake of others.

Notice the points Jesus makes after telling the parable:

> [9]"And I tell you, ask, and it will be given to you; seek, and you will find; knock, and it will be opened to you. [10]For everyone who asks receives, and the one who seeks finds, and to the one who knocks it will be opened." (Luke 11:9–10)

Wow! We can ask God for whatever we want, and He will give it to us? Is that what Jesus is saying?

This passage has been used and misused by Christians through the years. It has been used to promote what is known as the "prosperity gospel." It is often used to tell people if they just have enough faith, whatever they ask for, as long as it is in keeping with God's will, God will give it to us. Since God wants us to be blessed, He is just waiting for us to ask Him so we can receive the blessings we request. Unfortunately, it is used out of context, apart from the Lord's Prayer. This verse is often used to tell us that we can ask God for whatever we want, and we will get it. We can seek for our heart's desire and find it. We can knock on the door of our golden opportunity so that all the obstacles in our way will be removed.

Unfortunately, so many people have understood these verses this way, and then this happens:

- When they asked and did not receive, they were disappointed.
- When they searched and didn't find, they were disheartened.
- And when they knocked and the door stayed shut, they were dismayed.

You see, Jesus's command for his followers to ask, seek, and knock in prayer was given *after* he taught them to pray the Lord's Prayer. And if we truly learn to pray in the manner and spirit of the Lord's Prayer, what we ask for *will* be in line with God's will. What we seek will be, first and foremost, God Himself, to be transformed into His character. The doors we knock on will open divine opportunities for us to serve God and others.

Praying in the manner and with the focus that Jesus taught us will change what we ask from Him. It will change our notions of what we need in order to find purpose and fulfillment in our lives. It will change what we hope to accomplish and do with our lives. When that happens, we will be looking to become involved in what God is blessing rather than asking God to bless what we are doing apart from His character and apart from His kingdom.

Lessons about Persistence

We need to be persistent in prayer. But we need to understand the point about persistence in prayer that Jesus was making. The first lesson about persistence is that it is not about praying to get answers; it is about praying to get *perspective*. God's perspective! Persistence is not in order to wear God down and get Him to say yes to our requests. Instead, it helps us see our prayers and our lives from God's perspective. Are we praying to get Him to yield His will to our requests, or are we praying that we might yield to His will as citizens of His kingdom? Persistence in prayer is not about praying hard enough and long enough to get God to do what we want. Persistence in prayer is about having a life of prayer that creates in us a desire to become the person God created us to be.

Several variations of a story have been told about a magazine that hired a large firm to mail out reminders to people to renew their magazine subscription. One day the company's computer malfunctioned. A rancher in a western state received thousands of separate pieces of mail asking him to renew his magazine subscription.

Somewhere, in the midst of handling those pieces of mail, he had had enough. He dropped everything he was doing. He filled out the form. Then he travelled ten miles to the nearest post office and purchased a money order to pay for the renewal. He placed the money order and renewal form in the envelope along with a note that read, "I give up! Send me the magazine, okay?"[83]

Too often we portray God like the exasperated rancher, responding to His children's prayer request when He has been pestered into doing so.

- Persistence in prayer is not about getting God to answer our prayers; it is learning from Him so that we know what to ask.
- Persistence in prayer is not about changing God's mind; it is about changing our hearts
- Persistence in prayer is not about twisting God's arm to do what we want; it is about transforming our lives so that we will do what He wants.
- Persistence in prayer is not about getting God to give us our heart's desires; it is about desiring God with all our heart.

E. Stanley Jones made the following observation: "Prayer is surrender—surrender to the will of God and cooperation with that will. If I throw out a boathook from the boat and catch hold of the shore and pull, do I pull the shore to me, or do I pull myself to the shore? Prayer is not pulling God to my will, but the aligning of my will to the will of God." [84]

The second lesson Jesus wants us to learn from this parable in connection with the Lord's Prayer is that God is more willing to give us what we need than we are willing to ask.

---

[83] Whether the story is true or apocryphal, the story illustrates the author's point.

[84] Stanley E. Jones, *A Song of Ascents* (Nashville: Abingdon Press, 1968), 383.

> [11]"What father among you, if his son asks for a fish, will instead of a fish give him a serpent; [12]or if he asks for an egg, will give him a scorpion? [13]If you then, though you are evil, know how to give good gifts to your children, how much more will your Father in heaven give the Holy Spirit to those who ask him!" (Luke 11:11–13)

Let's look at what Jesus meant by evil parents. He is not contrasting God's holy and perfect generosity with the worst parents the world has ever known. He is contrasting the willingness and ability of God to care for His children and the willingness and ability of earthly parents to care for their children. God responds to our requests in ways that are consistent with His holiness. He answers our prayers in ways that are in harmony with His perfect heart of love and compassion. He considers our pleas out of His complete knowledge of our personalities and needs. And He does it all with His eye on eternal consequences. And whatever He does for us is accomplished through His grace. Earthly parents respond out of their own hearts with sinful natures and selfishness rooted deep within them. We respond with limited love, with damaged emotions, and with incomplete knowledge. All too often, we respond with earthly solutions and our eyes on earthly results instead of eternal ones. Not because we are so evil in our actions but because sin has infected our humanity. There is not a one perfect parent!

Do you see what Jesus was saying? If we, as sinful humans, know how to give, to the best of our abilities and capabilities, good things to our children, *how much more* will our heavenly Father, who alone is perfect, give good gifts to His children?

The third lesson Jesus had regarding persistence in prayer is found in His concluding remark on this parable found in verse 13:

> "If you then, who are evil, know how to give good gifts to your children, how much more will the heavenly Father give the Holy Spirit to those who ask him!"

The Holy Spirit is the ultimate answer to our requests! Whatever our requests might be!

The Holy Spirit? There is nothing in the Lord's Prayer that mentions the Holy Spirit! There is nothing in the context of the Lord's Prayer or the parable itself that even alludes to the Holy Spirit. Not even one symbol! No dove, no tongue of fire, no oil, and no other symbol of the Holy Spirit are in the parable. The Holy Spirit is only mentioned in what comes after the parable. So why does Jesus refer to the Holy Spirit? Because God is more eager to give, not just good gifts to His children but the best gift to us. The gift we need the most! It is the Holy Spirit who transforms and empowers us to live the Christian life and to minister to others. The fruit of the Holy Spirit is love, the sum and substance of God's character. The gifts of the Spirit are the spiritual abilities and divinely empowered talents to do ministry, to serve others.

It is when we recognize the connection between this parable and the Lord's Prayer that we are able to see Jesus was indeed responding to the disciples' real question behind their question. Because the disciples had not understood the role of the Holy Spirit in the life and ministry of Jesus, he had given them first the Lord's Prayer and then the parable of the persistent neighbor. He wanted them to see the contrast between a man who caved in and said, "Enough is enough, here you can have what you want!" and God who says, "I am willing to give you what you really need. I want to give you what you need the most!"

Just as bread was the eating utensil that enabled people of that time to eat their food, so the Holy Spirit was the essential power that enabled Jesus to accomplish his ministry. Jesus was telling them that if they were going to live godly lives, if they were going to preach powerful sermons and if they were going to perform mighty miracles in their ministry, then they would need the Holy Spirit to be given to them.

Much has been written about what we must do if we are to receive the gift of the Holy Spirit. Books have been written about the requirements we must meet if we are to receive the Holy Spirit. Could it be that the Lord's Prayer itself contains the provisions necessary for receiving the gift of the Holy Spirit? These provisions include:

- an intimate, trusting relationship with the God
- living in the awareness of our relationship with a holy God and our relationship with members of His family

- recognizing the principles of His kingdom and submitting our lives to His will
- requesting to receive the Bread of Life to sustain us and others spiritually, physically, emotionally, and socially
- asking for forgiveness and for the grace to forgive others
- seeking His protection—and victory—from times of testing and being kept from the evil one
- gratefully acknowledging that God is the source of our transformation and ministry to others

The Holy Spirit is given to us when we learn to live the life of prayer that Jesus lived.

Reflection and Application

Persistence in prayer is about regularly opening our lives to God so that our lives are being transformed. It is opening our lives to God so that we become givers and not just receivers of His love and grace. Persistence in prayer will allow God to use us in ways we never thought possible. True persistence in prayer will enable us, through the Holy Spirit, to become the disciples Jesus had in mind who will fulfill the commission to go into the world—the world in which we live—and make disciples of others.

As you think about the purpose of persistence in prayer, spend some time reflecting on the following:

Is the primary focus of your prayers on receiving answers or knowing God and His character?

How and why do you think persistence in prayer leads to receiving the Holy Spirit?

To what extent are you experiencing persistence in your prayer life?

What steps will you need to take to become more persistent in prayer as Jesus taught?

Prayer

Our Father in heaven, we long for our lives to reveal and reflect Your holy, compassionate character. Open the eyes of our hearts to understand more clearly Your generosity, compassion, and the nature of your holiness. Guide us when we study Your Word to understand the self-revelations You have made of Your character. When we read of Your interactions with the biblical characters, may how You responded to them and through them give us fresh insights into Your character. Help us to understand and apply Your teachings of the law, prophets, and wisdom passages of the Old Testament through the lens of the teachings of the gospels, letters of the New Testament, and prophetic passages of both Testaments. We know that only as we know who You are will we be able to relate and respond as Your sons and daughters.

We want our lives to be lived under the principles of Your kingdom. Renew our minds. Soften our hearts. Subdue our wills. We want to submit our lives to Your will. We want to give You loving obedience. We want to fulfill Your mission for the saving the lost.

Oh how we long to be sustained by Jesus! His words of life! His sacrifice, death, and resurrection! His life of servant leadership! His promise to give us the Holy Spirit! May we ever hunger after the Daily Bread that feeds our souls. May we also trust in You to provide for the daily physical, emotional, and social needs of our lives.

Forgive us for all too often attempting to live our lives on our terms. Forgive us for trying to live the Christian life by slight modifications of behavior instead of transformation of our characters. As we forgive others, may we see them through Your heart and eyes. To see them as Your children whom You love as much You love us. To see them with Your heart of compassion for what they can become through Your grace instead of through our nearsighted eyes that too often judge others by human standards of success or human failures.

Keep us faithful when we experience times of testing. Times when circumstances, events, or trials test our ability to trust You to guide, protect, or care for us and those we love. May we grow more confident as we trust in Your love, Your plan of salvation, and Your power to deliver us and give us victory over the devil and the evil of the world in which we live. Deepen our faith and give us the strength we need to live the prayer that Jesus lived.

I ask these things on behalf of those who read this book, my family, church members, friends, and for myself. And we will give You the praise and the honor for what You accomplish in our lives and through our lives.

In the character of Jesus. Amen.

Benediction

Now to him who is able to keep you from falling
and to present you before his glorious presence
without fault and with great joy—
to the only God our Savior
be glory, majesty, power and authority,
through Jesus Christ our Lord,
before all ages, now and forevermore!
Amen.
(Jude 24–25, NIV

Invitation

It was the day after I had written the first draft of the last chapter. I was taking my dog on her morning neighborhood walk. I was not consciously thinking about the book. We had just finished our little neighborhood loop when the lightbulb went on. I couldn't help but smile. It dawned on me that chapter 9, "Persistence in Prayer," takes us full circle from chapter 1, "The Priority of Prayer." The only difference? Chapter 1 revealed how persistent Jesus was in his prayer life. Chapter 9 challenges us to make prayer the same kind of priority in our life that Jesus made it in his. Persistence in prayer will only take place when prayer is a priority in our lives. They are two sides of the same coin!

So instead of making this a summary statement of what you have read, I want to make it an invitation. It is an invitation to continue learning to pray as Jesus taught his disciples to pray. An invitation to allow the example and teaching of Jesus, through his life of prayer, to inspire and inform how *you* pray!

Applying the principles of the Lord's Prayer to your prayers is not another method for getting answers to your prayers. Nor is it a simple formula that if you follow the steps, you will achieve success in prayer, whatever that may mean to you. You will be learning the process that the Lord's Prayer generates and not just the following of a pattern to reproduce.

Above all, you will be placing your life in the presence, plan, and purpose of your heavenly Father, who is so committed to you that He sent His Son to save you (John 3:16), so committed to you that Jesus knew he could ask the Father to guard and keep you (John 17:11, Jude 24–25), so committed to you that he gave you the gift of the Holy Spirit to dwell in you (Luke 11:13).

Prayer

Our Father in heaven, thank You that I can bring the readers of this book into Your presence. Even though I may not know them, You know them, for they belong to You. Therefore, we are united together as Your children. May it always be our desire that Your reputation and character be honored and glorified in our lives. Give each reader the desire to learn and embrace the prayer Jesus taught us that we, too, might live out the qualities of the spiritual life that Jesus taught us to focus on in our prayers to our Father.

We long for the principles of Your kingdom to be so established in our lives that they are seen in our interactions with all whom we know who are in our sphere of influence. We hunger and thirst for Your righteousness to be on display in our lives and in the way we treat others. May those principles be unmistakable evidences of Your mercy and grace at work in our lives. And may they become invitations for those who do not know You to "taste and see that the Lord is good." We want Your will to be accomplished in our lives, in how we live and how we cooperate with You in making disciples of others. I ask you to daily give each reader the spiritual food and nourishment they need. May they seek to follow Jesus who is the Way. May they seek to feed on Jesus, who is the Word of Truth. And in so doing, may they find Him to be the source of their eternal life, even as they live each day in Your presence. May they also depend on You and make wise decisions regarding the physical, emotional, and social needs of their lives.

Father, may they continually experience Your forgiveness when they fall short of the mark of loving You and loving others. May their failures never prevent them from wanting to be in Your presence or make them feel that You cannot forgive them. And may the mercy and grace they receive from You inspire them to forgive those who offend and hurt them.

We are living in difficult times. The devil is doing everything to discourage Your children, to divide us and to dissuade us from surrendering and submitting our lives to You. I ask you to keep Your children from the hour of testing that would destroy their trust in You. May we cling to Your promise to "be with us until the end of the age." May we trust in Your promise and power to "keep us from falling and to present us blameless before the presence of Your glory, which will give You great joy."

And we will acknowledge and declare Your character of love, righteousness, holiness, mercy, grace, faithfulness, and justice as we give You the praise and glory. Not just today but throughout eternity.

In the character of Christ. Amen.

Jesus invites *you*: "Pray then like this: 'Our Father in heaven, hallowed be your name … (Matthew 6:9–13, ESV).

Why not accept his invitation?

Addendum 1

Ellen White Statements on Jesus's Prayer Life

Found in Her Primary Books

The Ministry of Healing, page 52:

The childhood of Jesus, spent in poverty, had been uncorrupted by the artificial habits of a corrupt age. Working at the carpenter's bench, bearing the burdens of home life, learning the lessons of obedience and toil, He found recreation amidst the scenes of nature, gathering knowledge as He sought to understand nature's mysteries. He studied the word of God, and His hours of greatest happiness were found when He could turn aside from the scene of His labors to go into the fields, to meditate in the quiet valleys, to hold communion with God on the mountainside or amid the trees of the forest. The early morning often found Him in some secluded place, meditating, searching the Scriptures, or in prayer. With the voice of singing He welcomed the morning light. With songs of thanksgiving He cheered His hours of labor and brought heaven's gladness to the toil worn and disheartened.

Education, page 80:

Thus were spent the days in the earthly life of Jesus. He often dismissed His disciples to visit their homes and rest; but He gently resisted their efforts to draw Him away from His labors. All day He toiled, teaching the ignorant, healing the sick, giving sight to the blind, feeding the multitude; and at the eventide or in the early morning, He went away to the sanctuary of the mountains for communion with His Father. Often He passed the entire night in prayer and meditation, returning at daybreak to His work among the people. It was not on the cross only that Christ sacrificed Himself for humanity. As He "went about doing good" (Acts 10:38), every day's experience was an outpouring of His life. In one way only could such a life be sustained. Jesus lived in dependence upon God and communion with Him. To the secret place of the Most High, under the shadow of the Almighty, men now and then repair; they abide for a season, and the result is manifest in noble deeds; then their faith fails, the communion is interrupted, and the lifework marred. But the life of Jesus was a life of constant trust, sustained by continual communion; and His service for heaven and earth was without failure or faltering.

Thoughts from the Mount of Blessing, page 102:

The disciples had been for a short time absent from their Lord, when on their return they found Him absorbed in communion with God. Seeming unconscious of their presence, He continued praying aloud. The Saviour's face was irradiated with a celestial brightness. He seemed to be in the very presence of the Unseen, and there was a living power in His words as of one who spoke with God.

The Desire of Ages, pages 259–260:

The Saviour loved the solitude of the mountain in which to hold communion with His Father. Through the day He labored earnestly to save men from destruction. He healed the sick, comforted the mourning, called the dead to life, and brought hope and cheer to the despairing. After His work for the day was finished, He went forth, evening after evening, away from the confusion of the city, and bowed in prayer to His Father.

4 Testimonies to the Church, page 528:

When the cities were hushed in midnight slumber, when every man had gone to his own house, Christ, our Example, would repair to the Mount of Olives, and there, amid the overshadowing trees, would spend the entire night in prayer. He who was Himself without the taint of sin,—a treasure house of blessing; whose voice was heard in the fourth watch of the night by the terrified disciples upon the stormy sea, in heavenly benediction; and whose word could summon the dead from their graves,—He it was who made supplication with strong crying and tears. He prayed not for Himself, but for those whom He came to save. As He became a suppliant, seeking at the hand of His Father fresh supplies of strength, and coming forth refreshed and invigorated as man's substitute, He identified Himself with suffering humanity and gave them an example of the necessity of prayer.

The Ministry of Healing, page 500:

Christ gave no stinted service. He did not measure His work by hours. His time, His heart, His soul and strength, were given to labor for the benefit of humanity. Through weary days He toiled, and through long nights He bent in prayer for grace and endurance that He might do a larger work.

2 Testimonies to the Church, pages 202–203:

Through the day He labored earnestly to do good to others, to save men from destruction. He healed the sick, comforted the mourning, and brought cheerfulness and hope to the despairing. He brought the dead to life. After His work was finished for the day, He went forth, evening after evening, away from the confusion of the city, and His form was bowed in some retired grove in supplication to His Father. At times the bright beams of the moon shone upon His bowed form. And then again the clouds and darkness shut away all light. The dew and frost of night rested upon His head and beard while in the attitude of a suppliant. He frequently continued His petitions through the entire night. He is our example. If we could remember this, and imitate Him, we would be much stronger in God.

2 Testimonies to the Church, pages 202–203:

If the Saviour of men, with His divine strength, felt the need of prayer, how much more should feeble, sinful mortals feel the necessity of prayer—fervent, constant prayer! When Christ was the most fiercely beset by temptation, He ate nothing. He committed Himself to God and, through earnest prayer and perfect submission to the will of His Father, came off conqueror. Those who profess the truth for these last days, above every other class of professed Christians, should imitate the great Exemplar in prayer.

The Ministry of Healing, page 58:

In a life wholly devoted to the good of others, the Saviour found it necessary to turn aside from ceaseless activity and contact with human needs, to seek retirement and unbroken communion with His Father. As the throng that had followed Him depart, He goes into the mountains, and there, alone with God, pours out His soul in prayer for these suffering, sinful, needy ones.

Christ's Object Lessons, page 139:

Not for Himself, but for others, He lived and thought and prayed. From hours spent with God He came forth morning by morning, to bring the light of heaven to men. Daily He received a fresh baptism of the Holy Spirit. In the early hours of the new day the Lord awakened Him from His slumbers, and His soul and His lips were anointed with grace, that He might impart to others. His words were given Him fresh from the heavenly courts, words that He might speak in season to the weary and oppressed. "The Lord God hath given Me," He said, "the tongue of the learned, that I should know how to speak a word in season to him that is weary: He wakeneth morning by morning, He wakeneth Mine ear to hear as the learned." Isaiah 50:4.

Found in Book Compilations

Gospel Workers, page 255:

Because the life of Jesus was a life of constant trust, sustained by continual communion, His service for heaven was without failure or faltering. Daily beset by temptation, constantly opposed by the leaders of the people, Christ knew that He must strengthen His humanity by prayer. In order to be a blessing to men, He must commune with God, from Him obtaining energy, perseverance, steadfastness.

Gospel Workers, pages 255–256:

Frequently He continued His petitions through the entire night; but He came from these seasons of communion invigorated and refreshed, braced for duty and for trial.

Addendum 2

Aspects of the Kingdom

Ask God for grace to enable you to be authentic with Him about the ways in which the following aspects of the kingdom:

    a)   are present in your life—and thank Him for those ways
    b)   need to become more evident in your life
    c)   are missing in your life

1. The kingdom of heaven is *future*. Am I living in the expectation of the future coming of Christ in His kingdom?
2. The kingdom of heaven is *present*. Am I living with an awareness of being in His kingdom now?
3. The kingdom of heaven is the *reign and rule of God*. Am I submitting my life to His reign and rule? Are there aspects of my life I am still trying to control?
4. The kingdom of heaven is a place of *righteousness*. Am I living with an awareness of His robe of righteousness covering me while I am seeking, by grace, to live the life He has called me to live? What practices, habits, or sins in my life do I need to confess? What aspects of Christ's character do I want to behold that I might be changed?
5. The kingdom of heaven is made available through the *gospel of grace*. Am I living by the grace of God that forgives my sins, transforms my life, and empowers me to serve and lead others?

6. The kingdom of heaven is *available to all*. Am I willing to serve wherever and whomever God invites me to serve?

7. The kingdom of heaven is entered through *faith*. Am I willing to trust God to be the One who reconciles me to him, transforms my life, gives me gifts for serving him and to continue to do so regardless of circumstances?

8. The kingdom of heaven is motivated by *love*. To what extent does 1 Corinthians 13:4–8 describe my life? Is my love for others conditional or unconditional?

9. The kingdom of heaven involves *sacrifice*. What sacrifices of my time, talents, finances, or caring am I willing to give right now?

10. The kingdom of heaven includes God's *power over evil*. Do I trust that God is able to overcome the power of evil through miracles, divine appointments, and encounters that liberate others from the power of evil?

11. The kingdom of heaven expects *growth*. Am I expecting and open to spiritual growth in my life and in the lives of others and at the same time to numerical growth through my personal witness and evangelism?

12. The kingdom of heaven is *Jesus*. To what extent am I living with an awareness of the sufficiency, presence, and power of Jesus in my life?

Bibliography

Augsburger, David W. *Caring Enough to Forgive: True Forgiveness.* Scottdale, PA: Herald, 1981.

Augsburger, David W. *The Freedom of Forgiveness.* Chicago: Moody, 1988.

"Baker's Evangelical Dictionary of Biblical Theology." *Bible Study Tools.* N.p., n.d. Web. 13 Apr. 2016.

Barclay, William. *The Daily Study Bible Matthew.* Philadelphia: Westminster, 1975.

Bounds, Edward M. *Purpose in Prayer.* Grand Rapids, MI: Baker Book House, 1978.

Bunch, Taylor G. *The Perfect Prayer.* Washington: Review and Herald, 1939.

Chappell, Clovis Gillham. *Sermons on the Lord's Prayer: And Other Prayers of Jesus.* Nashville: Cokesbury, 1934.

Coffee Break with God. Tulsa, OK: Honor, 1996.

Crockett, Kent. *I Once Was Blind, but Now I Squint: How Perspective Affects Our Behavior.* Chattanooga, TN: AMG, 2004.

Crossan, John Dominic. *The Greatest Prayer: Rediscovering the Revolutionary Message of the Lord's Prayer.* New York Harper One Publishing, 2010.

Haloviak Valentine, Kendra. *Signs to Life*: *Reading and Responding to John's Gospel.* Victoria, Australia: Signs Publishing Company Victoria, Australia, 2013.

Jones, E. Stanley. *A Song of Ascents: A Spiritual Autobiography.* Nashville: Abingdon, 1968.

Keller, Phillip. *A Layman Looks at the Lord's Prayer.* Chicago: Moody Bible Institute, 1976.

Kittel, Gerhard, G. W. Bromiley, and Gerhard Friedrich. *Theological Dictionary of the New Testament.* Grand Rapids, MI: Eerdmans, 1964. Web.

Kittel, Gerhard, G. W. Bromiley, and Gerhard Friedrich. *Theological Dictionary of the New Testament.* Vol. 6. Grand Rapids, MI: Eerdmans, 1964.

McDowell, Josh. *Evidence That Demands a Verdict: Historical Evidences for the Christian Faith.* San Bernardino, CA: Campus Crusade for Christ International, 1972.

Murray, Andrew. *The Prayer Life.* Public Domain. Charles Rivers, ed. e-book.

Seventh-day Adventist Bible Commentary. Vol. 5. Washington, DC: Review and Herald Pub. Association, 1978.

Smedes, Lewis B. *Forgive and Forget: Healing the Hurts We Don't Deserve.* San Francisco: Harper & Row, 1984.

Smedes, Lewis B. *The Art of Forgiving: When You Need to Forgive and Don't Know How.* Nashville, TN: Moorings, 1996.

Strobel, Lee. *The Case for Christ: A Journalist's Personal Investigation of the Evidence for Jesus.* Grand Rapids, MI: Zondervan, 1998.

Temple, William. *Christian Faith and Life; Being Eight Addresses Delivered in the University Church at Oxford, February 8th–15th, 1931.* New York: Macmillan, 1931.

Trueblood, Elton. *The Lord's Prayers.* New York: Harper & Row, 1965.

White, Ellen Gould Harmon. *Christ's Object Lessons.* Washington, DC: Review and Herald Pub. Association, 1941.

White, Ellen Gould Harmon. *Testimonies for the Church.* Vol. 5. Mountain View, CA: Pacific Pub. Assn., 1948.

White, Ellen Gould Harmon. *Testimonies to Ministers and Gospel Workers: Selected from Special Testimonies to Ministers and Workers.* Mountain View, CA: Pacific, 1962.

White, Ellen Gould Harmon. *The Desire of Ages.* Mountain View, CA, Portland, OR: Pacific Pub. Association, 1940.

White, Ellen. *Thoughts from the Mount of Blessing.* Boise: Pacific Press Publishing, Boise, 1956.

Willimon, William H., Stanley Hauerwas, and Scott C. Saye. *Lord, Teach Us: The Lord's Prayer & the Christian Life.* Nashville: Abingdon, 1996.

Wright, N.T. *The Lord and His Prayer.* Grand Rapids, Erdman's Publishing, 1996 and Cincinnati: Forward Movement Publications, 1997.

Printed in the United States
By Bookmasters